MEN HAVE CALLED HER CRAZY

A Memoir

ANNA MARIE TENDLER

Simon & Schuster

New York   London   Toronto   Sydney   New Delhi

1230 Avenue of the Americas
New York, NY 10020

First Simon & Schuster hardcover edition August 2024

SIMON & SCHUSTER and colophon are registered trademarks of Simon & Schuster, LLC

Simon & Schuster: Celebrating 100 Years of Publishing in 2024

For information about special discounts for bulk purchases, please contact Simon & Schuster Special Sales at 1-866-506-1949 or business@simonandschuster.com.

The Simon & Schuster Speakers Bureau can bring authors to your live event. For more information or to book an event, contact the Simon & Schuster Speakers Bureau at 1-866-248-3049 or visit our website at www.simonspeakers.com.

Interior design by Carly Loman

Manufactured in the United States of America

1   3   5   7   9   10   8   6   4   2

Library of Congress Cataloging-in-Publication Data is available.

ISBN 978-1-6680-3234-3
ISBN 978-1-6680-3236-7 (ebook)

To the women who held my hand when I was lost.

Amanda
Carmel
Holley
Irene
Jill
Kylie
Lauren
Maria
Sarah

and

Petunia

One

First, they take my suitcase away from me. This is so they can search my clothes for drugs and weapons. Who are "they"? They are hospital staff, a specific check-in team that I never see again during my time here. They are warm, but not too warm, hardened from years of dealing with bullshit from patients who check in against their will, who are angry to be here, and who take their anger out on the first line of duty. However, they quickly accommodate their approach to you based on how you approach them. If you are difficult and have an attitude, like the young redhead checking in next to me, they will be short and direct. If you, like me, have chosen to be here, are relieved, even happy to be here, they will speak to you in soft voices, ask you if you're comfortable and offer you snacks. I only accept a paper cup of water.

I sit in a room by myself for five minutes. The room has beige walls, gray carpet, and a wood-carved sign hanging on the wall that reads HOPE. A friendly nurse in her mid-fifties comes to get me and brings me into an exam room, like one you would see at any doctor's office. She introduces herself, but it is unlikely anyone could remember a name under these conditions. I certainly do not. She asks me many questions.

"Why are you here?"

"Intense suicidal ideation, self-harm, disordered eating."

I try not to cry, saying it out loud for the first time in such a matter-of-fact way.

"What medications are you allergic to?"

"Sulfa."

The nurse then assesses me for suicide risk.

"Have you thought about taking your life in the past forty-eight hours?"

"Yes."

"Do you have the means to carry out this plan?"

"Yes."

"Do you experience feelings of worthlessness?"

"Yes."

"On a scale from one to ten, ten being the greatest, how great is your desire to die?"

"Eleven?"

Apparently, my risk is high.

I have entered the hospital on the recommendation of my therapist, Dr. Karr. She felt we had come to an "impasse" (her words), where she was at a loss for what to do with me (my words). I will participate not in their typical thirty-day program but in a new program that is only one week long and is designed to provide a psychiatric and psychological workup for patients who are struggling to get proper diagnoses elsewhere.

A psychiatrist enters the room. He is wearing a collared, button-down shirt that is a little too wrinkled, and khaki pants that have remnants of a coffee stain above the right knee. Though the hospital itself has no religious affiliation, this psychiatrist is Jewish. I know this because he is wearing a yarmulke. Jewish psychiatrists as a concept make sense to me. Judaism as a faith allows for doubt. It encourages its people to ask questions—of their relationship to God, of that which may be considered sacred. Jews love to analyze. I know this because I am one of those Jews. The psychiatrist, who identifies himself as

Dr. Samuels, asks a series of questions designed to illuminate possible psychosis or bipolar disorder.

"Do you hear voices speaking to you?"

"I do not."

"Do you ever have prolonged periods of elation?"

"No, but that sounds nice."

"Do you have long depressive periods?"

"Yes, but not in the way I think you mean."

I think that response is at least a little funny, but he jots down a note, straight-faced.

Within ten minutes I'm being asked to recount past physical and sexual abuse. I feel these should be Day 3 questions. However, it is often easier to tell these things to strangers, so I do. I tell him about more than one sexual encounter with older men when I was underage, but they were consensual. No matter how weird I feel about them now, they were, at the time, consensual.

"You seem to be making a point to tell me they were consensual," Dr. Samuels says.

I shrug.

Everything I explain to him feels vague, like it could be something, but it could also be nothing. Is any of it abuse? Is it kids simply exploring sexual boundaries they don't understand? Is it adult men simply exploring sexual boundaries they are conditioned to disregard? I feel stupid recounting these experiences in all their un-concreteness. I do not know what they mean. Maybe they don't mean anything.

The doctor makes me follow his finger with my eyes, *not* my head, to make sure I don't have a brain tumor. I do not. As he is about to leave the room, he pauses and turns around.

"Have you ever written a suicide note?"

"No. I mean, yes. I'm not sure. I think so?"

"When you wrote it was your intent to harm yourself after?"

"It was."

"But you didn't."

"Not in the suicidal sense."

"Can you elaborate?"

"I wanted to die, but I cut myself instead, and that cutting wasn't meant to kill me."

"What was it meant to do?"

"Relieve my pain."

"Did it work?"

"Temporarily, yes, it did. But now I'm here. So I guess . . . no?"

He finally laughs. "Have you been restricting your eating for a long time?"

"Not really," I say. "Summer 2020."

"Why did you start restricting your eating then?"

"I was experiencing very bad anxiety, exacerbated by the pandemic. So at first I wasn't eating because I was so anxious, I didn't have an appetite. Then it turned into a competitive game with my scale. A how-low-can-I-go situation, because I wanted to feel in control of something."

Dr. Samuels nods. "I understand. Thank you."

Then he is gone.

While I wait for the nurse to return, I think about that note—its absurdity, its self-involvement. It was largely about how no one around me seemed to be paying attention to my mental and physical decline. There was one particularly mortifying part about wearing a very sexy dress to a party and receiving no compliments about how hot I looked. The note was filled with venom and rage. I was so blinded by anger, I was ready to end it all over something as trivial as a leopard-print Norma Kamali dress. Underneath the vanity was a deep depression, a seemingly bottomless chasm of worthlessness and anxiety. I was a woman losing her grip on a life I was holding so tightly to. Consumed by embarrassment at the note's contents, I ripped the note into tiny pieces the following day and scattered it into various garbage cans inside my New York City apartment.

The nurse measures my height and weight: five foot two, eighty-one pounds in clothes. Her face shows no sign of reaction as she writes these numbers down. There are no mirrors in this room, but I know what I look like—emaciated arms, a massive thigh gap when I stand with my legs together, ribs and hips protruding, breasts nearly dissolved into my bony chest. She takes my blood pressure, which is eternally low, and I hear, as I always do at doctor's appointments, "Wow, you're going to live forever!"

If up until this point I had any illusions that I haven't checked into a full-blown psychiatric hospital, the nurse makes me undress to confirm I have no drugs hidden in my clothes or on my person. I do not. As the nurse rifles through my clothing, she apologizes and tells me, "It's not personal." I pee into a cup, a triple check that I'm not on drugs. I'm still very much not on drugs. The nurse does a visual body scan to assess the severity of my self-harm. It is quite severe. I pull the medical tape, which holds bandages in place over the cuts covering my arms and thighs, from my skin.

"What type of self-harm do you engage in?"

"I cut," I say, wondering why doctors and nurses seem to never debrief one another.

"What do you use to cut yourself?"

"Scissors."

She looks up at me from over her wire-framed glasses, her stoic expression breaking for a moment. "You did all this with scissors?"

"I did."

"At what age did you begin to self-harm?"

"Fourteen."

She looks over my arms and legs carefully, but with swift purpose. "Do you feel like any of these are infected?" she asks me.

"No, I take pretty good care of them," I say, and she nods, jotting something down on my chart. "I guess that's part of the ritual too," I add.

It has been about ninety minutes since I arrived, and now I'm fully clothed again and sitting alone in the waiting room. Another strange face pops his head in and says they are almost finished searching my bag and I should not have to wait too much longer. I'm wishing I had accepted the snacks offered earlier. I'm hoping he will ask me again if I want snacks. God, all I want are snacks. He starts to close the door and I find my voice, but only insofar as to croak out one word:

"Snacks?" Jesus Christ. At least I had the wherewithal to phrase it as a question.

"At the end of the hall. Help yourself." He smiles and leaves.

At the end of the hall there is a small table set up with chips, cookies, hot water, and a coffee maker. I pocket three packets of Swiss Miss Milk Chocolate with Marshmallow hot cocoa mix. *Treats for later*, I think to myself, smiling at my keen ability to plan ahead. I also take a bag of Cool Ranch Doritos. My absolute favorite junk food. I have not eaten much in the past seven months, but in truth, I do not like not eating. I feel like shit all the time—tired, weak, nauseous from my stomach trying to eat itself. I know it's doing nothing to help my mental health, but I find comfort in how bad not eating has made me look. Most of my life my outward presentation has not matched my inward reality, but with my body gaunt, my face droopy and puffy at the same time, I'm forcing the outside world to confront a more honest—and probably scary—version of my mental state. Now, today, I no longer have to convince anyone how bad I feel. I might as well eat the Doritos. Still, enjoying a flavor-bursting tortilla chip at my hospital intake feels somehow disrespectful to the gravity of the occasion. I decide I'm too tired to have a morality negotiation with my inner monologue. I open the bag and pop a chip into my mouth.

So far, the hospital is not so bad. This is an all-you-can-eat treat situation. Then they take my iPad, wallet, and my phone. For some reason, they let me keep my Kindle. I am given a tiny blue notebook with about ten blank pages and a super small pencil.

"It's for writing down anything you might want to write down," the nurse says.

It would be difficult to write anything beyond "I am at hospital" with these items. I'm relieved I brought my own notebook and pen.

I am loaded onto a small bus with my suitcase. I am the only person on the bus. The hospital is set up in six houses. The Main House is where everyone starts. You are monitored closely, you detox if you need to detox, and after about five days to a week you are filtered into one of the other houses based on your diagnosis. I am allowed to skip Main House because I do not require a detox. Dalby is female only, for patients struggling with addiction and co-diagnosis mental illness. Oscar is male only, for patients struggling with addiction and co-diagnosis mental illness. Forest is coed, for patients in the dialectical behavioral therapy program, non-addiction, co-diagnosis mental illness. Andrews is for patients with severe mental illness—mood and personality disorders—who risk being a danger to themselves or others. And lastly, there is Carlyle, a coed house for people who pay extra to be sequestered from the general hospital population.

I arranged ahead of time to be in Dalby because I absolutely refuse to be around men.

"I don't even want to look at them," I told Dr. Karr, our faces side by side in the Zoom split screen I had come to know so well over the past year.

"You should know that your medical team there is going to be largely men," Dr. Karr said. "A male psychologist, a male psychiatrist, and one female social worker."

"I don't like that."

"They're professionals. I would like you to give them a chance."

"I can do that. I don't like it. But I can do it."

"I've communicated to them that you are distrustful of men and that it's important for the female social worker to regularly check in with you."

"Thank you. I appreciate that. Fucking men."

"Fucking men," she repeated back to me.

Now, on the bus to Dalby, I have the terrifying realization that I'll be living for the next week with females who are strangers. I'm not sure why I hadn't considered this before, but I'm glad I had not; maybe I wouldn't have come—too scared at thirty-five to put myself in such an unfamiliar social situation. The women might be mean to me because I'm new, or they might be unpredictable due to mental illness. My anxiety hinges on the anticipation of the unknown.

I get off the bus and am greeted at the door of Dalby by a house manager, a brunette woman in her late twenties.

"You can leave your bag right here," she says, gesturing to a spot in the foyer. The house décor is plain but not clinical. The living room is cozy; carpeted, with two couches and a love seat. The kitchen has a large table with dining chairs. It feels like a modest New England vacation home. "We'll go over some rules and basic information, then you can grab your suitcase and I'll show you to your room."

At the kitchen table she starts right in. "There's no food or drinks allowed in the rooms. Don't go into other patients' rooms. Socializing must take place in the common areas. Feel free to go for walks throughout the campus. iPads, provided by the hospital, are allowed to be borrowed for one hour a day to check email. Your search history will be checked upon their return." She pauses. "Any questions?"

"Not at the moment," I say.

"Now we have to go over fire safety." She reads the confusion on my face. "It's protocol. How would you know if there was a fire in the house?"

This seems like a trick question.

"I'd hear a smoke alarm?" I say.

"What would you do if there was a grease fire in the kitchen?"

I'm so confused why I'm being asked this.

"I'd throw flour on it?" I vaguely remember learning this at fifteen in home economics class, the same class where I got a finger stuck in a sewing machine while sewing piping onto a pillow without the machine's safety foot. My machine jammed, making a horrible loud click, and I looked down to see the needle through the pointer finger of my right hand. It did not hurt immediately, but the pressure was intense. I raised my free hand.

"I just sewed into my finger," I said calmly.

"OH MY GOD!" a girl yelled. The entire class jumped out of their seats, gathering around the machine to which I was attached.

The teacher screamed and ran out of the classroom.

"Where the fuck is she going?" I said. "I literally have a needle through my finger."

The teacher reentered the room with the gym teacher, who was next door teaching a CPR class.

They walked up to my machine.

"If you turn the manual knob one way, the needle will go straight up and out," she explained to the gym teacher. "If you turn it the other way, it will go down first and *then* up."

"Which way do I turn it so it goes straight up?" the gym teacher asked. Why had the home ec teacher called on him to do this job? He seemed like a totally unhelpful addition to this equation.

"I don't remember!" Beads of sweat were forming on her nose.

"Can someone go to another machine and see which direction to turn the knob so the needle goes straight up?" I said, losing my patience.

A classmate popped over to the machine next to mine. "It's clockwise."

The gym teacher put his hand on the knob. "On the count of three I'm going to—"

"JUST DO IT!" I screamed. He did, releasing my hand from the machine.

I fainted on my way to the nurse's office, but I happened to be passing a friend in the hall and he got me to my destination. My mom picked me up and drove me to the local hospital.

"Hey," she said proudly, "this is the first time you've been back to this hospital since you were born. Not bad."

"Not bad at all." I was so happy to get out of school early.

The hospital I'm at today isn't the kind of hospital you go to for a tetanus shot after sewing through your finger in home ec class. And my mom didn't drive me here, I drove myself. When I told her over the phone I would be going to a psych hospital, she was confused. When she saw me in person she was no longer confused, she was relieved.

"You passed the fire safety test," the house manager says and takes me to my room.

The room looks exactly like the dorm where I spent ten months before dropping out of college: two single beds, each with a nightstand, two dressers for hanging and folding clothes, and two small wooden desks.

"The good news is no one has to have roommates right now. It's always very quiet here the first week of the year. There are only four other girls besides you. As new people arrive, we'll have them bunk up before you guys have to. Chances are highly unlikely you'll ever have a roommate."

"Oh, that's nice," I say as she leaves the room. When I close the door, I stand facing it, my forehead resting against the cool wood. "Thank you, thank you, thank you," I repeat, like an incantation for future protection.

I sit down on the bed, which is hard and sounds like it has plastic casing around the mattress. The sheets and blanket are extremely thin. I immediately become anxious that I will be cold at night. Since I've lost so much weight, I'm cold all the time. At home I wear long underwear under my clothes during the day and sleep in sweats under a big down comforter at night. Why would the sheets be so thin? It's winter. For clothes, I have only packed three sweatsuits, which I'd planned to rotate over this week, but I realize now that I forgot to pack pajamas. I designate one sweatsuit for sleeping. When unpacking my toiletries, I find they have confiscated my travel-sized bottle of contact lens solution, presumably so I don't try to kill myself by drinking it— not a thing I have ever entertained doing.

I sit on my bed and stare—at the empty desk, at the pilled blanket beneath me, at everything and nothing at all. My eyes are in a soft focus as I contemplate my situation. I'm in a psychiatric hospital. I will be here for eight days. I will have extensive psychological testing. I will live with strangers. I will hopefully get some help. I have no idea what comes next for me after I leave here.

The hospital was Dr. Karr's idea. She and I had first started working together five years ago. When she asked me during our first session why I was there, I told her I felt I was at a crossroads in my career, worried that I would never do anything worthwhile with my life. "Is that your main concern?" she had asked me. It wasn't. It was only one fear among many.

"My brain never stops," I said. "I have an internal monologue that is running all the time. I constantly weigh and analyze everything I do and say. I worry something bad will happen to someone I love. I worry my dog, Petunia, will die. I worry about whether or not to have children. I think no, but then, like, what if down the road I regret that? I worry about germs. Sometimes it's hard for me to get on the subway. When I'm near someone who's coughing, I panic."

"That is a lot to worry about all the time," Dr. Karr said. "It sounds very anxiety-inducing and heavy."

"Yes," I said with a loud exhale. "I feel it in my body. I feel dizzy a lot, or my brain feels foggy and out of it. Sometimes I feel like my whole body is tingling."

She asked if I'd ever considered medication, and I told her I'd prefer to exhaust all other options first.

"I was raised in a home where medicine was rarely used," I said. "My parents used homeopathy—natural medicine. I think I can count on one hand the number of times I've taken antibiotics. The idea was that Western medicine weakened your immune system overall."

"Did you go to doctors?" Dr. Karr asked.

"Yes, definitely. But I would have had to have been sick for many days before I was brought to a doctor. Normally things were just . . . toughed out. I remember getting strep throat a couple of times as a kid and I took antibiotics for that, but only if my sore throat hadn't gone away for three or four days. Same with ear infections."

"Three or four days?" Dr. Karr seemed shocked. "Would you be in pain during those days?"

I laughed. "Oh yeah, tremendous pain. I remember screaming because my ear infections hurt so much."

"Have you ever considered that there is a link between your intense fear of germs and these experiences you had as a child being sick and in a great deal of pain?"

I had not considered this.

"I think this is worth exploring more," Dr. Karr said. "Especially because I would hate to see you not take medication for anxiety, a medication that could change your life drastically for the better, because of a stigma you've picked up from your childhood."

Over the next three years I dismissed the idea of medication every time Dr. Karr brought it up. I gained more insight into the causes of my anxiety, but the anxiety did not decrease. I tried meditating, breathing techniques, exercising; none of it helped.

It was around this time that I was accepted into the Costume Studies graduate program at New York University. I had always been interested in the history of fashion, and of fashioning the body, and—after years of feeling lost professionally—thought perhaps a master's degree could lead me into a museum career. Going back to school at the age of thirty-three was terrifying. I was not a fast reader and had to analyze hundreds of pages of dense text. After the first two weeks, I had experienced three panic attacks, cried every day, and was ready to drop out.

"I can't do it!" I sobbed into my hands in Dr. Karr's office. "I should have never even applied."

"Anna," Dr. Karr said, "I promise you will get the hang of it, and you will learn how to do all the things you are afraid you can't do. This is the first thing I have seen you do for yourself to take control of your own life, to make something that is yours and yours alone. I think it would be a huge mistake for you to give up so quickly. I know you can do this."

I grabbed the last tissue out of a box next to me.

"This might not be what you want to hear, but I think you should strongly consider medication right now."

"I want to be able to do it without medication," I said.

"I've listened to you talk for three years. I've watched you try every other option. Still you are spiraling. Still you are living your life in a near-constant state of stress. At a certain point you need to decide whether the effects of stress outweigh the potential side effects of medication. As I see it, your anxiety is not merely situational, it is chemical. It has likely always been chemical. You may only see relief by taking medication. What if medication helped you get through graduate school? Would that be worth it to you?"

"It would," I said.

"My worry is that soon this anxiety will turn into a more serious depression. I see it holding you back in life and I really don't want that for you. I can put you in touch with a great psychiatrist, and please, just go talk to her. Will you do that?"

"I will," I said. I had exhausted all other options.

The way antidepressants changed my life so fast was comical. Within two weeks I had a sense of calm I had never experienced. My body stopped vibrating. It was not as if my anxiety completely dissipated, but the cyclical thinking, the inclination to bore into a thought or decision until it subsumed all rationality, stopped. I felt lighter, happier. My only regret was not doing this years earlier.

My first year of grad school was hard, but grad school is supposed to be hard. That's why not many people do it. I felt confident enough in my new path to defer my second year for a yearlong job in Washington, DC, with a textile conservator. We would be helping to mount an exhibition featuring female fiber artists at the Smithsonian American Art Museum. I felt my life coalescing into a form that made sense, one that gave me pride.

But as soon as I arrived in DC I experienced a severe regression in my mental health. I cut myself for the first time in thirteen years. I confessed this to Dr. Karr, who suggested I enroll in a six-month course of dialectical behavioral therapy, a structured program that taught skills for managing intense emotion, chronic suicidal thinking, and self-destructive impulses. I didn't cut during the six-month-long program, but as soon as it ended, the cutting started again. This time I did not tell Dr. Karr.

Six months into the job, Covid shut the world down. The museum exhibition was canceled. I returned to New York after lockdown to finish my final year of school, which would be held remotely over Zoom. My dog, Petunia, was suffering through a bout of pneumonia and a flare-up of a degenerative spinal disorder. My marriage was falling apart, and the more I tried to hold on, the faster it seemed to slip away.

I began cutting with more frequency than at any point in my life. I was nauseous all the time and had stopped eating. No one saw how thin I had become because I only saw people from the chest up through a computer screen. I was irritable and quick to get angry or cry. I would sit on my bathroom floor, my body heavy and unmoving, staring for hours at the wall. I thought I was losing my grip on reality. Thoughts of death and wanting to die consumed me. I had the will, a plan, and the means to carry out the plan. Suicidal thinking as an adult felt so much different than it had as a teenager. As a teen, it was about revenge. I wanted people to be sad I was dead. As an adult, I was not worried about anyone else. I just wanted an exit.

"You're sick, Anna," Dr. Karr said to me at the very end of 2020. "You need more help than I can give you. I urge you to get it in a hospital setting."

An hour of constant rumination passes. The house manager knocks on my door.

"Are you doing okay?"

"Yeah." But I'm not.

"It's six fifteen and everyone is leaving for dinner now. You'll take the bus with the other girls up to Main."

I throw on my boots and jacket and descend the stairs to meet the four other women in the house.

Caitlyn is tall, but her face looks very young. It is one of those visual incongruencies, whereby I am reminded how height is often inadvertently associated with age. People have always thought I am younger simply because I'm short. From the back I would likely guess Caitlyn to be in her mid-twenties, but straight on, I can tell she is barely an adult. She asks how old I am.

"Thirty-five."

"Oh wow, you look younger than that." A wide smile reveals dimples that make her look even younger. Her long glossy brown hair hangs past her shoulders in a plain blunt haircut that tells me she still sees her mom's hairstylist. Another marker of youth.

"I was like, she's either eighteen or thirty-five," says a short woman with thick black plastic-framed glasses. She has not yet put on her jacket, and I can see her arms are covered with tattoos. "I'm Kristin."

Saying thank-you to either of them feels weird, because these seem like neutral comments rather than compliments. So I just laugh nervously and say, "Oh yeah, thirty-five. How old are you guys?"

"She's eighteen. A baby!" Kristin says, pointing at Caitlyn. "I'm twenty-nine, and that's Mary; she's twenty-three."

Mary has dyed blond hair that has been pulled into a messy bun. I can tell she has been here for a few weeks by the ash-blond roots about a half-inch from her scalp. Her eyes are a little droopy and her speech is a tick slower than normal, like the friends I've had who take lithium for bipolar disorder. "You'll get used to things pretty quick," Mary says. "Don't be too nervous. Everyone who works here is so nice, if you have questions, don't be afraid to ask!" Mary is smiley, warm, and she immediately makes me feel more at ease. I bet she is the type of person who asks people how they are doing and genuinely wants to know the answer. "It's just been the four of us for the past couple days, so it's nice to have another girl here!"

The fourth girl appears at the top of the stairs. She does not smile at me. She is wearing sweatpants and an oversized parka with a fur-lined collar. "Hey," she says with a quick tip of her chin upward in my direction. "I'm Shawn." She gives nothing else. "What's up?" she says to the other women. Unlike Mary, Shawn does not genuinely want to know the answer, it's just her version of hello.

"This is Anna," Kristin says to Shawn. "She's thirty-five."

"Got it. Hi," Shawn says, making eye contact with me only for a second.

"How old are you?" I say. I feel stupid, like I've forgotten how to converse. Why are we all just telling one another our ages?

"Twenty-seven."

I like Shawn immediately. I am also a little afraid of her.

"You're here for the thirty-day rehab program?" Kristin asks me.

"No, I'm actually here for the weeklong evaluation program."

"So you're not here for addiction?" Kristin speaks rapidly, squints her eyes, and then looks at the other girls.

"I'm not." The girls exchange glances.

"Why aren't you in Forest House? That's for dual-diagnosis, non-addiction. Dalby is dual-diagnosis, addiction." Kristin's voice has a sharpness to it.

"I wanted to be in a living situation without men."

They nod.

Main, where the dining hall is, is only a five-minute walk from Dalby, but since it is below thirty degrees, we take a sixty-second ride on the hospital bus to dinner. On the way we pass a large white house that looks newer and nicer than the other buildings on campus. Inside, people are sitting on plush couches. A large-screen TV is on, and I can see someone cooking in what appears to be a very nice kitchen.

"That's Carlyle. The fancy house," Mary says, noticing me noticing the house.

"Rich people and celebrities go there and pretend they're getting help," Kristin says.

I laugh at this.

"They don't have to give up their phones. They get to use their laptops. They don't do groups with any of us," she says.

Mary looks at me with wide eyes. "They have a *private chef*."

"Oh, that seems like a good way to do rehab," I say.

Kristin scoffs in agreement at my sarcasm. I look at Shawn, sitting one row diagonally ahead of me. She is looking out the window, her face expressionless.

"Dinner is grab-and-go," Mary says. "We load up our food in a to-go container, get back on the bus, and eat dinner at Dalby."

"Is that what we do every night?"

"No, the houses switch off who eats in the dining room and who does grab-and-go. Some nights we'll eat in the dining room. It's because of Covid, so this way if someone has it, it's less likely to spread around the houses."

All the patients are tested for Covid before they enter the hospital, and I was told by both the check-in team and the house manager that thus far there hasn't been a widespread outbreak. The staff tests every day, and some of them even have one dose of the vaccine already. Still, my particular brand of anxiety is laced with germaphobia. I do not feel safe.

"I noticed no one wears masks here," I say.

"We're basically in a bubble," Caitlyn says.

On our way into the dining hall, we pass a group of seven or eight men leaving with to-go containers in their hands—Oscar House residents.

"We've got a new one!" Caitlyn says, pointing to me. "This is Anna."

They all look at me for too long. I mouth a silent "Hi" and avert my eyes, never breaking my stride into the large white building.

The dining room is small, just six tables. There is a salad station, soup, and a hot bar behind glass where we tell the cooks what we want and they load up our containers.

"Hi, Marty!" Mary says to one of the cooks. "Happy New Year! Did you have a nice day off yesterday?"

"Ma-RY! I did, thanks for asking."

The food looks homemade and not at all gross. I get salmon, rice with spices in it, and sautéed green beans. I walk over to a small dessert setup and survey my options.

"Oh my god, they have the gluten-free chocolate chip cookies again," Kristin says. Turning to me she adds, "These are actually the best desserts. I'm not even gluten-free."

"Facts," Shawn says. She reaches between us, grabs a cookie, and walks away.

I grab a cookie too.

As we leave the dining room, we pass four other patients coming in for grab-and-go.

"Hi, Jan!" Mary says to an older woman. "How was dinner? I miss seeing you every day!"

"Hi, Mary! It was good, thank you. I miss you too. You have a good night, now."

"Thanks, you too, Jan. You guys all have a good night!" Mary says.

As we hop back on the bus, Mary turns to me and says, "That was Forest House. Jan and I went through Main together. She's sweet."

The five of us eat dinner in the living room while watching a terrible Amazon Prime show called *Goliath*. This is my first meal of the day.

"Where do you live?" Mary asks me.

"I live in New York City," I say, but then correct myself. "I *did* live in New York City. I just moved back to Connecticut, close to where I grew up. I'll probably move back to New York soon though. I guess I'm not sure where I live right now."

"Oh cooool, I wanna live in New York City." Caitlyn looks at me, smiling, dimples fully displayed.

"What do you do?" Kristin asks. "For work."

"I'm an artist. And I'm in graduate school for fashion and textile history," I say, prepared to explain this specific field, as I find myself doing whenever I mention my grad program, but no one asks for follow-up.

Shawn addresses me directly for the first time. "You're an artist? That's what I want to do. So, you make *all* the money you need as an artist?"

"Yeah." I sit quietly for a few seconds before deciding to tell the truth. Who am I trying to fool? "Actually, I'm very dependent on my husband's income."

They all nod and turn their attention back to *Goliath*, but I want to keep the conversation going with Shawn.

"What do you do?" I say to her.

"I work freelance graphic design. But I want to work in music. Making music. Like, making beats other people can use and shit."

"That's cool," I say, trying to sound laid-back.

"I'm planning to take the LSAT when I get out of here. I really want to go to law school," Mary says.

"You seem like you'd make a good lawyer," I say with no elaboration. I don't know her; how do I know she'd make a good lawyer? I just want to say something nice.

"Do you know what you want to go to college for?" I say to Caitlyn.

"Literally no idea," she says, laughing.

"It honestly doesn't matter," I say. "Chances are whatever you go to school for you won't ever end up using."

Caitlyn nods, and I immediately regret giving such nihilistic advice to an eighteen-year-old.

The house manager calls us into a "wrap-up meeting." Here, we review our day and assess whether we have met the goals we made for ourselves during the morning meeting. The house manager hands me a printout with a script to read from.

" 'Hello,' " I say. " 'My name is Anna.' "

Everyone responds, "Hi, Anna."

Looking at the printout, I continue, " 'How many days have you been clean?' " I look at the house manager and say, "This one doesn't apply to me. What should I say?"

"You can just say 'This doesn't apply to me' and move forward."

"Got it. This doesn't apply to me. 'How are you feeling at this moment?' " I pause and try to identify my emotions from a laminated card with a rainbow wheel of "feeling" words. "At the moment I feel anxious. 'Did you complete your goals for the day?' " I look to the house manager again and say, "I wasn't here this morning, so I didn't make goals."

She nods.

"Actually, I guess I could say my goal was to check in, which I certainly accomplished." I gesture around the room, thinking I'm making a joke, but no one laughs. " 'What was the best part of your day?' I'm not sure I would say there was a best part today."

"Thanks, Anna," the house manager says. "Now you can pass the printout and the feelings card to Caitlyn."

After the meeting we go back to watching TV.

"Oh shit! He shouldn't have told her that," Shawn says.

"But do you think the guy will find out she's lying?" Mary says.

"Which guy?" Caitlyn says.

"You know, the other guy."

"Oh yeah, *that* guy."

"Oh shit, he might!" Shawn laughs, throwing her head back.

"I can't believe she did that!" Caitlyn says, pulling her knees up to her chest and covering her face with her arms.

The girls have been watching *Goliath* from season one. They are now on season three. They know what is happening and who "the other guy" is without needing to say names. I'm lost and I do not remotely know what is going on. All I can tell is that it's about a law firm and Billy Bob Thornton is the star.

In the hospital, what you watch has to be mutually agreed upon by everyone in the room. The policy is not to watch anything that might be triggering or otherwise upsetting to any of our fellow patients. There are certain things we are not supposed to watch without consent from everyone, like the news, and other things that we are flat-out not allowed to watch, like HBO's *Euphoria*. Disgraced lawyers played by known weirdo middle-aged actors, yes; teens with sparkly eyeliner who take Molly, no.

Since I cannot participate, I just sit there quietly, eyes never leaving the screen. I am becoming increasingly anxious the other girls might not like me because I am quiet. This has been a theme my whole life. I have been antisocial since puberty, preferring to watch others rather than participate. Or, even better, to get lost in my own thoughts and imagination, crafting made-up scenarios and arguments of which I am both the director and the only audience member. I have been trying to ask questions, but I feel like it is not enough. I create a scenario in my head where they interpret my lack of participation for bitchiness.

Sitting alone on one of the couches, Kristin has become increasingly more irritated, but it is unclear by what or who. She is exhaling deeply and audibly. She's fussing with her glasses repeatedly and scratching at her tattooed arms.

"I need to talk to the house manager or I'm going to explode," she says, getting up from the couch and pacing around the living room before returning to the couch. On the fourth repeat of this, Mary gets up and intercepts her near the front door. I watch them speak to each other in hushed tones, their bodies only inches apart. Then, Kristin knocks on the door of the house manager's office and goes in. I'm suddenly struck with panic that I have done something to make Kristin upset, but I cannot imagine what that could be. Perhaps just my presence. I get up off the couch and linger in the kitchen, pretending to make tea. I watch Kristin in my periphery as she speaks to the manager with exasperated gestures behind the glass walls of the office. Could merely being quiet make someone want to explode? I hate myself for not being more outgoing. I decide *that* will be my goal for the morning meeting, to be more outgoing.

Kristin leaves the office and blows past me, exhaling sharply.

"Do you want to do vitals?" the house manager says to me.

"What?" I regret how harshly the word exits my mouth.

"Vitals. You have to do them every morning and night. The house manager on duty, me tonight, will take your temperature, your blood oxygen, and your blood pressure. And give you your meds if you take any at night. Do you take any at night?"

I walk into the office and sit in a chair as she attaches an oxygen reader to my right pointer finger.

"I guess I'll take half a Klonopin. Also, how do I get my contact solution?"

"Oh." She rifles through a plastic bin and hands me my contact solution. "You can keep that in your room, actually. Since you're not here for addiction, you're allowed to keep all your toiletries in your room."

"Cool. Yeah, I'm not gonna drink my vitamin C face serum. Too expensive."

She removes the oxygen reader and wraps the blood pressure device around my upper arm, activating the pump with her hand. "Damn, ninety over sixty, you're going to live forever."

"Unfortunately, that's what they tell me."

Two

I cut myself for the first time at age fourteen. I showed Amanda two cuts as we sat in the minivan she had driven me home from school in. Looseleaf papers of half-finished homework assignments lined the floor by my feet. Amanda was a terrible student, but her teachers always passed her because she was so likeable.

"That looks bad," she said, looking at my wrist.

"I know. But it feels good," I said.

"I don't like to think of you doing that to yourself."

I didn't say anything.

"Do your parents know?"

"No. And I don't want them to. Please don't tell anyone."

"Fine, but you should stop."

"I probably will. Sometime."

Amanda was a junior in my high school when we met my freshman year, though I remembered her from middle school. She was outgoing, popular, and unpredictable. At a dance in our middle school gym, I remember her casually walking up to unsuspecting students and spastically dancing in front of them, while her equally popular friends looked on and laughed. Having eighth graders laugh at me was an embarrassment I knew my ego couldn't take, so I kept my distance from her.

I had already struggled socially in elementary and middle school, and was often ridiculed over my clothes, most of which were originally my mom's. My mom was an expert seamstress. She sewed all her own clothes while in high school, and the myth goes that she never wore the same outfit twice during a school year. In the late 1960s, she received a full scholarship to the Fashion Institute of Technology in New York City. Her father, a man formed by the economic values of the Great Depression and conservative ideas on women's ambition, wouldn't let her go. It was instead decided for her that she should be a teacher, and she remained in rural Pennsylvania, attending a local college for a teaching degree in art education. My mom saved most of the clothes she made for herself and bequeathed them to me when I was finally big enough to fit into them.

In contrast to the American Eagle, Gap, or Abercrombie my classmates wore, in my mom's clothes, my personal style read as flamboyant and dramatic, looking like a *Rumours*-era Stevie Nicks crossed with Fairuza Balk in *The Craft*—black dresses, dark brown lipstick, and pentacle chokers around my neck. "Please don't put a voodoo kurse on me," wrote a male classmate next to my eighth grade yearbook photo. But I did not want to be ordinary or fit in. I wanted to be exceptional, special. I leaned into how different I appeared, knowingly instigating my own ostracism. If I could not be accepted, fuck it, I wanted to be hated.

Amanda was not deterred by how I looked. She was intrigued. It made her want to know me. A few weeks into my freshman year she messaged me on AIM.

PunkyBoobster: yo, you made me late for class
TNT1999: what?
PunkyBoobster: is this Anna?
TNT1999: yea . . .
PunkyBoobster: this is Amanda, i'm a junior. you made me late for class.

TNT1999: i know who you are. i was home sick today.

PunkyBoobster: exactly

TNT1999: ??

PunkyBoobster: you pass me in the hallway every day between 5th and 6th period. i usually hang in the hall with people because who wants to go to world history? mrs. garvey is nutty. when i see you pass me, i know it's time for me to go into the classroom. but you didn't pass me, so i didn't get into the classroom before the bell rang and now i have a detention.

TNT1999: i'm sorry? but i don't really think i can apologize for that. seems like your fault.

PunkyBoobster: so true

TNT1999: i also have mrs. garvey this year. she is totally nuts.

PunkyBoobster: wanna hang out?

TNT1999: sure

Amanda and I became so inseparable that people at school thought we were dating. We spent every Friday and Saturday night together, either at her house or mine or going to local punk shows. She would rent R-rated movies for us that my parents would not let me see, like Harmony Korine's *Kids* and Todd Solondz's *Welcome to the Dollhouse*. Often we would sit on the floor of her bedroom threading thin cords of elastic with round, neon rave beads and various styles of letter beads, while in the background a TV played reruns of *Blind Date*, a dating game show hosted by a man with hair dyed too dark named Roger Lodge. We made bracelets with our favorite bands' names, each other's names, and inside jokes. FLAT IS BEAUTIFUL read one of Amanda's, a reference to a T-shirt she had picked up at Goodwill that had the same slogan printed across the front. The shirt was advertising a local landscaping company, but we never got over how funny it looked on Amanda, stretched across her large chest. We did not anticipate how many older men would comment on the shirt. She eventually stopped wearing it. The bracelet could remain a joke just for us.

The bracelets had the added bonus of hiding my cutting. Committing to long sleeves would have interfered with my personal style, an absolute non-option, but moreover, it would have been unbearable during humid New England summers. I simply refused to be uncomfortable in that way. Instead, I would be uncomfortable with stacks of cheap plastic Mardi Gras beads pressing into fresh cuts and tender scars. It made perfect sense to me.

I am not sure how I landed on cutting or where I first encountered it in society or pop culture as a coping mechanism, but I am certain I would have found my way to injurious behavior eventually. I danced seriously from age seven, at a prestigious preprofessional ballet school that funneled its students into the best dance companies in the world. Dance was my first love. It was my outlet, the place where I felt my true self expand. It taught me discipline; to show up even when I might have not felt like it; to be inside my body, not divorced from it. It also taught me how to gracefully push through pain. In my teen years I was forced to accept I was not skilled enough to make it as a professional. It crushed me, stripped me of my identity. Who would I be if not a dancer? Dance fell away from my life, but finding comfort in pain did not.

Keeping self-harm wounds hidden from my parents was easy. Their attention was consumed by the unraveling of their marriage, which began before I was even born. Childhood was marked by blowout verbal fights between them that happened everywhere—at home, in public, in front of friends, while on vacation. The concept that parents would keep their disagreements behind closed doors while remaining united in front of their children was completely foreign to me. My mom would scream in fits of rage, while my dad fought back with quiet passive-aggression. They were two people who never should have gotten married, wrong for each other from the outset. By the time I was in high school, my mom was using all her energy to hold together a marriage she frequently threatened to leave, while my dad had already checked out.

My melancholia, unlike my cutting, was impossible not to register, even for my parents. I was not rebellious—too afraid of my mother's rage to act out against her. I did not scream or cry. I just went numb. I retreated into myself. I stopped talking except for when I was with Amanda.

"What's *wrong* with you?" my mom said. "You're just moping around everywhere."

"I don't feel good."

"What doesn't feel good?"

"I don't know, I'm just tired."

"Well, I'm sick of you walking around here looking like you're miserable. You have nothing to be miserable about. Maybe you have food allergies."

"Yeah, maybe." I was pretty positive allergies didn't cause intense anger and a desire to harm oneself.

Sitting in the allergist's office on a plain gray upholstered chair, I looked over the stack of papers I had to fill out. They had lists of symptoms grouped by body system. I checked no on most of them. I had no incentive to lie. I checked yes on the ones I did experience— headaches, fatigue, body aches, foggy brain, and depression.

"Why did you check that?" my mom said, pointing to depression. I had felt her eyes on the papers as I marked off the checks. "Don't check that, you're not depressed."

I x-ed out the check in the yes column.

A few weeks later I found out I was allergic to eggplant and peppers.

"Maybe you'll feel better now, cutting those out of your diet," my mom said.

Unsurprisingly, this did nothing.

Three

Checks happen every two hours during the night. An overnight house manager opens my door and shines a flashlight at me to make sure I haven't escaped. The whole situation feels very *Girl, Interrupted*, but there is no hot male orderly and, as far as I can tell, none of the girls are stashing rotisserie chickens under their beds. Surprisingly I'm not cold during the night, despite the thin blanket. I owe this to the full leopard-print sweatsuit I slept in. And the long-sleeve shirt under that. And the wool socks.

At seven thirty a.m. a new house manager knocks on my door and tells me I have to go for blood work. I do not change my clothes. I have my vitals checked, take my seventy-five milligrams of Zoloft, and I'm out the door to the nurse's lab. Blood work is standard procedure in the hospital. I'm not afraid of needles, so having blood drawn has never bothered me.

"Do you faint?" the nurse asks me.

"No. Though I haven't eaten anything since last night. So maybe? I doubt it."

She skips small talk, which no one needs at this hour, and inserts the needle. Within sixty seconds she sends me back to Dalby.

"That was fast," the house manager says.

"I'm a fast walker," I say.

"I guess that's what happens when you live in New York City."

"Yeah, I think it's more because my mom is a really fast walker.

She used to go on these neighborhood walks, and I always wanted to go with her when I was a kid, but she told me I couldn't come unless I could keep up with her. She didn't want to be slowed down. I started walking really fast so she would let me go on the walks. And then it just stuck."

"Oh." The house manager gives a friendly laugh.

I have no idea why I told her that.

Since Covid, breakfast gets delivered to the houses instead of patients eating in the dining room or doing grab-and-go like we do for lunch and dinner. This does not make sense to me, but I do not ask questions. All I know is breakfast is *not* a meal you want delivered. It is supposed to arrive between 7:45 a.m. and 8:30 a.m., because that is how long it takes the kitchen staff to make the rounds to all the houses; it is pretty easy to deduce what the 8:30 a.m. eggs will taste like. Today, Dalby's breakfast arrives at 8:37, and it's not even lukewarm.

"Ew." Caitlyn is flicking a soggy piece of perfectly round pork sausage with her index finger. "I guess we were last."

I take a brick of congealed scrambled eggs and an oily hashbrown square out of a plastic to-go container, put them on a small plate, and walk into the living room for the morning meeting. The five of us go around and say how we are feeling and our goals for the day. I go last.

"Physically, I feel . . ." I scan the laminated card with the color-coded feeling words, the same one I held last night when I said I was anxious. "Tired. Emotionally, I feel . . ." I pause again, trying to find the correct word. "Numb. My goal for the day is to . . ." I've been planning all morning to say that my goal is to be more outgoing, that I realize my introversion can be interpreted as bitchiness, which is an effective defense mechanism, but one that ultimately makes me feel guilty and isolated. "Go for a walk" comes out instead.

Next, on the TV we watch seven minutes of a TED Talk whose topic is "gratitude." Following the video, the house manager asks if we want to share any thoughts we might have on gratitude. Mary says she is grateful for her doctors at the hospital who dedicate their time and energy to helping people. Caitlyn says she is grateful for people in her life who have not deserted her, especially parents, friends, and teachers. Mary agrees with her; she is grateful for this too. Shawn does not share. I listen with festering anger. "DO BETTER!" I want to scream at them. "THE PEOPLE YOU'RE SO GRATEFUL FOR LOVE YOU, AND YOU'RE FILLING THEM WITH A PAIN SO INTENSE IT FEELS LIKE DEATH. YOU'RE CREATING A TORNADO OF DESTRUCTION WHERE EVERYONE LOSES SOMETHING." Yet I stay silent, of course, because you cannot scream at people you do not know, and because in reality, I do not know any of their situations. What I do know is that they, like me, are all women, and being a woman is hard. I also know addiction is a motherfucker. I breathe in through my nose for three seconds and out for six, a relaxation technique I learned in a yoga class that stuck with me. In for three. Out for six. I repeat that two more times. I ease into listening to everyone else talk, knowing I will not share. I cannot share. I have nothing to share. Gratitude is a feeling I am unable to access at this present time in my life. All I feel is anger that I'm thirty-five and back to cutting myself, and that my life feels like a series of bad mistakes.

At the close of the meeting, I decide to immediately meet my day's goal. I zip up my jacket, pull on my boots, and begin walking the grounds. The campus is small, and I am unclear where I'm allowed and not allowed to walk, so I circle the walking paths between the houses and the perimeters of the parking lots over and over again. It's cold and no one else is outside. The grounds are still and as quiet as winter itself. While I am walking, I close my eyes and pretend I am hiking in Hunts Park with my mom. Hunts is a state park that I grew up hiking in. I know the paths so well, I can trace them in my mind. Photo albums my mom used to keep during the '80s and '90s are peppered with images of me at Hunts—my cousin and me with our arms stretched high above our heads, standing on an enormous granite boulder; me, standing on a pedestal with life-sized statues of wolves cast in oxidized metal that mark the trailhead; standing at the edge of the reservoir with my brother, us hugging, like we often did in photos. "Should we take the long way or the short way," either my mom or I will say to each other at the start of our walks. We always take the long way.

I open my eyes to make sure I am not about to walk into a car, or a bush, or a lamppost. I find myself in the parking lot of the intake building, where my car is parked. I walk over and stare at it. It's filthy. Dirty snow, ice, rain, and about a year without washing it has left a dingy film on its exterior. I run my fingers along the trunk and stand for a while with my fingertips resting lightly on the hood. In that moment it feels like a friend, or a familiar face, or perhaps simply a link to a life that feels as if it is rapidly receding. Metal and plastic, glass and rubber, a sturdy thing. The only sturdy thing. My eyes fill with tears. I continue on my walk.

There are cute wooden gazebos outside each building on the hospital grounds. These are the designated smoking areas. It strikes me as an unfortunate way to ruin such an otherwise quaint structure. It also strikes me that I would love to be smoking a cigarette right now. I realize, out of nowhere and apropos of nothing, that not having access to my phone has sent thoughts, sentences, and fully formed paragraphs flooding into my head at rapid speed and with seemingly no end. My brain is percolating with activity and is narrating every single move I am making. I am glad I brought a notebook with me to the hospital. What if I fill the notebook? What if I cannot get any more paper? Worse, what if I am having all these thoughts and I *do not* fill the notebook? That would be embarrassing. Or maybe it would just mean that the notebook had too many sheets to fill in only a week's time. It *is* college ruled. Who could fill a college-ruled notebook in a single week? But then again, the notebook is not standard size. It is small, around six by seven inches. I should be able to fill it without running out of paper. I hope. Am I a bad writer? Probably. I am likely very bad. What if this narration is some serious mental illness poking through, an illness only my phone was keeping at bay? No, that doesn't make sense. What if I am actually a genius? What if I am great at writing but I *also* hear voices? I wonder what that life will be like. It is possible for someone to discover they are a genius at thirty-five, right? To be honest, it does feel like something that would have been identified in my childhood. This walk doesn't feel very fun anymore.

I head back to Dalby to meet the other girls for lunch. Caitlyn is sitting on the porch steps with her knees pulled up to her chest, making her look childlike. She smiles her wide, dimpled smile and says, "You're right on time!"

Instead of feeling nervous to engage, I feel happy to see her.

Lunch is grab-and-go with the men's house.

"Why do we have lunch with Oscar House today?" I ask Kristin, who seems to have recovered from the previous night's aggravation. She is being totally friendly, which makes me happy, because it means it likely was not me that was upsetting her. Then again, I am worried that thinking it was about me is a symptom of soon-to-be-diagnosed narcissism. Sometimes, geniuses are also narcissists.

"We do all our meals with Oscar, actually," she says.

"But yesterday we weren't in the dining room with them. We only passed them on our way in."

"Probably because they walked to dinner and we decided to take the bus, so they got in early or something. But it's freezing and so dark at night, who cares how short the walk is. You'll see, most nights they'll take the bus with us. Our DBT and group meetings are with them as well. I'm not sure if you'll go to any of those because of the program you're in, but if you do, you'll see them."

"You know a lot about how this place works," I say.

"Yeah," Kristin says totally unselfconsciously, "this is my third time through their thirty-day rehab program."

I feel nervous that I've inadvertently walked her into this confession. If I apologize, it implies some sort of shame in her seeking help on multiple occasions. I know recovery does not always stick the first time and I don't want her to think I am forming a judgment, so instead I just nod and focus on being so utterly annoyed that we have to do everything with the men's house. I chose Dalby because I thought it would save me from interacting with men. I feel like someone should have warned me about this. Technically I don't know who would have done that, and I doubt that it is anyone's job. All Dr. Karr relayed to the hospital was that I did not want to live with men, and the hospital honored that request.

While Caitlyn, Mary, Kristin, and Shawn discuss group meeting with the guys in line for the hot bar, I speak to no one. I silently but *with attitude* pack my grab-and-go bag—a salad, butternut squash soup, cracked pepper potato chips, and one of the gluten-free chocolate chip cookies. These men may have done nothing to me personally, but I hate them and I hope the force with which I'm packing my lunch conveys this to everyone. I look around, ready to go. Everyone else is happily enjoying their conversations.

On the walk back from lunch, one of the guys, Adam, starts talking to me even though I'm walking ten paces ahead of the group.

"You look like you're going to a fashion show," he says.

I give him a nearly expressionless smile. This is the exact type of comment I hate. It is not a compliment, but it is not an insult, either. I would know what to do with an insult. This is just a subtle dig that is meant to make me feel othered. I am wearing a sweatsuit that I slept in. My underwear is clean, but that is it. I did not even change my socks. Besides, I feel personally offended that someone thinks I would go to a fashion show in a sweatsuit, even a leopard-print one.

"I also really like your jacket."

Okay, maybe the fashion show comment was a compliment after all. Loosen up, Tendler.

Then he adds, "And pink hair. Look. At. You."

I hate him. I hate him so much. None of these are compliments. Why is he commenting on the way I look? Why is he still even talking? Words cannot describe the antipathy I have for this conversation. The walk feels interminable. In this moment I am suddenly overcome with gratitude that I am in the female-only house. Thinking back to this morning's meeting—apparently, I do have the capacity for gratitude after all.

"I'll probably wear jeans on Monday," Kristin says to me and Adam. It's Saturday and she is also wearing sweats. "Weekends here are more laid-back."

I immediately regret only bringing sweats.

The confluence of the pandemic and my slipping mental health has robbed me of my personal style. Where once I lived almost exclusively in carefully sourced vintage dresses and Gucci from the early days of Alessandro Michele's maximalist reign, now I wear only roomy jumpsuits, pants with an elastic waist, and one pair of Levi's so worn in, its cotton twill is now closer to flannel than denim. During lockdown, a group text chat with my best girlfriends quickly became a hub for sharing our favorite shapeless garments.

At Dalby, Caitlyn, Kristin, Mary, Shawn, and I circle around the living room coffee table to eat our lunch and watch another terrible episode of *Goliath*. I find this routine, only two days in, incredibly comforting, even if I do not know what is going on in the show.

"How's your soup?" Mary asks me cheerfully.

"It's good. Thanks." Tears crest my lash line and drip down my cheeks. The girls notice, but let me cry without saying anything.

One of the afternoon activities available to patients is yoga. My mom is a yoga teacher, and when people find this out they tend to assume that I, too, love yoga. I don't love yoga, I hate yoga, but I will do yoga sometimes because I know how to push my body through discomfort, mental or physical, for the sake of exercise. It's a skill I learned from my many years practicing ballet and modern dance. In yoga, holding poses is boring to me. It feels like a waste of my precious time. I like moving. There is a moving type of yoga, vinyasa, but I don't like vinyasa classes. My experiences have shown me most teachers are not well enough versed in proper alignment to be teaching vinyasa in a way that is actually safe. Alignment is everything; it is how you protect your body from injury. I learned that from dance too. My mom, a truly great teacher, practices Iyengar yoga and teaches in a style inspired by this technique. Iyengar is all about holding poses in proper alignment, so while I hate holding poses, the proper alignment piece of it makes it the only type of yoga I'm willing to do. Though sporadic in my yoga practice, I still manage to be very snobbish about it—exercise-related snobbishness is also a holdover from dance. This whole scenario means I mostly avoid yoga, though today I have nothing else to do, so, yoga.

The class is held in a rec center that has a pool and a gym. Strangely, yoga is held in the pool room, not the gym. The room has floor-to-ceiling windows and is filled with light. The air is thick with warm humidity and the smell of chlorine. I roll out a mat, hoping some of the other girls from Dalby will show up, but only Adam walks in. I am furious. To deal with my anger, I focus my attention on doing every pose perfectly, as if I am going to get special recognition for being so good. I am not even that good at yoga—I lack the flexibility I used to have in my ballet years. Besides, this is barely yoga. It is closer to interpretive dance, swinging our arms around while we occasionally find our way into a two-second Downward Facing Dog or Triangle Pose. The teacher is a lanky woman with a breathy voice and frizzy hair. She is wearing a scarf and blinks very slowly and with great intention. She is not at all concerned with alignment. Adam is not good at yoga. I am better than him, and this makes me happy.

"Close your eyes," the teacher says. "Imagine yourself as a tree or a plant moving in the wind." I close my eyes but then squint one eye open to watch her sway manically with her arms stretched high above her head. I do not want to laugh, so I shut my eyes tightly.

I picture a small fern, low and compact. I have always liked ferns, their triangular fronds with tiny but hearty leaflets, their deep green color. If I am small like a fern, I am less exposed than a tree with high-reaching branches; the wind cannot whip me around. Yet, I am also more susceptible to being stepped on. Which is worse? I stop envisioning myself as a fern.

During Savasana, lying on the yoga mat that smells of disinfectant, the sun pours through the windowed room, enveloping my body in warm light. I feel incredibly calm for the first time since I arrived at the hospital. I don't even mind that Adam is lying only five feet away from me. I feel lucky to be lying on that floor instead of lying on the floor of my empty house in the woods, as I have been doing since I moved there from New York City two weeks ago. I feel lucky that I do not have a phone and that I can only check my email once a day. I feel lucky to be in a place where I cannot hurt myself and where hopefully I will glean some insight into what is wrong with me. The teacher ends Savasana and tells us to open our eyes. Adam and I sit up to see a flock of eleven wild turkeys directly on the other side of the glass walls.

"Oh wow." The words fall out of my mouth.

"It looks like they're watching us," Adam says.

I've never seen a wild turkey lit by a low winter-afternoon sun. Their feathers are beautiful and amazingly varied, iridescent in the light. The three of us sit and watch them in silence for a few minutes, until the teacher starts setting out illustrated cards in a serpentine path along the floor. This, for sure, has never happened in any yoga class I have taken.

"Walk along the path and look at the cards. Really look at them closely, but try not to read the words on them. Pick up the cards whose illustration resonates with you. Then read the words once you've picked one."

I walk the path a few times, allowing myself to give in to this weird practice. The words on the cards are small, and even if I wanted to read them, it would be impossible from five feet, two inches up. The images were likely paintings in their original form but have been shrunk down to fit on three-by-five cardstock. They are colorful abstracts, with people, animals, and plants. I keep coming back to a card with a woman's face surrounded by green leaves. I pick up the card and notice the leaves are ferns. The inscription reads YOUR SELF-WORTH CAN ONLY BE DEFINED BY YOU, NOT BY OTHERS. I'm not so sure about that.

"Does anyone want to share what came up for you during meditation or when you look at this card?" the teacher asks.

I sit silently, staring at the floor, as if by averting my eyes from the teacher she will forget I am there. Adam shares. He talks about his wife and his baby, how he misses them and wants to do better for them. He expresses his gratitude for being able to come to the hospital and go through the rehab program. It is heartfelt and honest and it is obvious to me that at this time, emotionally, he is way far out in front of me.

"Good job," he says, holding out his clenched fist for a fist bump at the end of class. I very tentatively give the fist bump back to him, laughing nervously, saying "thanks." I feel embarrassed, at first for him for fist-bumping me, but then for myself for being so anxious, so cold, so judgmental that I cannot accept a gesture of kindness for what it is. Adam seems like a nice person. I cannot be angry at him simply for being a man. I want to say "Good job" back to him and tell him that I think it's impressive that he came to yoga. None of the other men did. But I cannot get the words out and the moment passes.

Before we leave the room, we both walk up to the glass where the turkeys had been, trying to catch a last glimpse of them, but they have already retreated into the surrounding woods.

"It's cool we got to see them," Adam says.

"I agree, it really is."

When I return to Dalby, I go into my room to take a nap. Drifting in and out of sleep I hear music playing, a violin, but we are not allowed to have iPods, or phones, or speakers. I assume it's coming from the TV, but it has the crisp tonal quality of being not filtered by speakers. Also, why would someone be watching a TV show of a musician playing scales on a violin over and over? Now very confused and wide awake from curiosity, I decide this music is definitely not coming from the TV and is being played live. How can that be? I get up from bed and open my door.

The music is coming from the room next to mine—Shawn's. She is playing violin, and she is playing it very, very well. I am afraid she will hear me lingering outside her room and will stop playing. I don't want her to stop playing. I want to listen. I tiptoe slowly backward into my room and close the door, holding the knob with the latch retracted so it does not click. Shawn starts practicing a very intricate classical piece that sounds familiar but I cannot place it. I lie down on my bed and listen to Shawn play through the walls.

* * *

In the evening, a guest speaker comes to the house to talk about her experiences with Alcoholics Anonymous and to share her recovery story. Her name is Betty. Attendance to evening speakers is not mandatory, especially for me, as I am not in the hospital for addiction, but I decide to go. In the months leading up to the hospital I had begun attending Al-Anon and Nar-Anon meetings. Al-Anon and Nar-Anon are for the people whose lives are altered by the addictions of people close to them. Like Alcoholics Anonymous and Narcotics Anonymous, they are step programs, following the same principles and steps. When I started, everything was online because of Covid, making it easy to try out meetings, dip out of ones I did not like, and make a weekly commitment to the one I did. Since I would miss my meeting while in the hospital, I figured I could attend this one and practice the often-discussed AA, NA, Al-Anon, and Nar-Anon skill of taking in what serves me while letting the rest go. Kristin and Shawn do not participate. I get it. AA and its offshoots can skew very religious, so if you, like me, are not religious, the meetings can sometimes be difficult to sit through and hard to connect to. Yet Betty has shown up to our house on a very cold night, just days after the New Year. I sit and listen to her.

Betty talks about her slow decline into alcoholism, one that took many years. It started with a glass of wine before bed to sleep, then two glasses, then three. Next, she was getting blacked out at office parties and dinners, until finally she was jobless and driving drunk on a daily basis. She had "hit rock bottom." Betty's alcoholism was not just affecting her, it was ruining the lives of her wife and daughter. She sought out help, attended rehab programs, and did AA. She eventually got her job back and made amends with the people in her life whom she had hurt, namely her family.

The trajectory of Betty's story is a common one in meetings. We hear the stories over and over again, and often in the retelling of one's darkest moments, they flatten, bleeding into one another. "And then one day I got better"; "Then one day I stopped drinking," or "using," or, I suppose, "cutting." It sounds like something miraculous and otherworldly happened, a random epiphany that made a person turn things around, when in fact it was an incredible amount of hard work. The magical quality makes recovery feel unattainable, and after a while some of us—I—stop listening.

After getting sober, Betty's life got better, but not easier. Betty's daughter developed her own serious issues with addiction, for which Betty felt responsible, both genetically and by setting the example. She tells us that right before Covid, her wife died of pancreatic cancer. It took her life within six weeks of a surprise diagnosis. Then, in the thick of lockdown in summer 2020, her daughter passed away from drug- and alcohol-related health complications. The two people she loved most in the world were dead within a year of each other.

I sat, curled on the couch, waiting for what would inevitably come next in Betty's life: a relapse. Because how could anyone survive that sort of loss without turning to their vices? Followed by a recommitment to AA and the step program. Followed by perhaps four to six months since her last drink.

"Not long after my daughter died . . ." Betty pauses, her eyes filling with tears. Her hand clenches a small paper napkin that doubles as a tissue. Betty regains her composure. *Here it comes*, I think.

"Not long after my daughter died," Betty continues, "I celebrated twenty-five years sober."

The room is silent for a full minute.

Betty invites the three of us to share. Caitlyn and Mary tell brief versions of the events that immediately preceded them each checking into the hospital, a tiny but illuminating glimpse into what they've endured, what they are enduring. While listening, I realize something I have been picking up on since I checked in—we do share our stories with one another, but not in their totality. Specific details or comprehensive backstories are rarely offered. Instead, we speak in fragments and euphemisms. Quickly calibrating when I share, I'm careful to say "self-harm," not "cutting"; "suicidal ideation," not "I'd really like to die." Though slightly sanitized, it is the first time I'm revealing this information to any of my housemates.

Mary and Caitlyn are so young, but I can tell they understand they have their whole lives ahead of them. They are kind and not cynical. They appreciate their time in the hospital and their nearly thirty days sober. They have goals—to attend college, to become a lawyer—and as I listen to them talk, I am filled with so much emotion, so much hope for them, so much gratitude to have been able to share this brief time with them that I cannot help but cry.

"I wasn't sure I would get much out of this meeting, but I'm glad I'm here." I address Betty directly. "I'm so sorry about your wife and daughter. I can't imagine how devastating that must have been. For me, it's inspiring to hear you talk about facing such adversity without turning back to self-destructive behavior. I've had a really bad ye—" The words get stuck in my throat as I choke back tears. I so want, in this moment, to be able to get my words out without being sidelined by my overwhelming emotions, something that has been difficult lately. "Year," I finish. "My life feels like it's falling apart. Everything I thought I knew about my world is unraveling, and I feel powerless to stop it. I don't know how I'm ever going to feel better. Some days I feel utterly hopeless. My wish for myself is that one day I'll reach a place where I can face hardship—because I fear the worst is still to come—without trying to destroy myself."

Betty looks me in the eye and nods.

Four

"Hey, what's your name?"

I was walking up the stairs to freshman English class when a very popular senior put his arm around my shoulder and asked this.

"Anna," I said, not looking at him.

"Anna. You have a cool look, Anna. It's different."

"Okay." I was still walking.

"I'm Ethan," he said.

"I know who you are," I said. Ethan was a jock and traditionally hot. The type of guy who would look right past me if we had been in middle school together. Ethan's approval of me could significantly help my reputation. It could also make the girls who had made my life hell for the past three years seethe with envy. The latter appealed to me.

"Alright, Anna, I'll see you tomorrow." He peeled off me and walked into a classroom. I walked to third period smiling.

The next day I felt Ethan's arm drape over me.

"Fancy meeting you here," he said.

"Imagine!" I said.

"You're pretty. But you dress crazy."

"I thought I had a cool look?"

"You do, but you'd be prettier in, like, some more normal clothes. Maybe some pants that weren't so . . . baggy?"

"I like my pants. My mom made these pants when she was in college." They were a pair of high-waisted khaki corduroys, perfectly fitted in the hips and butt, with wide-cut legs. I was wearing them with burgundy Doc Martens boots and a black Doc Martens baby tee printed with a photo of two young boys hugging and text that read SOLE BROTHERS. I'd bought the shirt a year earlier at Yellow Rat Bastard, a clothing shop on lower Broadway that existed in a time when SoHo was still cool.

"Yeah, but, like, who wears their mom's clothes?" he said.

"I guess I do."

He laughed, removing his arm from my shoulder, heading down a flight of stairs as I continued straight to fifth period.

That Saturday morning Ethan showed up at my house with no warning.

"Hi," I said, opening the door. I was still wearing pajamas, a blue tank top–and-shorts set. I had my period and felt disgusting.

"Hi," he said, still straddling his bike on my lawn.

"What's up?" I stalled, not knowing what to do. My parents weren't home. I didn't know what letting Ethan into my house might mean to him or for me.

"Don't you want to hang out?" he asked as if I'd already slighted him.

"Sure," I said.

"Can I come in?"

"My parents aren't home. I don't know when they'll be back. Could be any minute."

"Cool." He opened the door and walked through with confidence. "Cool house." He looked up at the tall, vaulted living room ceiling.

I hated my house. It was contemporary-style architecture with white walls and sharp angles. I thought it was ugly, cold, and unwelcoming. My parents had it built, and we moved in the summer before I started fifth grade. They fought about the cost of it constantly.

"Let's sit down," Ethan said. I led him into the family room.

Ethan kissed me the second we sat on the couch. I suppose I knew this would happen. It was why I brought him to a room whose windows didn't face the driveway. The kiss was hard and messy and unpleasant. I wanted it to stop, but I also didn't. It was the validation I needed, that I'd never gotten from guys at school.

So far, only older men had noticed me. A year earlier, I was shopping at a vintage store in SoHo when two men in their thirties approached me.

"Hi," one of them said to me, standing very close.

"Hi," I said quickly, while continuing to shuffle through the rack of clothes.

"My friend and I were wondering how old you are?"

"What?" I said. I had heard him, but I panicked and didn't know how or even if I should answer. My question bought me a few seconds to think.

"How old are you?" the other one said, sliding to the opposite side of me so I was between them.

"I'm thirteen."

"Anna!" My mom called my name from across the store. The men turned to see her.

"You look really good for your age," one of them said, the other signaling with his head toward the door.

"Thanks." I didn't make eye contact. They left the store.

"What did they say to you?" my mom asked, meeting me where I was looking at vintage band shirts.

I was embarrassed but told my mom what they had asked and what I had said.

"You did the right thing," she said. "Just be friendly enough to not make anyone mad, but don't ever give anyone more information. Try to end the interaction as quickly as possible."

"Okay," I said. I knew by "anyone" she meant "men."

Ethan pushed me onto my back and got on top of me, trapping my small frame beneath him. My head was pinned to the couch cushions by his tongue sharply entering and exiting my mouth. He used his knees to open my legs. He pushed himself against me until I felt his erect penis jamming against my crotch through his shorts. As I lay underneath him, I wondered if he could feel the maxi pad in my underwear. I didn't want him to know I had my period, for fear he would be disgusted. After ten minutes Ethan got off me as abruptly as he'd pinned me. I sat up, relieved.

"I gotta go. It was nice to see you," he said.

"You too," I said.

I walked him to the door, we hugged, and he biked away.

The next week in school Ethan again threw his arm around me when we passed each other in the hallway.

"You should come to the mall on Saturday night. I work at Abercrombie and I can get you a discount," he said.

"There's no way I'm wearing Abercrombie."

"Fine!" he said, laughing, "but if you dressed more normal you'd be totally datable. Come by anyway. I'm done at nine thirty; we can hang out after."

"I don't understand why you are going to the mall so late," my dad said. He was driving me to meet Ethan at nine p.m.

"I told you, my friend doesn't get off work until nine thirty. We are meeting after he's done and going to Jessica's house with a bunch of other people." There was no one else besides Ethan I was going to meet, and I didn't have any idea what we'd be doing after he closed Abercrombie.

"Call me if you need anything or if plans change," my dad said.

"I don't need anything! These are the plans!" I exited the car.

I'd been in that mall a hundred times, but never that late at night. Its emptiness was eerie and unnerving. Entering Abercrombie I saw three salesgirls, all young and pretty.

"Is Ethan here?" I asked one of them.

"Um, yeah? I think he's in the back."

She disappeared behind a door, then quickly reappeared.

"He'll be right out," she said, returning to a table where she had been folding T-shirts.

Ethan exited the door and looked at me, surprised.

"Hey, what's up?" He seemed embarrassed.

"What's up with you?" I said, confused but playing cool.

"Just, you know, work. We're about to close though, so I can't hang out."

"Oh, got it. Do you want to hang out when you're done?"

"Nah, I can't tonight. I have plans."

I nodded.

"What are you doing at the mall?" he said.

"I was here with a friend, but I'm taking off soon." I knew he knew it was a lie.

"Thanks for stopping by. I gotta finish up now."

"Have a good night. See you Monday." I walked out of Abercrombie. I sat on a plastic chair at a table in the food court. The table was still dirty from someone's pizza. I got up and dropped a quarter into a pay phone nearby.

"Hello?" My dad answered the house phone on the second ring.

"Hey, it's me. So, my friend had an emergency. His parents called him and said he had to come home right away and babysit his brother." Ethan didn't have a brother. "I'm so sorry, I know you probably just got home. Do you think you can come get me?"

"Sure, do you need me to take you to Jessica's?" my dad said.

"What?" There was a short pause. "Oh, no, that's okay. I'm pretty tired. I'll just come home."

"Are you sure?"

"I'm sure," I said.

Fifteen minutes later I was back in my dad's car.

"I'm sorry your plans got messed up," he said.

"That's okay, it happens." I turned my head to count the street-lights as they passed my passenger-side window. Even though it was dark, I did not want my dad to see my face, fearing it was written with embarrassment. Though I am sure he saw through my story about Ethan's babysitting emergency, he graciously did not pry.

After I hit puberty, my dad disconnected from my life significantly. It wasn't that our relationship was adversarial, we were just strangers to each other. He worked as a school psychologist in a public elementary school, and that was the demographic where he excelled. Once I was in middle school, it felt like he could no longer relate to me. Conversely, the older I became, the more my mom treated me like a friend. She and I spent so much more time together that I believe my dad came to see me as an extension of her. In pulling away from her, my dad also pulled away from me.

Our love of music was still something my dad and I shared, though. Driving home that night, he popped in the *Simon and Garfunkel's Greatest Hits* CD and skipped a few tracks until it landed on "The Boxer." We both sang along.

Ethan and I stopped talking at school after that, but a month or so later, on another weekend morning when my parents happened to be out of the house, my doorbell rang. I crept downstairs on my tiptoes, entering a bathroom that had a small, curtained window facing the front lawn and driveway. I stood close to the window, my eye up to a slit in the curtains. Ethan's bike lay on its side on my lawn, one of the tires still slowly turning. I shifted my position slightly so I could see my front door. He rang the doorbell twice, then three times. I waited, breath held. After a third ring he turned from the door, jumping over the three small stoop steps onto the grass. He picked up his bike and I watched him ride down my long driveway until he disappeared behind the trees.

Five

I'm sleeping terribly here. A recurring dream has plagued me for the past year and it comes to me now on my second night in the hospital. In the dream, a claustrophobic room thrown into shadow by low light resembles a detective's office from a 1940s noir film. There is a faceless man in the room. All I can hear is his voice, and we are arguing. It is an argument I'm not winning.

"I'll tell everyone I'm not crazy," I say to the voice, with little confidence in my own.

"Who will believe you?" the voice asks.

"I'll convince them! People will listen to me!"

"You *are* crazy."

"I'm not crazy!" I am now yelling, as if yelling will convince him.

The voice just laughs, and I am left alone in the room. The door disappears. There is no way out.

When I awake from the dream my sweatshirt is damp and stuck to my torso with sweat. I'm hyperventilating. I lie in bed for a while, trying to calm down before I finally get up for breakfast. I take my Zoloft and do vitals with the house manager. It is the same woman from my first day, so she does not comment on my low blood pressure. It's old news now. I eat an orange and a granola bar, the kind that crumbles into a thousand bits when you take one bite. I make myself green tea from microwaved tap water in a paper cup that reads NOT MICROWAVABLE. As I am finishing my tea, a man from the kitchen staff shows up to Dalby with a spare coffeepot that will allow us to boil water on the extra burner of the coffee maker. The original coffeepot the girls used to boil water broke weeks ago, long before I ever arrived. In my first two wrap-up meetings I heard the girls request a new pot, noting that they had been asking over and over with no result. "I know, I'm sorry it's taking so long," the house manager had responded sympathetically. "I'll ask again."

"We got a spare coffeepot!" I relay to Kristin while trying to peel my orange in one unbroken ring.

"Oh my god, *finally*!" Kristin says, punching the air above her head.

Shawn walks into the living room, rubbing moisturizer on her face in small circles. "What happened?" she asks.

"We got a coffeepot for hot water!" I say.

"FINALLY." Shawn sits down on the couch next to me, still massaging her face. "Mary, we got a coffeepot!" she yells as Mary enters the room.

"Oh wow! We can finally make tea. Or, you guys can make tea, I don't really drink tea, but I'm happy for you!" She is genuinely happy for us. "Caitlyn!" Mary says as Caitlyn walks into the kitchen.

"Mary!" Caitlyn says back to her.

"Look what's on the counter."

"Whoa! Finally! I'm gonna make hot chocolate later."

"Oh, me too," I say, remembering the packets I swiped from the snack table at intake.

Being the bearer of good news to the rest of the group, to join in this celebration, no matter how small, makes me feel like I am part of their team. In this quotidian exchange, they allow me into something I am barely a part of, and they do so enthusiastically. They do not question my own excitement over the new coffeepot—I having suffered without it for less than seventy-two hours—instead they match my excitement with their own. I feel the energy of our group change instantaneously. We are no longer four women plus one new girl; we are five.

After breakfast I walk to the Doctors Office building. Why it is called this I do not know, since there seem to be doctors working in every building. The building is small, like a colonial house from the 1700s still commonly standing in New England today. The only thing modern about it is the intercom outside the front door, which allows someone inside to screen the person buzzing and unlock the door.

"Hello," a crackled voice comes through the speaker.

"Hi, this is Anna. I have an appointment with Dr. Philips."

"Come on in and have a seat on the couch, he'll be right down."

I hear the lock click and I push the door open to find a room even more New England-y than the outside. It is decorated in Federalist style, a design and architectural movement unique to the burgeoning United States in the eighteenth and early nineteenth centuries. It looks nothing like Dalby or Main, or the building where I did yoga yesterday. The carpeting is a patterned navy blue; the furniture is dark mahogany and looks beautiful but not comfortable. An old grandfather clock ticks loudly in the otherwise quiet room. It is nine a.m. on the dot. I am never late for anything—a consequence of growing up with a mom and brother who were perpetually late for everything. Getting out of the house was an anxiety-ridden affair of people yelling at each other for their tardiness, the effect of which never made anyone move faster but instead made the whole situation more frantic and stressful.

I take a seat on a shallow settee upholstered in green chintz fabric—the historical accuracy is impressive. I recently renovated the interior of my own home—the one I just moved into in Connecticut—from a neutral Restoration Hardware advertisement to a sort of haunted Victorian dollhouse. I wallpapered every wall. I painted every ceiling. One of them I even tiled, an ode to Rafael Guastavino, the famous

Spaniard who tiled the ceilings of Ellis Island and Grand Central's Whispering Gallery. Each piece of furniture I own is an antique carefully chosen from a dealer or rehomed from my grandparents' house. There is no overhead lighting in most of the living spaces, as was custom in old houses. Instead, low, warm light glows from sconces and lamps, many of which I have made. I took inspiration from the Aesthetic and Arts and Crafts movements of the nineteenth century. The Arts and Crafts movement, spearheaded by designer William Morris in England, embodied the ethos that rooms should be entire environments, every inch considered. If a wall was white it was purposeful, not the default as it is today. There is not a single room in my house that does not feel like its own cocoon. Settees are plentiful.

This settee I'm sitting on is across from a fireplace with a roaring fire. There is a painting of a ship at sea above the mantel. If you overlook the four boxes of tissues scattered throughout the room, it looks more like a house museum than an office at a psychiatric hospital.

"Hello, Anna." A man in a shirt and tie enters the room. He appears to be in his early fifties. He is soft-spoken and immediately calming. "I'm Dr. Philips, the head psychologist here. I'm going to be performing your psychological testing today. Why don't you follow me and we will get started."

"Thank you," I say in a small voice, and follow him up a narrow, creaky set of stairs to a plain conference room suited to an office building from the 1980s. The table is Formica, not wood like the furniture downstairs. It looks wholly bland and out of place among the rest of the building.

"You can have a seat here." He gestures to a disappointing, worn-in desk chair. I think about asking, "Can we bring up that settee from downstairs real quick? I'd be more comfortable in that." I decide not to. This doctor doesn't know me and therefore doesn't realize that an antique settee truly *is* something I sit on regularly. He might think I am making a different joke—that a settee is uncomfortable or even ridiculous. I'm unwilling to provoke a laugh at the expense of an antique settee, especially one upholstered in a historically accurate chintz.

Dr. Philips explains the test will have many sections and it will test my general cognition, memory recall, ability to solve puzzles, arithmetic knowledge, and vocabulary. The whole thing will take about three hours. I am nervous, but at the same time excited. It has been a long time since I have taken a test. This could be the moment when I discover I'm a genius. Or at least very, very, very, very smart. I wish I had slept better.

The first test is to draw a series of nine images exactly how I see them from a card Dr. Philips is holding up in front of me. The images are basic line drawings, easy to replicate, but I want to get them perfect so I pay close attention to all the details. I take my time so my drawings look *exactly* like the ones on the cards. I am really excelling at this. It is so easy.

When I we get through all nine cards, Dr. Philips hands me a fresh sheet of paper.

"Now draw as many of those images as you can from memory," he says.

Fuck. How did I not see that coming? I panic, having focused so hard on getting each drawing perfect that I did not attempt to commit the shapes to memory. My anxiety further blurs the simple line drawings, making them impossible to recall. I draw seven of the nine, but I have no idea how accurate they are, and Dr. Philips gives no indication of how well I've performed.

Next, I am given a set of red and white blocks. I do a series of timed exercises where I arrange the blocks to match designs printed on a page. I laugh because of its striking similarity to a scene from my favorite movie, *The Royal Tenenbaums*.

"You're quite fast at this," Dr. Philips remarks. The patterns continually get more difficult, but I am surprising even myself at how fast I'm moving. Until I get stuck, reversing one of the blocks. My brain is unable to correct how it fits into the space, and I end up just sticking it randomly onto a white block. My design does not look like the photo.

It is now time for a Rorschach test. I have always wanted to do a Rorschach test. They, too, remind me of movies, like when a forensic psychologist is trying to diagnose a sociopath. The Rorschach, or ink-blot test, involves a series of abstract ink designs from which I must interpret what I see. Dr. Philips pulls the first card, and I am disappointed that I can only relay the world's most cliché answer: "It looks like a mask."

From that point forward I see a variety of dynamic scenes: two woman making pottery, connected by an energy field at their heart chakras; an elk standing by a lake in a field speckled with wildflowers; a map of Paris, complete with the Eiffel Tower and the long promenade of the Tuileries Garden; a man, shot in the back, lying face down, blood seeping into his clothes; a sinister pair of pliers with bursts and splatters of blood. I also see a lot of vaginas.

Following the Rorschach, I am presented with a series of illustrations for which I must provide a story with an approximate beginning, middle, and end. Technically this test is called the Thematic Apperception Test, and it is used to measure one's perception of interpersonal relationships, but I will not learn this until later. Right now I naively think it is measuring my storytelling abilities. I worry this will be difficult, but it is in fact remarkably easy. Black-and-white drawings of ambiguous scenes involving people and places immediately call to mind rather complete stories of who these people are, what they are feeling, and the circumstances of their world. Most of them center around women. In one image I see a young girl who is leaving her family home on a farm to attend school. She's the first of her family to leave, let alone be educated, and she feels the ambivalent pull of her situation. Now she will separate herself both geographically and intellectually from her family, the weight of responsibility sitting cozied to the lightness of freedom. It reminds me of the path my mom never got to take. Another image portrays to me a woman consumed by anguish upon discovering her unfaithful husband. In another I see a woman haunted by a cloaked figure who hovers behind her wherever she goes. I describe to Dr. Philips how the figure uses the woman's increased paranoia against her for his own gains. It is a striking resemblance to my recurring dream, the one I had again last night. In one image I see a woman who is grief-stricken to find that her sister has, in the wild throes of mania, hurled herself down a flight of stairs. In the last I see a poet, in beautiful and quiet solitude overlooking a European city at night, full of hope.

The storytelling portion of the testing ends, and we move on to the section that is most likely to prove that not only am I not a genius, but I might not even be that smart: numbers, arithmetic, and puzzles. First, I must memorize number sequences, which does not go well. Next, I must solve increasingly difficult math problems. Dr. Philips instructs me to do this "without the help of pen and paper." To which I respond, "This is going to be very bad." It doesn't matter that I can't use pen and paper, they wouldn't help me anyway. Aside from figuring out a 20 percent tip on a restaurant bill, I have not done math in decades. My academic arithmetic career ended after my junior year of high school and I never looked back. I add, subtract, and multiply numbers using the calculator on my cell phone, like any person in the twenty-first century does. After two questions I freeze, my brain completely blank. I am unable to proceed further.

"I'm very bad at math," I say to Dr. Philips as he turns the page to puzzle sequencing.

I think I correctly identify at least three of the puzzle sequences, but it is entirely possible I've identified zero. In examining the last few sequences, I have no idea what I am looking at.

The following puzzle subtest requires me to look at a shape and choose three smaller shapes that can fit together perfectly to form the one larger shape. I do twelve of these. Some are easy, some are not, all are anxiety-provoking.

"How was that?" Dr. Philips asks when I finish.

"You tell me."

He laughs. "Your answers were mixed in quite an odd way. You got some very easy ones incorrect, but you also got some very difficult ones correct, and clearly not as a fluke."

"Interesting." I nod, trying to think about what this might mean.

We reach the second-to-last section of the test, in which Dr. Philips provides a word and I supply the definition.

"You have a strong vocabulary," he says to me, which I appreciate because I have never considered myself a person with a particularly strong vocabulary.

We come to the last word: *palliate*.

"That one I don't know," I say sheepishly.

He nods and puts the card down.

"What does it mean?" I ask.

"It means 'to ease' or 'to make more comfortable.' You've most likely encountered the word in relationship to the medical field, as in 'palliative care.'"

"Ahh yes, of course." I had heard that word used many times when my grandmother was dying of cancer. I know with confidence that I will never forget what "palliate" means now.

The final part of the test involves answering random trivia questions. Like the puzzles and math before, not my forte. I feel embarrassed when I cannot remember who wrote *Sherlock Holmes* and relieved when I remember that Lewis Carroll wrote *Alice in Wonder-*

land. I feel nothing when I cannot recall the circumference of the earth. Why would I ever know the circumference of the earth offhand? I wonder what percentage of people answer *Walt Disney* to the *Alice in Wonderland* question.

The entire test takes three hours and thirty minutes, but Dr. Philips gives me three more written tests to fill out on my own time today. I walk back to Dalby feeling neither particularly like a genius or like an idiot, but like a woman who is anxious and depressed, who loves stories and drawings but hates math and puzzles.

At the house I immediately fill out the take-home tests. They have very official names—NEO Five Factor Personality Inventory, Personality Assessment Inventory, and Trauma Screening Inventory. Each of them asks a series of questions or poses situations for which I choose a number from zero to five that rates how closely I identify with it. For example: *I get violent urges to cause someone bodily harm.* I fill in the bubble marked zero—*Do not identify at all.* Conversely, to *I prefer to be alone rather than in a social setting*, I answer five—*Strongly identify.* I am very anxious about answering the questions accurately and honestly, which makes the tests difficult to complete. There are times when I *identify strongly* with a situation, but other times when I only *somewhat identify* with that same situation. Which do I choose? What if my answers summate to a description of me that is inaccurate, rendering this entire evaluation purposeless? What if I overstate my mental anguish and I end up looking insane? Worse, what if I understate it and everyone thinks I am fine? I check and recheck my answers.

I take a break. I bundle up in a T-shirt, long underwear, sweats, and my jacket. I walk to the rec center for a Tai Chi class that is listed on the TODAY'S ACTIVITIES board in the living room. Tai Chi sounds relaxing. Once in the rec center, I take off my jacket, sweats, and long underwear top, until I am wearing only a T-shirt and long underwear bottoms. I roll out a yoga mat and take a seat. No one shows up to the class, not a teacher, not another student. After fifteen minutes, I re-dress in all my layers, roll up the mat, and walk back to Dalby.

At 4:45 p.m., Kristin, Mary, Caitlyn, Shawn, and I do art therapy. The therapist gives us each a sheet of white paper and dumps a bunch of markers onto the kitchen table.

"Close your eyes and make a line scribble with your nondominant hand until I say stop."

By the time she says stop it feels like we have been scribbling for a long time.

"Now," she continues, "create a drawing from the scribbles by adding lines, erasing lines, and adding color."

I cannot see any discernable image through my scribbles. I turn the paper a few times. At one angle I see a penguin wearing sunglasses and a scarf. Eventually three serpents emerge, which takes me by surprise. I have, and have had since childhood, a severe snake phobia. I cannot look at them in movies or even see photos of them. Once in Manhattan while walking in Washington Square Park, I saw a man holding an enormous snake, and I had to backtrack and walk around the park instead of walking through it, as a way to bypass the snake. The outskirts did not feel far away enough, though. I dissolved into a panic attack. Even clothing with faux snakeskin print makes me nauseous.

My drawing becomes an aerial view of a pond. Two serpents coil around each other in the water with their red forked tongues, the third is removed and on its own.

We go around the table and share our drawings—a fish jumping out of the ocean, a field of sunflowers with a rainbow arching over it, a clown—and our own interpretations of them. They are all so different, and equally fascinating.

I go last.

"Why three snakes?" the therapist asks me.

"I don't know, really. This is simply what presented itself to me. I hate snakes. But these snakes don't really feel malevolent to me, I suppose."

"What does the number three mean to you?" she says.

I'm reaching for an answer, trying to satiate her need for an explanation.

"I guess I like astrology, and usually when you look at a person's astrological chart you look at three placements—the sun sign, the moon sign, and the rising sign. Maybe that's it?"

"Maybe," she says, unconvinced. "Anything else?"

"There are three members in my family? Me, my husband, and my dog. I really don't know. It could literally be nothing." She gives me an annoyed look, unsatisfied. I assumed everything we said in art therapy would be a right answer. I guess not.

As the therapist packs up her box of markers, Caitlyn, Mary, Shawn, Kristin, and I dissolve into an excited conversation about astrology and our respective birth charts. We are so engrossed in one another that we don't even notice the art therapist walk out the door.

After grab-and-go dinner, everyone receives phone calls from family and friends on one of the landline phones in Dalby House. Phone calls always happen in the evening, after dinner but before the wrap-up meeting. When it rings, whoever is closest to the phone answers.

"Hello?"

"Hi, is Caitlyn there?"

"Sure, one second." The answerer holds the phone away from her ear and yells, "CAITLYN!" Caitlyn runs to the phone and then disappears to a more private area of the house. This pattern repeats itself six or seven times, each time the caller asking for a different girl. It feels like high school, when the phone would ring and you would have no idea who was calling until you answered it. Were I a different person I might feel nostalgic watching this antiquated scene play out, but I do not. I love to screen my calls.

I have not given the Dalby phone number to anyone. I told my girlfriends to contact me by email. Their emails are sweet, but also hilarious, because my friends know laughter is the best thing for me at this moment. Before I checked in to the hospital, I was working my way through the best movies of 1999 in virtual watch parties with my friends Carmel and Sarah.

Anna, We are thinking about you so, so much and hoping everything is going as well at the hospital, one email from Carmel began. We also wanted to remind you of a few dozen social commitments you made to us upon your return. This was followed by a list of twenty movie titles from 1999. Another friend wrote me: You know that healing candle I started burning for us the day you went into the hospital?? Well it finished burning! We're all done healing!

My mom also emails me regularly. Very regularly. Ten times in the first three days to be precise. Her emails are funny too, but in a less purposeful way than my friends'. Exactly twenty-four hours after I'd checked in, I emailed my mom to tell her everything was going okay, that I liked the girls I was living with, and that I hoped Petunia—my French bulldog she was babysitting—wasn't being too bad. I ended this last sentence with an exclamation point to show it was a rhetorical joke. Petunia was definitely being bad. She was a dog with a lot of behavior issues, but I assumed my mom would shield me from this information so as not to make me feel guilty about asking her to watch Petunia.

Anna! my mom responded. I am so happy to hear from you! I have been worried. Petunia was terrible yesterday, Friday. She bit your brother once and growled at him twice. She got a time-out in her room, the den. I think she was upset leaving you and her home. She just needed time to settle in. She has been really good today. Then two minutes later she sent a follow-up email that simply read, No problems feeding Petunia today.

The next morning, at eight thirty a.m., she sent an email that said, I am at your house. The alarm went off. Three hours later she sent a follow-up. I am sorry to bother you. After the alarm went off, a police officer came to the house. He was okay with my story, that I am your mom. The alarm company called, but they could not tell me how to turn off the alarm. I told them the code, but they said there was also a word code. I did not know that. Also, if you are able to, I think you should turn down the heat in the house. When away, you can keep the house at sixty.

The frequency, mundanity, and abundance of unnecessary information contained within my mom's emails were the reasons I didn't give my mom the house phone number. I worried she wouldn't not be able to call. I didn't give it to my friends because I wanted to try as much as possible to sequester myself from the outside world. I wanted pure healing with no interruption. Still, seeing the excitement on the girls' faces when they receive their nightly calls makes me wish I had not isolated myself in this way. What was I trying to prove? I bounce back and forth between my room and the living room, trying to find a place where I feel like I am neither hiding nor intruding on people's phone calls. For a while I sit at the top of the stairs and listen to the other girls' conversations. They all sound happy, which makes me happy and also sad.

In my room I pick up my drawing from art therapy. Now, I do not think it has anything to do with astrology or my family. It is just the best I could do with a scribble of lines.

Six

My sophomore year I was in love with a junior named Julian. We met when I was "manager" of the boys cross-country running team. Manager of any high school sports team was a fake job, albeit one that earned you a varsity letter jacket should you want to pay for one; I did not. Being the "manager" meant I recorded the boys' finish times at practice and at races. There were no other duties. The title itself was bestowed upon me in an act of pity by the coach, who noticed I was always hanging around at practice, waiting for my friend Elaine, who was on the girls team.

"Why don't you go home? Where are your parents?" the coach said to me one afternoon as I was sitting on the bleachers.

"They're at work," I said.

"You look like you'd be a fast runner. Do you want to join the team?"

"I can't run. I'm a dancer. I might get injured."

"Well at least make yourself useful," he said, waving me down to the track. "Here"—he handed me a Seiko stopwatch, a clipboard, and a pen—"record their times when they get to this yellow line."

"Sure."

"You're the boys cross-country manager now. You'll do this at practice and at races."

The title and responsibility made me feel important, even if it just meant clocking a time and writing it down. Now the boys would have to come to me to see if they had done well or totally whiffed it. I had power. Or at least, my presence wasn't superfluous.

The boys and the girls cross-country teams were all close friends, spending most of their time outside school together. I was folded into that group, though remained very much on the outside. On weekend nights we would drive around to different parking lots and just . . . sit. Some nights we would watch Peter, the team clown, binge eat—two hot dogs, a large bag of Smartfood popcorn, an entire to-go order of penne alla vodka, a bottle of blue Gatorade, and a carton of 2 percent milk—to see how long it took for him to vomit. It was utterly gross, watching someone puke out the driver's side of their Toyota Corolla in a 7-Eleven parking lot for laughs, but I endured it to be close to Julian.

I liked Julian because he seemed different from the other guys on the team, a little weirder, a little more offbeat, though this assessment hinged largely on the fact that he was quiet. He paid attention to me—not overtly, but I would catch him looking at me, our eyes connecting for a moment before they averted. He listened when I spoke and he laughed when I said something funny. I took this to mean that he thought I was interesting and funny, which in turn made me think he was interesting and funny. Julian was nice and he was smart, though it is difficult to describe him, or what drew me to him, in anything other than vague terms. Perhaps that is because in high school, our desire for another person *is* vague and nondescript. As teens we rarely know why we like someone, just that we do.

At one a.m., after one of these group nights out, I received a long email from Julian. The contents offered his thoughts on cars, movies, and clothing I had worn that he liked. These emails became a common recurrence. They were creative. Background skins of

Angelina Jolie. Multiple font styles. Silly subject lines. They took effort, the kind you allocate to someone you have a crush on. In person and at school we rarely spoke. I understood implicitly that he did not want to be romantically linked to me in public at our small-town high school.

One night, he brought me along to a game of Magic: The Gathering that a few guys from the team played. I figured some of the other girls would be there, but when I arrived, I realized it was just me. It felt like a test—not for me, but for the guys. How would they react to my presence? Would they have thoughts about Julian and me being together outside the boundaries of the greater group? Might they have unkind things to say about me, perhaps teasing Julian for bringing me along? The answers to these tests would be calculated and digested outside my presence, of course. Data to be analyzed only when the boys were alone, none of it ever explicitly communicated to me. I silently watched while sixteen- and seventeen-year-olds sat at a folding table and traded cards illustrated with therianthropic characters. *Fyndhorn Elder; Creature—Elf; Add (two little icons of trees) to your mana pool.* I was furious that these boys would dictate my position in Julian's life.

Julian's attitude toward me in the following months remained distant in the presence of his teammates. At the end of parking lot nights, Julian would often drive me home, though rarely did we go straight there. We would drive around for an hour, on a continuous loop snaking through the winding roads of our town and the surrounding towns, sometimes talking, sometimes not.

"Second," Julian would say as we approached a curve. He'd press the clutch and I would move the stick shift into second gear for him.

"I don't think you should trust me to do this," I said. I didn't know how to drive a stick.

"I trust you, you can do it. Fourth," he said, his voice calm and measured as I upshifted. Julian was a good driver, but fast. We never discussed our drives with other members of the team.

I can recall us kissing one night, me sitting between his legs, his arms wrapped around me on a huge granite boulder above the suburban sprawl of a small city neighboring our even smaller town. From our vantage point we could see the bright lights of two strip malls dotted with mom-and-pop shops and restaurants—a framing shop, an electronics store, the Thai restaurant where my mom had gone into labor with me in June of 1985. It was the perfect crystallization of a pocket-sized metropolis come of age in the 1990s. I am not sure if the kiss actually happened. Perhaps it has always been my subconscious giving me the memory I wanted.

"Anna! We need a fitting," my mom shouted down the hall.

I had designed a dress to wear to the Ring Dinner dance. My mom drafted a pattern and sewed it. The dress was skintight and impossibly sexy. Made from pink stretch velvet, it had a front slit that ran up my right leg and ended inches below my crotch. The fully open back dipped just above my butt. Its straps were a simple thin string of rhinestones. We worked on the dress for weeks, her sewing machine churning in my brother's old bedroom as I sat in my own room doing homework.

I slipped on the half-sewn dress, trying to avoid being stuck with pins that held the other half together. Her critical eye scanned her work for imperfections or areas that needed further alterations. "Do you feel comfortable? Can you move in this? Should it be shorter here? Longer here?" She asked questions like a couture designer.

"Oh my god, it's incredible," my mom said when I wore the finished dress for the first time. She was standing behind me as we both looked into a full-length mirror. "You could walk onto a red carpet in this."

I turned around, admiring myself. "Thank you so much. I love it. It's exactly what I wanted."

It was not until my friends from the cross-country team, in long gowns with poofy skirts and square necklines, showed up at my house for photos with their dates and parents that my mom realized she was sending her sixteen-year-old daughter to a school dance in a dress inappropriate for a high schooler.

"Wow, that is *quite* the dress," one of the other parents said to her.

My mom's face reddened with embarrassment. "I can't believe I made the back that low and the slit that high," my mom whispered to me as I got into Julian's car.

"It's a perfect dress and it looks amazing."

"Yes." She smiled. "It does."

A month earlier I had asked Julian to be my date to the dance. We stood in the basement hallway of our high school, the one spot our paths intersected between classes. It had been months since the cross-country season ended, and months since we'd last talked. Our relationship had fallen away when fall turned into winter.

"Um, sure," was how he responded. He was too nice to say no, and who knows, maybe part of him wanted to go with me.

We barely spoke at the dance, and we danced together only once, to "Back at One" by Brian McKnight, in a forced state of body proximity that felt unwelcome from his side and uncomfortable from mine.

After that night, stolen glances in the school hallway turned to purposeful avoidance. I wished I could have shown him how great I was, how essential, even, to his happiness. I stopped chasing Julian, but I didn't stop chasing. Instead, I cemented my role in relationships as a pleaser, a convincer, a girl who, well into adulthood, would contort and conform to the desires of a man, overlooking his easy dismissal, and dampening her self-worth, all to be loved.

Soon I would discover I only had to look outside high school to find boys who would pay attention to me.

Seven

In the early morning I am awoken by one of the room checks. The door opens, then closes. Standard procedure. But a minute or two later it opens again. I remove the pair of leggings draped over my eyes that I call my sleep mask, lift my head, and say "Hello?" I am worried I have slept through my alarm.

"I'm sorry," the night-shift house manager says in a too-loud voice. "I couldn't tell if you were breathing, so I went to get a flashlight, but then I couldn't get it to turn on. Obviously you're breathing. Sorry again."

Now I understand why the blankets are so thin.

I never get back to sleep. I feel incredibly tired and heavy with sadness this morning. I miss my house, its cocoon of aesthetic beauty, its woods, its solitude. I have five hours of therapy scheduled today and I don't know how I'll get through it. I force myself out of bed and move to Dalby's kitchen, where I sit alone eating an orange, staring out the window. I wonder what I look like to the other girls. I imagine I seem very depressed, which would be an accurate assessment.

Shawn comes into the kitchen and makes herself coffee without speaking. In the house, especially in the mornings, we use our intuition to know when to talk and when not to. I still, however, feel self-conscious that I am too quiet.

"Everyone keeps telling me there's a flock of wild turkeys here, but I haven't seen them yet," Shawn finally says while looking out the sliding glass door.

"I saw them. Two days ago. They walked past the windows of the yoga room."

"Oh my god! I want to see them so bad," she says. "Everyone has seen them except me. It's so fucking annoying."

"They were so much more beautiful than I thought they'd be. I bet you'll see them before you go."

"I hope so." Shawn is massaging her shoulder and moving her head from side to side. Her eyes are closed, her brow furrowed. "Motherfucker," she says quietly.

"Did you get hurt?" I ask.

"I slept weird on my neck a couple nights ago. It still fucking hurts. They will only give me two Advil a day. And a fucking heating pad that does basically nothing."

Shawn leaves the kitchen before I can respond. I like Shawn and I wonder if she likes me. She is easily irritated, but she herself is not at all irritating. She seems angry, like me, and I like that.

A male nurse comes into the house and asks if I am Anna. "I am," I say back to him. He proceeds to check something that was apparently put under the skin of my forearm during intake. You would think I would remember something being put under my skin, but I have no recollection of it. I can't even remember if it hurt.

"What is that for again?" I say as he checks my skin with what appears to be a small black light.

"It tells me if you have tuberculosis."

"If I did have it, wouldn't I have already infected everyone else in the house?"

"No. Not necessarily. Also, no one ever has it."

Imagine if I died of consumption. This is very funny to me in the moment, though I am sure actually dying of consumption is horrific. In my graduate program we spend a lot of time talking about consumption, especially in our 19th Century Dress class. Women with consumption during the nineteenth century were thought to be the epitome of beauty. They are described in books and depicted in paintings as being luminescent with their milk-white skin and red lips. This is how men saw them, anyway. The perfect woman— impossibly pale, impossibly thin, lips tinted red (from coughing up blood), too tired to speak, too weak to move. All she can do is sit and stare out the window, incandescent as life leaves her body. A woman was thought by many to have contracted consumption due to some moral failing, so while her beauty was fetishized, her character was denigrated. Fucking men.

At ten a.m. I meet with my social worker, Beth. I am relieved to be talking to a woman. The meeting lasts two hours and I am reduced to tears only once. I feel proud of myself for that. It seems like I am crying constantly. Today I am crying about school, how I have fallen behind in the past month. Up until the very end of the semester I had been able to work to the peak of my ability despite my mental health decline, but recently this has fallen apart. I cannot read, or research, or string together a cohesive sentence. All the things you need to be able to do to write a master's thesis. I am afraid I will not be able to finish the program, which triggers the greater fear that I will never be able to finish anything. My life feels like a series of starts and stops, walking road after road, hoping to find the one that leads to something mean- ingful. Yet when I come to an intersection, instead of walking straight, I unfailingly turn left, beginning all over in a new direction.

I spent most of my childhood training to be a dancer, but I wasn't good enough to be a professional and so I changed focus. I went to cosmetology school but failed my state board exam and never got my license. I started art school but became very depressed and dropped out after one year. I cut hair illegally in people's apartments but got bored and stopped. I became a makeup artist but realized that I hated being on sets and eventually ended that path too. My financial situation has always been precarious and, I am embarrassed to admit, made stable by the security of my romantic partners.

I had, in my mid-twenties, eventually finished my bachelor's degree, which allowed me to apply to graduate school, but that feels like a minor victory in the midst of constant failure. I have never felt truly good at any of the things I started, so I abandon them when the weight of mediocrity—or worse, inability—becomes too overwhelming. Graduate school, I believe, is something I am good at. For it to become another thing I do not finish, cannot finish, would be devastating.

I explain all this to Beth, plowing my way through a box of tissues.

"You seem very conscientious and dedicated," Beth says. "I really think you'll be able to finish." Her faith in me that I lack in myself only makes me cry more. Jesus Christ, why can't I stop crying?

The air is frigid walking to the next building, and this leopard-print sweatsuit is doing little in the way of wind protection. It is a different leopard-print sweatsuit than the one Adam thought I might wear to a fashion show. This is the "nice" one, meaning I am trying not to sleep in it. I enter a new doctor's office building, where I am to meet with the hospital chaplain. This place has none of the character or charm of the building where I did my psych testing; not a settee in sight. It is a basic-but-nice municipal building—a reception desk, offices, classrooms, laminated flooring, and a waiting room with some upholstered chairs. My focus zeroes in on a hot-water dispenser and white pouches with small red lettering, tucked behind rows of individually wrapped tea bags. Please be hot chocolate, please be hot chocolate, please be hot chocolate. It's hot chocolate.

Meeting with the chaplain is standard protocol of my evaluation. She will assess my spiritual and religious background, as well as how spirituality affects, or does not, my current day-to-day. For patients in the hospital's other thirty-day programs, the chaplain runs groups and is available to people for whom religion is an active part of their life.

She comes to get me from the waiting room, smiling warmly from behind blond bangs, and leads me into a classroom where all the chairs are pushed to its perimeter except for two facing each other, six feet apart. It is one of those ever-present reminders of Covid, like grab-and-go dinner.

"Let's start by closing our eyes and taking an intentioned deep breath and exhalation," the chaplain says, her voice soft.

I breathe in as deeply as I can, first allowing the air to expand my stomach, then my chest. In for three. Out for six.

"We are going to spend the next hour talking about your spiritual life. Does that sound okay?" she says.

I nod, taking a sip of my hot chocolate. Scalding liquid fills my mouth. My instinct is to spit it out, but it seems unwise to spit hot chocolate on the floor in front of a woman I have just met and who is analyzing my mental state. Instead, I swallow, charting its fiery descent down my esophagus.

"How old are you?" she asks me.

"Thirty-five."

"Oh, you look much younger than that."

This exchange is almost verbatim my initial conversation with the girls at Dalby, and I love it. I have not felt this good about my appearance since last summer when I got carded buying cigarettes at a bodega. "Wait," I said to the cashier, as I slid my license across the counter to him, "you think I'm *under* eighteen?"

"You could be," he said.

"I could be, or you think I *am*?" I said, smiling mischievously.

"You could be."

"You know what, I'll take that. Have a great day!" I grabbed the pack of Marlboro Lights and skipped down Fourteenth Street.

The chaplain clasps her hands and rests them in her lap. "I'm curious what spiritual or religious climate was in your home growing up?"

"I was raised culturally Jewish. Not religious. I'd say there was an appreciation for latkes over an appreciation for God. We celebrated the High Holidays, but not the minor Jewish holidays. We also celebrated Christmas with my mom's parents, but, like, presents and Santa Claus Christmas, not Jesus Christmas."

"Did you enjoy celebrating the holidays?"

"When I was a kid I loved it. My Jewish grandmother was an amazing cook."

"You two were close?"

"Yeah. She died in early 2019. Of cancer." *Palliate.*

"Can you think of something in your life that has made you feel close to spirituality?"

"When I was dancing, I suppose. Specifically, when I got to perform. It was the happiest and most in tune with myself I ever felt. My body moved without my mind having to work. All motion felt purely intuitive. Everything else in my mind disappeared."

"A flow state." She nods.

"A flow state," I repeat. "I loved learning choreography and rehearsing it, knowing the payoff would be to perform it. Once, I think I was eleven, when dance was still fun and not yet heartbreaking, I remember having a rehearsal on my birthday and being so happy. A five-hour rehearsal was exactly how I wanted to spend my day. I wasn't even annoyed it was Saturday. I was just excited."

"When did dance become heartbreaking?"

"Around thirteen."

"What happened?"

"I was injured, took some time off, then came back to suddenly realize I wasn't one of the talented girls. In that short amount of time everyone had surpassed me. Their turnout was better, their legs went higher, they were clearly stronger. I couldn't catch back up to where I needed to be to be taken seriously by any of my teachers."

"Dance was your first great loss," she says.

"Oddly, I don't think it was. I think it was my second."

She looks surprised. "What was the first?"

"I wanted to be an actor before I wanted to be a dancer. My brother, he's five years older than me, was a really successful commercial actor when he was a kid. A lot of my early childhood was spent going into New York City multiple times a week with him and my mom for auditions and jobs. When I was in fourth grade I asked if I could start auditioning too. My dream was to be on Broadway," I said.

"And did you get to audition like your brother did?"

"I did, for a little while, but then my mom was tired of that taking up her entire life with both my brother and me, so I had to stop."

"Do you remember what that conversation was like?"

I laugh. "Yes, quite vividly. I was in fifth grade and I had been auditioning for a Broadway play. There had been two callbacks, which meant I was in a very small pool of girls being considered for the role. The night before I was due to have another callback, my mom told me she wasn't sure if she could do this all over with another kid. If I booked the role, she would have to drive me in and out of the city six days a week. It would have been a major commitment for both of us. She told me she would think about it that night and the next day. I would go to school as planned and she would call the school to let them know if she was picking me up early to go on the audition or if I should take the bus home. If I got word to take the bus home, that meant I wouldn't be going in on the callback, and I understood that meant I would stop auditioning altogether."

"You were waiting for that call all day? What did that feel like?"

"Incredibly anxiety-inducing. I was only eleven, so it felt like my entire life was hinging on a single phone call. Around noon the classroom phone rang, the one that connects to the main office or other classrooms, and my teacher told me I should take the bus home."

"Did the teacher have any idea what was going on?" the chaplain asked.

"No, she was just relaying the message from the office," I said.

"What did you do when you received this news?"

"I went to the bathroom and cried."

"Was there any further conversation from your mom when you got home from school?"

"She said she was sorry. She understood how disappointed I would be. I stopped auditioning and put more time into dance. My dance school was thirty minutes away from my house, not an hour thirty, like Manhattan."

"That's a pretty major blow for a child. I can understand why the memory has stuck with you in such a visceral way all these years later. You had two huge losses very early in life."

I can't stop running my hot chocolate–singed taste buds back and forth along my teeth. "I guess I did," I say.

It is finally our turn to eat dinner in the dining room. We do this with the men from Oscar House, which I hate, but none of the other girls seem to mind. Everyone makes small talk as they fill their plates with food, but thankfully, we do not intermingle our tables. All the girls sit at one, all the men sit at another.

"How do you feel about tomorrow?" Mary asks Kristin. Tomorrow Kristin is leaving and transitioning to a sober living facility. Not everyone goes to sober living when they leave rehab, but it is considered a helpful step in transitioning out of the rigidity of a thirty-day program and back into real life. In sober living you have more freedom, usually you can come and go, you have access to your phone, you are able to work, yet at the same time it allows you to live with people who are also newly sober.

"I feel good about it," Kristin says. "I'm ready to go. I'm not sure what to expect in sober living, so that's scary. But otherwise, yeah, I feel okay."

"You're doing the right thing though by going there, ya know?" Mary says back to her. "I think you're gonna do amazing."

I want to be more like Mary in these exchanges—to confidently offer encouragement and support and not feel embarrassed, or anxious, or worried that I sound disingenuous. I make a mental note to work on this while I'm here.

Back at Dalby, sitting on the living room couches, we do our wrap-up meeting and then a Rock Ceremony for Kristin's last night. At a Rock Ceremony, the person who is leaving picks from a collection of small, tumbled stones that have words engraved on them. They pick a rock with a word that resonates. Then, each person passes around the rock and says a few words to the person who is leaving. Mary, Caitlyn, and Shawn have been with Kristin much longer than I have, so when it is my turn to speak, I feel bad that I don't have something more personal to say.

I hold Kristin's rock in my hand, feeling its weight, running my fingers along the engraved letters that spell HOPE. "I've only known you a few days, but I'm glad that we got to overlap, and I wish you so much luck on your journey outside of here" is all I have to offer her. My words might not be as encouraging as Mary's, but I hope Kristin knows I really mean them.

Eight

Brian: I'll drive to you.
Me: Ok. We can go to the movies or something.

I texted him from the back row of junior-year French class, my hand obscured inside my backpack, feeling my way across the keypad of my phone. I was so good at T9 I did not even have to look.

Brian: Want to see Lord of the Rings?

I did not.

Me: Sounds good! I'm going to tell my parents you're 19.
Brian: Haha ok

Brian was twenty-three. I met him at a local punk show in Pough-keepsie in 2001. Amanda and I were not even there to see his band. The show was in a very small room with no backstage. The bands hung out in an unpartitioned alcove with a few threadbare couches when they were not playing. "Good set," I said to Brian. I was leaning casually against the alcove wall. He looked up at me from the couch where he sat cradling his electric guitar and smiled. That was all it took. I left the show that night with his AOL Instant Messenger handle: BlinkyFizzz888.

My parents had finally decided to separate. I was relieved at first, but the separation proved at times more volatile than their marriage. This was due to their wildly differing opinions on why things were ending in the first place. From my mom's vantage point, my dad had had an affair. She believed he was giving up despite her renewed commitment to work things out. My dad would tell you no affair took place, that his new relationship began only after he and my mom had decided to separate.

I held yet a different opinion—that my mom's aggression and unchecked anger had pushed my dad away until he found solace in someone who was her opposite. That by the time his new relationship began, my dad was so done with my mom that to him it felt as if the overlap never occurred.

My mom's rage lived outside her. It could be directed at anyone—a cashier not accepting her coupon at a grocery store, a customer service representative who couldn't help her over the phone—but it was often directed at her family. She had strict and seemingly arbitrary rules that if broken, even accidentally, could be met with intense, explosive anger. I got in trouble for spilling food on my clothes and for not doing crafts at the correct table. I got in trouble if I broke something, if I cut my Barbie's hair, if I didn't want to do something that scared me. "I'm an Aries!" she would claim as justification. "Fire energy!" In my mom's defense, I saw how my dad's propensity toward condescension and competition activated my mom's worst qualities. But these behaviors were more covert and therefore more difficult for me to identify when I was a child.

Immediately after my parents' separation, my mom became more rageful. She also at times became despondent. As the only other person left at home, I was the sole absorber of her unpredictable emotions. She was angry when I would see my dad and didn't hold back in saying so, yelling at me to rebuke him in support of her.

"He chose to leave this marriage!" Her voice was so loud it echoed off the high ceilings of our living room. "He shouldn't get to see you."

I only saw my dad once a week to spare myself my mom's reaction. Other times, depression overtook her. She cried when I would leave the house to hang out with Amanda, pleading with me to stay home with her instead.

"He ruined my life," she would wail. "Sometimes I just wish I were dead." I feared her rage, but the depression was even scarier. When I did go out, I was terrified I might return home to find she had taken her own life.

"I'll be back later!" I yelled hurriedly as soon as I saw Brian's headlights making their way down my long driveway. I headed for the door, not wanting to see my mom cry as I left, but also to stave off any possible interaction between her and my twenty-three-year-old date. I could not risk her seeing him. He looked like Sid Vicious, with piercings, spiky hair, and tight black jeans. This was clearly not a high school student.

"Hi. How are you?" I said, settling into the passenger seat.

"I saw a really bad accident on my way here, actually." It had been torrentially raining all day.

"Oh, I'm sorry."

"An eighteen-wheeler was driving without taillights and a car going ninety drove right into the back of it."

"Jesus, did you stop?"

"No. What could I have done?"

Call 911? I thought, though did not say.

I had witnessed a fatal car accident, or rather the immediate aftermath of one, a year earlier, a vision that returned to me as I sat in the car with Brian. Driving with my mom, dad, brother, and cat to my grandparents' house in rural Pennsylvania for Christmas, the family car came to a wall of crawling traffic. We inched along for hours. I was listening to the Eve 6 album *Horrorscope* from my Discman when the cars parted to reveal a motorcycle accident. A body lay under a white sheet, deep red where the head would be. Blood soaked the pavement all around. A man's arm protruded from the sheet. A motorcycle lay on its side. My vision and hearing left me. I couldn't breathe. It felt as though I were descending to the bottom of a vast, dark body of water. My cat's small body, curled peacefully in my lap, felt all at once unbearably hot, and my legs began to sweat underneath her. I switched off my music and closed my eyes, hoping to trick my brain into believing I'd seen nothing, asleep the whole time. The car fell silent, except for a mournful "Oh god" from my dad. My mind filled with images of the deceased's final moments. Did he feel terror? Did he even know what was happening? Did death come quickly? Or did he suffer? The weight of these questions was made heavier by the holidays. In an instant someone had lost a husband or a father, a brother, or a friend. He was no doubt someone to somebody, and that somebody was about to have the worst holiday of their life. I remained silent and still, my cells entombing the implosion of panic.

No one in my family mentioned the accident until two days later when my dad brought it up at Christmas Eve dinner, hoping, perhaps, to banish the grisly scene from his memory by speaking it into evaporation.

My consciousness pivoted from the motorcycle accident, returning to Brian's car. If I had just witnessed a fatal car crash, I likely could not go on a date afterward.

"Are you sure you want to go to the movies?" I asked Brian. "We can find something else to do."

"No, I'm totally good."

I'd underestimated this man's desire to see an elf movie.

I fell asleep twice during *Lord of the Rings* and made a bathroom trip around the two-hour mark. Having grossly underestimated the length of the film, I ran to replace an already overtaxed tampon, only to find blood soaking the crotch of my underwear. I stuffed a wad of toilet paper between my legs to keep the blood from leeching on to my jeans and walked back to the theater. By the time this movie was over, the blood would be dry enough for me to ditch the toilet paper. Three arduous hours of orcs and CGI waterfalls. I had seemingly found myself at another game of Magic: The Gathering, only live-action, and this time I had paid money to be there.

It was eleven p.m. when we finally left the theater. I did not have to be home for an hour. I was not about to bring Brian back to my house, so in a throwback to my boys cross-country manager days I suggested we sit in a parking lot. I directed him to a park ten minutes from the theater. Almost immediately we started making out. I had calculated that we could do this for about twenty-five minutes before he would need to begin the drive back to my house. Brian reached down below the driver's seat and yanked a lever, throwing the seat backward. I straddled him, my right leg cramped against the door, my left knee pressing down on the hard plastic of the seatbelt. I never thought to voice my bodily discomfort.

Brian unbuttoned my pants and pulled down its zipper, trying awkwardly to push his hand beneath the band of my underwear. Nothing about this felt good, but I was thrilled at the fact that a boy, no, *man*, found me attractive enough to want to finger me. Brian was not just any man, he was a musician—a guy who played electric guitar in too-skinny jeans to nine-hundred-person-capacity theaters. Fuck Ethan, fuck Julian, and fuck all the boys at my high school who did not value my undeniable cool. This . . . this was winning.

His finger obliviously jammed against my tampon, forcefully slamming it against the side of my vagina and my cervix with bursts of pain. I did consider warning him about the tampon, but I did not anticipate him actually trying to put his fingers inside me, given our time

87

constraints. Once it was happening, I felt the warning opportunity had been lost.

"Does that feel good?" he whispered breathlessly into my ear.

"Yes," I said. It did not.

Blinding headlight beams filled Brian's car at close range. "Oh fuck," he said. I looked into the direction of the lights, but my field of vision was a blanket of white. I crawled off Brian and sunk into the passenger seat, quickly buttoning up my pants.

"What are you kids doing here?"

"So sorry, Officer. I'm just home from college visiting my girl-friend."

The lie left his lips so quickly, so smoothly, sure to mention college so as to obfuscate his true age.

"Well, go do that somewhere else."

"Yes, sir."

Back in my driveway, Brian kissed me and said, "Let's talk soon."

I messaged him on AIM and tried emailing him a few times after our date, measuring my tone to be as casual and laid-back as possible, but I never heard from him again.

Nine

Caitlyn, Mary, Shawn, and I gather around the kitchen table at Dalby. A woman enters the house pulling a Radio Flyer wagon filled with plants. Horticulture therapy is one of the enrichment activities here in the hospital, and unlike art therapy, you do not have to talk about your feelings or your trauma. You do not have to talk at all. The only requirement is to learn a few facts about a particular plant, fill a small plastic container with soil, and plant some clippings. For this reason, everyone loves horticulture therapy. The plant we are propagating today is called Cuban oregano. It is sometimes called Mexican mint, Spanish thyme, or Indian borage, though it is none of these things, nor is it oregano. It is part of the *Lamiaceae* family—or mint family, if you are not a botanist—but one inhale of a Cuban oregano leaf and you will understand, it is no mint. Its small, green, velvety leaves smell of pungent oregano. We all have the same reaction when we put the leaves up to our noses and crush them between our fingers.

"Whoa!"

"Oh my god, it's so strong. I love it!"

"Oh wow."

"Damn!"

We can't stop massaging the leaves and breathing in their scent as the horticulturist, Sandy, hands out small plastic cups with holes on the bottom and places a large bag of potting soil in the center of the table.

"I have gloves if anyone wants them, for the soil, but I like getting my hands in the dirt," Sandy says.

None of us opt for gloves.

The Cuban oregano, Sandy informs us, is a semi-succulent. It likes warm weather and sunshine. It is a hardy plant that grows quickly and easily.

"I hope I don't kill her," I say, reaching into the bag of potting soil. Dirt envelops my hand. I wiggle my fingers around for a few seconds before clenching my fist around the cold earth.

"These are pretty hard to kill. You only have to water them once a week," says Sandy.

"What happened to the plants at the houses during lockdown?" Shawn asks.

"Most of them died," Sandy says. "After a couple weeks I came back to the hospital and took the ones home with me that could be revived."

"So you're saying the Cuban oregano survived?" I asked.

"It survived and thrived!" Mary adds.

"It certainly did." Sandy gestures to the large plant.

We each choose a few clippings from a pile in the center of the table. I try to choose the ones closest in size, anticipating that if all three sprouts do not stand perfectly erect at roughly the same height, I might go crazy. Symmetry is important to me. It keeps everything else in line and contained, even when I do not know what "everything else" is.

Sandy shows us the planting protocol: First, stick a finger in the dirt to make a hole about two inches deep. Second, dip the bottom of the clipping in a powdered growth fertilizer. Third, place the clipping in the hole in the soil. Fourth, fill in the hole and pat the soil around the plant.

Mary, Caitlyn, Shawn, and I repeat these steps until we each have two or three clippings in our cups.

The growth fertilizer looks like caster sugar, the extremely fine white sugar that is used for baking French macarons. I think back a few years to when I became obsessed with baking the notoriously difficult-to-master dessert. On my first try I nailed it. A crunch on the perfectly inflated cookie shell, but with a chewy center. Each macaron the exact same size. They were perfect and beautiful and delicious, and not so hard to make after all. A week later I made macarons again. This time the cookie shells sunk in on themselves when I removed them from the oven. I threw them in the trash and started over again, but the outcome was the same. These, too, ended up in an ugly heap at the bottom of my trash can.

I tried making macarons three more times. Each attempt proved a new and unique failure to the previous batch. I threw them all away before even sandwiching the cookies together with buttercream icing. I vowed never to make macarons again, seeing their defeat against me as symbolic of some greater personal deficiency. I refocused my attention—once again turning left—and started baking choux pastry, a confectionary delight much harder to fuck up.

I survey all four of our newly potted plants. Mary has one sprout that is small and sticks straight up, and another that is long and leaning heavily over the edge of its cup. *It should have been planted deeper in the soil*, I think. Caitlyn plants her two clippings off to one side, not at all evenly spaced to take advantage of the cup's surface area. Mine, on the other hand, has three perfectly spaced clippings of equal size, properly supported by their depth in the soil relative to their height. I have followed directions exactly, and the result is equally exacting. Symmetrical, balanced, nice to look at. Nothing could go wrong today, or possibly ever again, now that I have potted the perfect plant.

Sandy hands out a couple of Sharpie markers for us to write our names and decorate our plastic cups with words or phrases we find meaningful.

"What does that mean?" I ask Caitlyn. She has written "LOOK UP" in all caps on her cup, making the *O*s into wide eyes with long eyelashes.

"It's what we say in volleyball. You always have to be paying attention to where the ball is. We write it on our shoes so if we ever look down, it reminds us to look up."

"I really like that," I say. I sit for a minute trying to think of something worthwhile to write on my cup. My version of "LOOK UP." In the end I write my name, the date, and "CUBAN OREGANO."

"Can you tell me about the last year of your life?" Dr. Samuels says to me. Dr. Samuels is the psychiatrist who did my day-one intake and is the lead doctor on my case. He will be the one who writes my report and diagnosis at the end of the week. I haven't seen him since I checked in. His small office, which looks like it belongs to a high school guidance counselor, has a faux-wood desk with a mess of paperwork, a sad swivel chair, and brick walls covered in very thick white paint. If I were to put my nails up to the wall and press, I could make five small half-moon indentations. It would feel satisfying to do this, but of course I don't.

"How much time do you have?" I say.

He points to a large clock on the wall. "An hour," he says, smiling in mutual recognition that a year of one's life cannot possibly be truncated into sixty minutes.

There is a lot of repeating yourself at the hospital. You have to tell the same stories of your life to numerous different clinicians. I want to say, "I explained this on Sunday to Dr. Philips, can you maybe have a chat with him and then we'll pick back up here?" but I also understand recounting events to various people is likely part of the psychological evaluation itself. If I told one version of events to one doctor, and a totally different version of events to another doctor, they would likely meet up at the end of the day, compare notes, and say to each other, "For sure, this one's crazy." I accept that repeating myself will only paint a more complete picture of my emotional and psychological state, thereby in the end benefiting me.

"You have experienced a significant amount of what is called 'strain trauma' over the course of your life. Are you familiar with the term 'strain trauma'?" Dr. Samuels says.

"I'm not."

"Shock trauma is the type of trauma most people are familiar with. It's the sort of trauma that occurs when someone is in war combat. It causes flashbacks, disturbing dreams, violent outbursts, the behavior we commonly associate with severe PTSD. Strain trauma, on the other hand, happens over long periods of time, when a person is in an environment that consistently puts them in a state of anxious arousal."

"Okay . . ."

"Take, for example, your home life growing up. Your mother was emotionally volatile. She had rage issues, and it seems she had trouble attuning to your needs because they were so different from her own. You didn't know what might set her off or what might get you in trouble. You couldn't trust that emotionally you would get what you needed when you needed it. Additionally, it doesn't seem like your dad did much to protect you from her anger."

"Sure." I feel myself getting defensive.

"Living in that state of fear and uncertainty could be extremely detrimental to a child."

"But she was also a good mom. She made dinner every night and packed my lunch every day. She drove me to school so I didn't have to wake up early to catch the bus. She was always doing creative things with me. She didn't control how I looked or how I dressed. She let me pierce my ears nine times, she helped me dye my hair pink and blue.

She read the entire Anne of Green Gables series out loud to me over the course of three years!"

"I'm sure those things are also true. Both can be true. She can be both a good mother in some ways and a mother who created a volatile environment in other ways."

"I believe she was doing the best she could, given the circumstances she grew up in. Her own childhood was traumatic and at times very abusive."

"I don't doubt that. These cycles are often repeated generationally," he says.

"And she's much different now. She isn't like the person I knew when I was a kid."

"That's very lucky, for both of you. That also doesn't mean the things that occurred in your childhood didn't have an enormous effect on you and continue to affect you as an adult."

"I understand," I say, and I do. I also feel incredibly guilty for having this conversation about a woman who devoted her life to raising me; a woman who I love very much, despite her challenging complexities.

I wish Dr. Samuels could see a more three-dimensional version of my mom, but I know that is impossible because the only information he has about her is coming from me. I get what he is saying. I do not believe a person should scream in rage toward another person, especially a child, the way she did at me frequently when I was growing up.

"I want to show you what it feels like to be spoken to the way you speak to me sometimes," I once said to her when I was seventeen. I sat in the passenger seat while she navigated a winding country road.

"Okay," she said tentatively.

"THIS IS WHAT IT FEELS LIKE TO BE SCREAMED AT. THIS IS WHAT IT FEELS LIKE WHEN YOU RAISE YOUR VOICE AND TELL SOMEONE ALL THE REASONS WHY THEY DID SOMETHING WRONG." I felt her flinch, but I kept going. "IT'S NOT VERY FUN TO BE SCREAMED AT, IS IT?" I screamed as loud as I could, even though the force of my own voice felt alien at that volume.

Silence.

"I'M ASKING YOU A QUESTION! DOES THIS FEEL GOOD TO YOU?"

"No," she said finally, "it doesn't feel good."

"Then I need you to stop speaking to me this way."

"Okay," she said.

"Okay," I said.

She would not raise her voice at me again until I was twenty-one, when we were making plans for the Thanksgiving holiday. My mom did not want me to see my dad; she felt as the parent who did not want the divorce, she was owed Thanksgiving. I felt no one was owed anything, but my life would be significantly easier if I gave my mom that day. I informed her I would spend Thanksgiving Day with her and then go to my dad's house the following day, thinking this would be a compromise both parents would be happy with, but she lost it. The day was not enough; she wanted the entire weekend. She did not want me to see my dad at all, and she relayed this at the highest, most intense volume a voice can reach.

"Mom," I said, my voice calm. "I'm going to stop you. If you keep screaming at me I'm going to hang up the phone. I will not speak to you when you are screaming at me."

"I WAIT FOR THIS ALL YEAR AND YOU'RE ONLY GOING TO COME ONE DAY. DON'T TELL ME HOW I CAN AND CAN'T SPEAK. IF YOU WON'T COME FOR THE WHOLE WEEKEND, THEN MAYBE I DON'T WANT YOU TO COME AT ALL."

At this point I was holding the phone far away from my ear. She was screaming so loud I could have heard her through a closed door.

I cut her off. "If you don't want me to come that's your decision, but I'm going to hang up now. If you want to talk about this calmly, you can call me back when you're ready to do that."

I hit end on my flip phone and sobbed. I had mastered keeping calm in front of people, only to break down in private.

We did have the calm conversation a few days later. She told me she wanted me to come, and I told her I would be there on Thursday and would go to my dad's on Friday. She was not happy, but she accepted it and she never screamed at me again. Ever.

That New Year's she attended a ten-day silent meditation retreat in northern Massachusetts. She returned with a sense of peace I had never seen in her before. The following summer she went to India for six weeks. After spending four weeks at the Ramamani Iyengar Memorial Yoga Institute in Pune, in a yoga workshop known for its rigorousness, both physically and mentally, she traveled through the country—to Agra to see the Taj Mahal; to Bodh Gaya, the site of Siddhārtha Gautama's great enlightenment; to Varanasi; and to the caves of Ellora and Ajanta. She navigated her way through India on overnight trains, packed into small sleeping quarters with strangers; she trekked through a remote village and to the top of a mountain to visit a shrine for Ganesha. She made offerings to the dead from a wooden rowboat on the Ganges. She did this all alone at fifty-seven years old.

My mom wrote me beautiful emails detailing her travels through India. I was moved by her bravery and by the care and understanding with which she depicted this new world, so vastly different from the one she was used to. For my mother's fifty-eighth birthday I had all her emails from India printed into a book, along with the beautiful photographs she had taken on her journey.

Sitting now in Dr. Samuels's office, I understand what he is trying to explain to me. Parents can be our greatest allies, they can fiercely love us, but they can also be the cause of our trauma. My mom helped create an environment for much of my childhood that deeply impacted my emotional well-being. Though I believe she did this unintentionally, she did do it. Still, I wish Dr. Samuels could experience all the ways she had softened and evolved when I became an adult. If I could, I would show him that book of her emails from India and say, "Look at this. This is her too."

In the evening, after dinner, Mary, Caitlyn, Shawn, and I continue our arduous trek through episodes of *Goliath*. I imagine when Dalby is at capacity, agreeing on what to watch would be nearly impossible and highly frustrating. It's only five days into the New Year; we still have the luxury of it only being the four of us. In the outside world, people's resolutions and best intentions have not yet worn off. But they will, and by mid-January the house will be full of patients. Mary, Caitlyn, Shawn, and I are all laid-back about what we watch, everyone is agreeable, and no one is trying to make life more complicated than it needs to be. Caitlyn says it wasn't like this in the Under-18 House, where she'd been originally placed before transferring to Dalby.

"We could only watch cartoons, because anything else was 'triggering,'" she said, putting air quotes around "triggering."

"So it was a bunch of teenagers watching cartoons?" I asked.

"Yeah. It was so weird. I never spoke and I asked to switch to this house immediately."

"Why didn't you speak?"

"Because everyone was triggered by everything. You couldn't say the word 'ice cream' without someone saying they were being triggered. It was a nightmare."

"I guess, good for them for being able to speak up for themselves?"

Caitlyn gives me a look like, *Are you fucking kidding me?* I laugh.

Caitlyn reminds me of me, but not in the way Shawn reminds me of me. Caitlyn is nearly twenty years younger, but when I talk to her, I can't really feel a pronounced age difference. When she mentions high school or talks about applying to college, I feel it, but when she sits across from me at dinner in a Sublime T-shirt, the one with the illustrated sun from the *40oz. to Freedom* cover, my brain is tricked into seeing overlap in our pop culture references, which by default makes her seem more mature. This shirt, a shirt she likely bought off the internet in 2020, is no more reliable a signal of her maturity than the Joy Division shirt I bought from Hot Topic in 2000. I think of Caitlyn as she is now, at eighteen. Then I subtract two years. I think of her meeting a guy who is twenty-eight. Then think of him having sex with her five months later.

"Anna." The house manager walks into the living room. "Dr. Philips is here to see you."

I look toward the front door and see Dr. Philips, the doctor who did my psychological exams a couple days ago. I get up from the couch and we have a seat in a room off the kitchen.

"Hi, Anna, how are you doing this evening?" he asks in his calm, steady voice.

"I'm pretty good." I cannot remember if I am wearing the same sweatsuit as testing day, and I worry he might think I have not changed or showered.

"I wanted to see if you'd like to discuss your test results, if you might find that helpful? You mentioned in the testing that you studied psychology in undergrad, so I thought you might appreciate having a discussion instead of just reading it in a report."

"Oh." I feel surprised and grateful that he is taking this approach, speaking to me like an intelligent adult who can grasp psychological concepts instead of like a crazy woman having a breakdown. "Yes, I would appreciate that very much."

"All right then, let's begin. Your results demonstrated some significant anomalies. I would say they are inconsistent. Verbal comprehension, for example, was high-average and very organized. You scored in the ninety-first percentile. On the Rorschach test, you took the entire picture into consideration, which is highly ambitious. You are clearly capable of rich, abstract thought. Does this resonate with how you perceive yourself?"

"Yes, it makes total sense."

"That's good to hear. Your working memory falls into the average range, however the bottom falls out drastically on arithmetic and puzzle identification."

"I'm terrible at math," I say quickly.

"Yes, you said that at the time of testing as well. You froze when you started to doubt whether you could solve the problem. Your anxiety became so great that you could not recover. I think this has less to do with your ability to perform arithmetic and more to do with your extreme anxiety interfering with your ability to reason. In other words, if the anxiety was removed, you likely could solve the problem."

"I don't know about that."

We both laugh.

"Well, there is a way in which you lose your center when your anxiety is activated. You are highly conscientious. In fact, you scored in the ninety-eighth percentile. You have tendencies toward orderliness, persistence, careful deliberation, and focus. You are cautious, detail-oriented, and try to actively manage situations and tasks. My assumption is you are also very reliable and dependable. Does this make sense?"

"More than you know."

"In neuroticism, which sounds jarring, but really just means your proneness to negative thoughts and feelings, you scored in the ninety-ninth percentile. You likely react very strongly to situations that have the potential to evoke fear, anxiety, sadness, guilt, and shame. You doubt yourself and also blame yourself for negative outcomes. When you feel you might fail at something, or like you've let someone down, your anxiety becomes so overwhelming that you shut down." He pauses and then asks, "How does it feel to hear this?"

I'm so stunned I almost don't know what to say. "That sounds like my exact experience of life."

"Would you like to continue or should we stop there?"

"I'd like to continue."

"You are in the high-average range of openness. This indicates that you are a person with wide interests, who enjoys being imaginative and insightful. You appreciate the arts, adventure, unusual ideas, and a variety of experiences. At the same time, you scored extremely low-average—in the first percentile, in fact—in extraversion and social detachment. Maybe you're an anti-extrovert, far beyond an introvert, so I can understand your intense desire to isolate."

At this point tears begin to fall from my eyes, not because I am sad or angry, but because I have never had these dueling aspects of my personality mirrored back to me in such a matter-of-fact way. I have, at so many times in my life, felt unknowable, but here I am having me explained to me as it feels to be me. One three-hour test and I finally have objective words to demystify a tumultuous and ambivalent life experience.

"We will leave it here, but I have one last thing I would like to say. The Rorschach and image testing reveal evidence of trauma associated with very early childhood development. I see a preoccupation with blood, morbidity, dismissal, and power struggles. There is a way in which you present as very sturdy to the world, yet inside you are carrying an incredibly heavy weight. There is a you *inside* who feels invisible to those looking at you from the outside. I feel an incredible amount of compassion for how hard each day feels for you."

"Thank you," I say, my voice quiet and quivering with emotion. "I really appreciate this."

"Yes," he says, "I believe you really do."

Ten

Leaving a punk show one night, Amanda and I found two windows smashed out of her car and the trunk open. There wasn't much to take, but they took it all. Three dollars in coins, Amanda's TI-89 calculator, and a vintage purse my mom had crocheted in the 1970s, the contents of which included a hairbrush, some makeup, a pair of underwear (why?), and the fourth Harry Potter book. I was lucky the bouncer at the club let me bring in the manual Nikon camera my mom had given me, otherwise that would have been gone too. There was glass all over the car, the broken windows promising a freezing ride home. We called the police, figuring they could at least help us clean out the car, but it was impossible to know how long we would have to wait for them, a mere car break-in being considered a low priority for city crime. We were parked not far from the band's tour bus, so when we saw the guitar player loading on equipment, we ran over and asked for help.

"Hi! We were just at your show. Her car got broken into." I pointed to Amanda.

"There's glass everywhere," Amanda said. "You don't, by any chance, have anything we could clean it up with or, like, anything we can cover the windows with? We have a long ride home."

"I got you. Where's your car?" He introduced himself as Todd.

We pointed to the navy blue Saturn.

Within minutes Todd returned with a shop vac, duct tape, and a roll of plastic tarping. He vacuumed up all the glass and taped the broken windows shut. We awkwardly made conversation.

"Where are you guys from?" I asked.

"Long Island," Todd said.

"We are going to a show on Long Island this weekend!" Amanda offered, naming the lineup.

"My little brother, David, is playing that show. He's only a couple years older than you guys. Say hi to him. I'll tell him you're the girls with the fucked-up car." Todd applied the last strip of duct tape, sealing the plastic in place where a window should have been. "I'm pretty sure it's illegal to have your windows covered in plastic, but at least you won't freeze on the drive."

"Yeah, it's going to be so cold. I wish we had extra sweatshirts!" I was trying to get free band merch. It didn't work.

Todd was correct; it was indeed illegal to drive with your car windows covered in plastic. Somewhere on the Taconic Parkway we were pulled over by a cop, who strangely ended up knowing our story.

"Ohhh, you're the girls with the car break-in outta Poughkeepsie. Okay, well, I'm not going to make you take the plastic off in this weather, so just get this taken care of as soon as possible."

We thanked him, then blasted the heat to compensate for the missing windows.

Over the hour-long ride home, Amanda and I played Starship's *Greatest Hits (Ten Years and Change 1979–1991)* cassette tape I found at my feet on the passenger side.

"Where the fuck did this come from?" I said. I had not played a cassette tape since 1995.

"I bought it at Trash. It was fifty cents." Trash was an alternative record store in the town next to us, and this was exactly the type of ridiculous thing Amanda would spend money on.

We never made it past the first song, "We Built This City," rewinding it over and over.

The next weekend Amanda, our friend Elaine, and I went to that show on Long Island and met Todd's brother, David. Soon after, David joined Todd's band. While touring the country in support of a more established punk band, David invited us to see them play in Philadelphia. He offered me a press pass so I could take photographs of the band while they played. At sixteen, I saw myself as Annie Leibovitz or Linda McCartney. I did not see myself as a teenager, but maybe this was because so few people treated me like I was one.

David's band was one of the few from the early 2000s emo-punk scene with any moral compass pertaining to underage girls, something I would only realize in hindsight. Being in high school did not deter other musicians in the scene from inviting us backstage, or inviting us on their tour buses, or inviting us into their hotel rooms. One time, a bass player from one of our favorite bands—a man with a wife and two children—tried to share a hotel bed with Elaine, who was fifteen at the time, while Amanda and I lay in the other double bed three feet away. Eventually, Elaine crawled in with us. "I think we should go," she said. We left and pooled our money to book our own room.

That weekend in Philadelphia, we mostly hung out with David. We never saw the guys from the headlining band.

Except for Sam.

Sam was twenty-eight. He was warm and friendly, though I did not speak with him much that weekend. When I was back home in Connecticut, David texted me:

David: So great to see you! Sam was very into you and asked me for your number.

Me: Give it to him!!!

David: Are you sure? He's almost 30.

Me: I don't care. Great to see you too.

David: Ok, if you want.

I did not care that Sam was nearly thirty; I only cared that an older man, in a popular band, thought I was worth his time and attention.

Sam and I began texting regularly and talking on the phone. I would fight sleep waiting for a middle-of-the-night text from Louisville, or Cleveland, or Portland that would spiral into an hours-long conversation, wrecking me for school the next day.

Sam: I showed our tour manager Robert the photograph you sent me. He said, "Oh wow, she has no idea how pretty she is, does she?"

Me: Aww that's so nice :)

Robert was forty-five.

Sam: I told him no one would ever guess you were sixteen. You seem so much older for your age.

Me: Thank you! Everyone tells me that!

Five months had passed between when I first started talking to Sam and when he invited me to Los Angeles. I told my parents I was visiting my brother in San Francisco, but once I got to Northern California, I boarded a plane south without them ever knowing.

"Play anything you want," Sam said as we exited Los Angeles International Airport in his small red sedan. I spun my thumb around the wheel of the iPod that played through his car speakers by way of a cassette tape attached to a cord.

"I really want one of these."

"It's amazing to have all your music in one place and not have to carry around CDs. You should get one."

"They're expensive. I don't, like, have an income." I put on the Sunny Day Real Estate album *Diary*, hoping to impress him. If I had played Fleetwood Mac, or the Rolling Stones, or Paul Simon he would know I had good taste in music, but only in proximity to my parents' taste. No one's parents were listening to Sunny Day Real Estate in 2002. *I* was not even listening to them, really. Amanda had introduced me to the album a couple months earlier, and I only knew the second song.

"God, this song is so good."

"I know," I said, smiling.

"Are you hungry?"

"Yes, very."

"Do you like pizza?"

I was pretty sure everyone liked pizza.

We drove to a strip mall and ate pizza at the counter of an empty storefront clearly designed for a takeaway business.

"I normally get sick when I'm going to meet someone romantically," he said. "I didn't get sick this time. You must be special."

I must be special.

When I envisioned this trip, I imagined going to the beach and taking walks among stately Beverly Hills mansions, but our only major outing was to Grauman's Chinese Theatre, that famous location where old Hollywood stars enshrined their hand- and footprints in cement. I held my own hands up to the impression of Judy Garland's. They were so small, like a child's. She was my age—now seventeen—when she'd left those prints, the words "All Happiness" scrawled above them. I wondered who she was trying to convince.

We spent most of our time that week sitting on Sam's couch watching reruns of *Reno 911*.

Over fast-food tacos the first night he asked me: "Your parents won't suspect where you are at all?"

"No. I literally never lie to them. They would have no reason to suspect I'd ever do something like this."

I popped a stale tortilla chip from the flimsy to-go container into my mouth.

"Your brother won't tell them?"

"Nah, he's cool."

A little after midnight we headed to the second floor of his house, stalling between two bedrooms.

"You can sleep in the spare bedroom if you'd be more comfortable with that. Or . . ."

"Or . . ."

"Or you can sleep with me, but I don't want you to feel like you have to."

"I'll sleep with you."

I have very little recollection of the sex except that I was on the bottom. I cannot remember if the moment of insertion was painful, or how long it lasted, or if I felt anything at all. When it was over, he walked to his bathroom sink and I watched him fill the condom with water.

"What are you doing?"

"I'm checking it for holes."

I walked downstairs to the kitchen, filling a glass with tap water. I drank the water while staring at the bottled water cooler next to the fridge. "No one in LA drinks tap water," he had told me earlier that day. The image of young women inspecting themselves in the mirror after their first sexual encounter popped into my head. I had seen this in countless movies. I thought about doing it, wondering if perhaps it was an important part of the virginity ritual, but I did not. I already knew I looked exactly the same. I was me, just with a vagina that now hurt.

The following morning, I woke up to an empty bed. Upon standing, I saw a bouquet of flowers on the floor.

"I wanted you to see them right when you woke up, so I put them next to the bed. I don't have a vase."

"Thank you so much! They're so pretty." It struck me as a kind but odd gesture.

He sat on the bed and kissed me.

I felt an obligation to tell Sam that before last night I had been a virgin, but I feared he would be mad at me for not saying something sooner. I also wondered if he could feel I was a virgin and that's why he had bought me flowers. I specifically did not mention my virginity because I did not want him to not have sex with me because of it. At seventeen I felt I was old enough to make this decision for myself, and that my sexual history was my business, not his. Now I felt he should know.

"I have something to tell you." Never a good way to start a sentence with someone you have just slept with. I know this now.

"Okay . . ."

"I was a virgin."

"What?! No way!" He seemed surprised but not angry. "Are you serious?"

"Yes." I smiled, sensing I was not in trouble. His was the first penis I had ever seen. I kept that to myself.

"I can't believe it!"

"You thought I was not a virgin? I'm seventeen."

"You're just so mature for your age. I figured for sure you were having sex."

"Oh, thank you."

I so very clearly remember that "thank you"—remember the pride I felt in being viewed by a man in his late twenties as equal. I also felt confused as to why Sam might assume I would be so sexually experienced at only seventeen. In the moment, however, pride superseded confusion. It is clearer to me now, having spent the last twenty years clawing for equality in my romantic relationships, equality that thus far evades me, why he had not asked about my sexual history before that night. He did not want to know. By knowing, he might face a greater moral dilemma. I doubt he even felt he *needed* to know. Real consequence was not something he had to consider.

"Wow, well, I'm honored it was with me. I hope you feel okay."

"Yeah, I feel good."

"I think the age of consent here is eighteen, so maybe, like, don't tell anyone about this," he said, laughing.

"Oh really? In New York and Connecticut it's sixteen." I knew this because Amanda and I had looked it up right before I had left for California. Doing this made me feel powerful. Pop culture had taught me that being the Lolita meant being in control. It meant being bad in a cool way. I wanted to know, numerically, how bad I was being. I never considered how bad he was being.

"Am I gonna go to senior prom with you?" Sam would say, laughing, on our nightly phone calls. We both knew this was a joke.

In May I texted David, the one who introduced us.

Me: Will you go to my prom with me?

David: Absolutely not.

Me: What?! Why not??

David: I'm 20. There's no way I'm going to a high school prom. Are you still talking to Sam?

Me: Yeah but he can't go to prom with me because he's in LA and too old.

David: It's really fucked-up that you guys are even talking.
Me: Why?
David: Because he's 12 years older than you and you're 17.
Me: I'm almost 18! I'm mature for my age. You just don't get it.
David: Whatever. I just think it's really weird.

In the end, I took Amanda to prom, proud that my boyfriend was too old to be seen at a high school dance. I wore a long dress with cap sleeves made from cream crepe silk with a pink floral pattern. Like for all the dances before it, I designed the dress and my mom made it. Neither Amanda nor I thought my relationship with Sam was weird or inappropriate. We were coming of age in a culture saturated with older man/younger woman relationships—Michael Douglas and Catherine Zeta Jones, Jack Nicholson and Lara Flynn Boyle, Hugh Hefner and every single Playboy Bunny. Girls were expected to date older men and taught to view boys their own age as immature. "It makes sense when I see you guys together," Amanda had said, further reinforcing this view.

My senior year I was accepted to a five-year dual program at Parsons School of Design and Eugene Lang College in Manhattan to study photography and psychology. I hated high school. Even though I did well, the rigid bureaucracy of it tested my limits with authority. The idea of going straight to college was unthinkable. I needed a break. I convinced my parents to let me defer college and move to Los Angeles for one year to attend the Vidal Sassoon Academy for cosmetology. If this sounds incredibly random it's because it was. I was trying to think of anything to get out of college for the year and anything that would bring me closer to Sam. I had always been interested in hair and I was good at it. While my friends went to salons before school dances, I did my own. With a cosmetology license I was setting myself up with a trade that could always bring in money. At the end of the year, when I returned to New York City, I could cut hair while in college to help support myself.

It was not without importance that California was the farthest I could go to get away from home. I told my parents I had found a free place to stay, a friend with an extra bedroom. A welcome arrangement given their mounting divorce expenses. They agreed with no follow-up questions. That friend, of course, was Sam.

Eleven

A dog named Biscuit comes to visit the house. Everyone loves her. Biscuit is a therapy dog, but she's pretty hyper. She tears all over the downstairs of Dalby, going from me to Caitlyn, back to me, to Shawn, over to Mary, back to Caitlyn, back to me. She never stays at one person's feet more than three seconds. She jumps on the couches and then quickly jumps down. She runs into the kitchen, but when she finds no one there she circles the table and heads back to the living room. Biscuit is a mini Australian shepherd who doesn't know how to settle the fuck down.

"Biscuit, come here!" Caitlyn says, patting the couch cushion next to her. Biscuit runs full speed to her and leaps onto the couch. She pants forcefully three times directly in Caitlyn's face and is gone from the couch as quickly as she arrived.

"Ew," Caitlyn says, wiping her face. "She's so cute though."

"Oh my god, Biscuit!" Mary walks into the living room. Biscuit runs into her legs, runs back into the kitchen, circles the table for the fifth time, and then runs upstairs.

"Biscuit! BISCUIT! BISCUIT!" Biscuit's owner, a dark-haired, middle-aged man, is yelling as he heads toward the stairs. "Am I allowed up there?" He's looking at me. I shrug. Biscuit comes racing down the stairs.

"There's another dog that sometimes comes here," Mary says to me. "Her name is Lady. She's a black lab and she's"—Mary pauses—"calm."

"Biscuit can do tricks!" Biscuit's owner says, fully exasperated. "Doesn't anyone want to see Biscuit do tricks?!"

I want to tell him to relax, we all like Biscuit.

"I want to see!" Caitlyn has had a huge smile on her face since Biscuit arrived.

"Super! Biscuit, come here." The owner addresses his dog in an authoritative voice. The shepherd runs to him and sits, staring at him with her wild blue eyes that appear to be looking in slightly different directions. Her little nub tail is moving side to side vigorously. "Lie down, Biscuit." Biscuit lies down. "Roll over, Biscuit." Biscuit rolls over. "Biscuit, play dead." Biscuit leaps off the floor and jumps onto the couch where Shawn has just sat down, a towel wrapped around her freshly washed hair. Biscuit licks Shawn's face. This is the opposite of playing dead.

"Oh my god." Shawn pulls her body back to escape the dog.

"I guess Biscuit didn't want to do that last trick," says the owner with a nervous laugh. "She's a puppy, we're still training her."

"She's very cute," Mary says.

At this point I think we are providing support to Biscuit and her owner, not the other way around.

After Biscuit leaves, Caitlyn says, "I miss my dog."

"Me too," I say.

"You have a dog?" Shawn says to me, looking excited. "What kind?"

"She's a French bulldog. Her name's Petunia."

"I love those; she must be so cute. I wish we could see a photo!" Mary, Shawn, and Caitlyn all talk at the same time, piling up on one another's words.

"She's the best. Not to be mean, but she's cooler than Biscuit in every way."

"Can she do tricks?" Caitlyn asks.

"She can. She knows sit, lie down, roll over, high five, and stay. She sort of knows stay, I guess."

"I want a French bulldog," Shawn says.

"I have to be honest, I wouldn't recommend it. They have so many health problems. I'm at the vet constantly with her. It's crazy expensive. Once Petunia is no longer on this earth, I will become a staunch anti-bulldog-breeding activist. We shouldn't keep making more of them."

"I bet you love her so much though," Mary says.

"She's the literal love of my life."

Today's creative arts therapy is jewelry making. As with horticulture therapy, jewelry making does not require us to do any therapy. The therapy is making the jewelry.

"Laurie, the woman who runs this, has *so* many beads. It's really fun," Mary says to me as we all take a seat around the kitchen table.

Mary is not wrong. Laurie unloads ten plastic containers that each have twelve compartments of various beads.

Laurie has curly blond hair and is probably in her early forties. Her voice is chipper, but not condescending. "I have clasps for bracelets, necklaces, or earrings. Make whatever you want!"

I decide to make a bracelet. After I stopped wearing stretchy rave bracelets to cover my cutting, I rarely wore bracelets again. It's an accessory I have missed out on due to my bone structure. My wrists are so small that clasped bracelets never fit me. On the rare occasions when I have worn bracelets, I felt like they got in the way of everything. Sweaters get caught on them. They unclasp and fall off easily. Am I supposed to take them off when I wash dishes or my hands? If yes, that seems annoying and not worth their added aesthetic value. Yet I simply cannot resist the opportunity to make a bracelet that fits my child-sized wrist. I survey the beads. There are so many.

"Oh my god, I love letter beads," I say, fishing around in a container of small white oval beads with black letters printed on them. "They remind me of high school."

Sifting through the letter beads at Dalby, I pull out an *A* and two small red hearts to flank it. Very inspired stuff.

"What are you making?" I ask Shawn.

"I'm gonna make a necklace. The last time we did jewelry, I saw these blue beads that were kinda like scarabs. I'll use those and then maybe some of these green ones." She holds up a small green bead to the light, which when backlit is iridescent and laced with glittering purple swirls.

"I like those." Our heads are tilted toward each other, taking in the fractured light behind the bead.

I throw back the *A* and the hearts. I pull two different shades of green glass beads and alternate them a few times before spelling out the phrase "NEW YEAR" with the letter beads.

"Why 'NEW YEAR'?" Shawn asks.

"I keep saying, 'This is going to be a bad year,' and I realized that's too pessimistic this early in January. We're only six days in. So instead of thinking 'bad year,' I'm going to think 'new year.' Who knows if it will be bad. It just might not be what I'm used to. New."

Shawn nods.

The house manager interrupts jewelry making to tell me I have to leave for an appointment with my social worker, Beth. I look down in a panic at my nearly finished bracelet, and then back at the house manager. How can I leave behind this masterpiece?

"I'll finish the clasp for you!" Laurie says.

"Thank you, I would appreciate that."

"Let me see it on your wrist so I can make it the correct size. Christ, they're so small!"

* * *

I walk to the Doctors Office building and check in at the front desk, where two friendly women tell me to have a seat in the waiting area. I notice the radio is on at the front desk, or maybe it's a TV. I can only hear it.

"This is really unprecedented, and information is coming in piece by piece as we get it from inside the Capitol," says a voice whose cadence can only belong to a news anchor.

I turn to the front desk, which is partitioned from the area where I am sitting by plexiglass. There are never TVs or radios playing in common areas, and we are not really supposed to watch the news. It can be triggering, and news is so politicized now it leaves little room for people to agree on which channel to watch. I still cannot see where the news anchor voice is coming from, but I see the two women at the front desk sitting very still with their heads tilted down, the way one would if they were really concentrating. I do the same, closing my eyes in hopes that blocking my sight will heighten my hearing.

"We don't know how many people are inside at this moment, however we do have word that members of Congress have blockaded themselves in their offices. Some offices have been completely ransacked by the mob."

I cannot make sense of what I am hearing, so I walk up to the front desk. "Hi, excuse me, what's going on?"

"We really aren't supposed to discuss the news," one of the women says, turning the volume down slightly on what I can now see is a phone. She breaks immediately, though. "A mob of people stormed the Capitol Building and got inside."

Just then Beth comes out and invites me into her office. I inherently trust her more than the other doctors simply because she is a woman, which is not to say I do not trust the other doctors, I do. I just feel that a woman can listen to my issues, my stories, my traumas and not pathologize them from a man's point of view.

"I'm curious if you've been witness to physical or sexual abuse?"

"I mean, when I was a kid my mom spanked me a few times. I remember one of those pretty vividly. But that's it, and I wouldn't call that physical abuse."

"Can you tell me about the circumstances of one of those times?"

"It was my birthday, I think my seventh or eighth birthday. My family was visiting—both sets of grandparents and my two cousins who I only got to see once a year at best. My mom had baked me a cake and we were all sitting down to eat it. She wanted to take my photo, but I didn't want to have my photo taken. She was getting madder and madder at me, but I refused to smile for a photo. I rarely tested her anger; it's strange that in that moment I decided to. But she grabbed me by the arm and took me upstairs to my bedroom. My dad followed, which was also strange because he wasn't the disciplinarian at all."

Beth dutifully takes notes and nods to show she is listening. Beth's face remains neutral with a small, pleasant smile. Beth is simply keeping record of the facts. She seems very diligent and organized. I wonder if Beth is a Virgo. I want to ask but I continue with my story instead.

"So we are in my room, and by this time I know I've fucked up. She's screaming at me. I'm now crying and apologizing. I can tell something is coming but I don't know what exactly. I say that I'll let her take my photo if we can just go back downstairs. She pulls me over to her, lays me across her lap, and spanks me three or four times as hard as she can. I'm screaming and crying, and she just holds firm in her rage. Then she and my dad make me stay in my room and tell me I'm not allowed to come downstairs to say goodbye to my cousins before they leave. They all eat my birthday cake while I'm in my room, and my aunt, uncle, and cousins leave to go back home. Eventually my mom lets me out of my room, but I'm not allowed to eat any of the remaining cake."

"And to clarify," Beth says matter-of-factly. She pauses, looking over her notes briefly, and then asks, "This happened because you didn't want your photo taken?"

"Yes."

"Anything else?" Beth asks.

"I had a sexual relationship with a much older man when I was a minor. It was definitely consensual, so I wouldn't file this under sexual abuse in any way. But it was weird, and I've felt weirder and weirder about it the older I've gotten."

"Weirder in what way?"

"Now, in my mid-thirties, I think it's super odd that a twenty-nine-year-old man would have sex with a seventeen-year-old, even if it was consensual."

Beth nods to let me know she's listening as her pen moves rapidly across her notebook. "Anything else?"

"Nope, that covers it."

"I and the other doctors on your case would like to make the recommendation that you stay at the hospital after this evaluation is finished and do the thirty-day in-patient dialectical behavioral therapy program. It would be an opportunity for you to do intensive DBT training while remaining in the safety of the hospital. Going back to an empty house might not be the best thing for you right at this moment."

I start to cry.

"What's coming up for you right now?"

"If I stay, I'll derail my master's program even more than I already have. We are in the middle of working on an exhibition. I don't want to miss that, and I don't want to let my classmates down by backing out of my responsibilities. Also, I can't ask my mom to watch my dog for another thirty days."

"Yes, I understand your concerns. Is it something you'd be willing to think about? You don't have to decide now."

"I'll think about it."

But I already know I am not staying.

When I leave the building, the women at the front desk are still listening to the news about the Capitol, and I do not stop to ask any more questions. I walk quickly back to Dalby. Shawn is sitting in the living room with Mary and Caitlyn.

"Did you hear what's happening at the Capitol?" I say.

Shawn picks up the remote from the coffee table. "Yeah, but only partially. I'm just gonna turn the news on."

After a few minutes the house manager runs into the living room. "Wait! Hold on, we are not supposed to be watching the news."

"I think we can all handle it." Shawn is annoyed.

"Is everyone okay with this?" the house manager asks.

Everyone nods.

We all sit, watching something play out that is hard to make sense of. It reminds me of walking into high school chemistry class on the morning of September 11.

"Someone flew a plane into the Twin Towers," my friend Elaine said to me.

"What an idiot. Did he die?" I was picturing a small prop plane flown by a single, inexperienced pilot.

"I think a lot of people died," Elaine said. "It wasn't a small plane, it was, like, a really big plane."

"Oh shit."

The chemistry teacher wheeled a big, boxy TV on a metal stand into the room and turned it on, flipping between static and low-channel news. The reception was terrible, and sound was not coming through the speakers, but we could see a shot of downtown New York City. One of the Twin Towers had a massive hole in its side and smoke was pouring out. The internal school phone in the classroom rang; the teacher answered it, saying simply "okay," and then turned the TV off, inciting an instant verbal revolt from the students.

"What the fuck!!"

"Turn it back on!"

"We want to know what's happening."

Everyone was yelling.

"Please, everyone, go to your seats and sit down. I have been instructed not to turn on the TV. We are just supposed to wait for further instruction."

"This is total bullshit," someone said, but then we were all quiet.

Within minutes we were directed to return to our homeroom classes, but were provided no other information. We sat for about an hour before we were told that the school day was over, and we were all to return home. I found Elaine outside the school, and we walked to her car while military planes, likely en route from the naval base in Groton, flew overhead toward New York City.

I had no idea both towers had fallen until I arrived home. My mom called me from the yoga retreat she was at and told me not to watch the news.

"They're just going to show the planes crashing and towers falling over and over and over again. Don't watch it. Do you want me to come home?"

"No, don't come home. I'm okay here. You don't need to come home."

"All right. If you're sure." She was crying.

I turned on the TV anyway. She was right. The same footage of the crashes and their aftermaths was recycled on a loop with little other information coming in. I quickly changed the channel to MTV, hoping for reruns of *The Real World*, but it was also a news broadcast. Grabbing a stick fashioned with a small stuffed mouse hanging from a string, I silently played with my cat because I did not know what else to do.

After a bit, it is just Shawn and me still watching the news. Finally we turn off the TV.

Mary, who has wandered into the kitchen, says, "Anna, Laurie left your finished bracelet on the table; don't forget it."

I walk to the table, pick it up, and put it on. It's way too big.

Twelve

"How come you cry every time we have sex?" Sam asked me as we drove down the 5 freeway. It was New Year's Eve and I had been living in LA for four months.

I paused, trying to formulate an answer. I had never asked myself this question. Sam was the first person I had ever slept with, and I did not realize this was not normal.

"Mmm, maybe because I'm just, like, having a release of emotion when I come?"

I had never had an orgasm when we had sex.

"I just wanted to make sure nothing was wrong."

"No, nothing's wrong."

And nothing was wrong, technically. I had a nice place to stay. I was enjoying my time at Vidal Sassoon and was making some friends. But things with Sam were becoming difficult.

"Look at this," he said one day, his voice filled with a mixture of anger and disappointment that was becoming more common. "It's ruined. I've been looking for this everywhere, and you ruined it."

The Thomas Guide in his hand was stained brown, and crispy the way wet paper becomes once dry. The Thomas Guide was a road atlas people used in California before GPS and which I was sure was very replaceable.

"I'm sorry," I said quietly. "Where was it?"

"On top of the refrigerator. But you obviously stuck some apples up there and forgot about them and they went bad and leaked all over. You didn't smell it?"

"I'm really sorry. I just forgot. Can I buy a new one?"

"That's not the point. This is just careless and lazy. You have to take better care of people's stuff. This is something a child would do."

I did not want Sam to be disappointed in me. I did not want to be childish.

I had come to feel trapped in a situation that felt at best untenable and at worst oppressive. When Sam was home from tour, I felt acutely aware that I was living on his turf. There were certain times of the day he would not leave his house because he did not want to contend with traffic. Going to a movie between the hours of two p.m. and seven p.m. on any day of the week was out of the question. When he was away, I did whatever I wanted on my days off, at whatever time of day, but in his presence I felt a self-imposed pressure to be home with him. The time he had free was minimal, and so I took it upon myself to alter my way of living to take advantage of whatever he could give me.

I did not have internet at Sam's. Occasionally I could connect to a weak signal coming from the neighbor's house, but most of the time if I wanted to check my email or use Instant Messenger, I visited an internet café down the street from Vidal Sassoon. That is where I was one afternoon when an IM from David popped up on the computer screen. We had not spoken much since I had moved to LA. He knew I was living at Sam's and disapproved.

David: How's it going out there?
Me: Hi David! It's ok.
David: Just ok?
Me: Yeah

David: Are you all right?

Me: I don't know. I just really want to go home.

David: Are you still with Sam?

Me: Yeah but he's away on tour for the next couple months.

David: If you're in a bad situation you should get out of it.

Me: I don't think I'm in a bad situation. Besides where am I supposed to go?

The internet crashed, abruptly signing me out of IM. I tried to sign back in, but all I got was an "Internet Unavailable" window.

"Excuse me," I said to the barista. "The computer I was using just signed me out and won't let me reconnect."

"Yeah, sorry, sometimes that happens. I don't know what to tell you. Grab another computer, I guess."

I turned back toward the "internet" part of the café. It was a bleak row of five PCs on the edge of breakdown, bodies slouched in front of every screen except the one I had been using. I turned back to the barista, but he was gone. Sitting at the computer, I reinserted my debit card, but I still could not connect to the internet. I hit the enter key with force, over and over again, until the man at the station next to me looked in my direction, eyes wide. I grabbed my things and left, blinking back tears.

Texting was my most reliable link to friends, but I had already overused my monthly text allotment, which I learned by way of a very annoyed phone call from my dad.

"You can't text all the time. This is costing me money! You have to be more careful."

"I'm sorry, I can pay you back," I said, but this was an empty promise. I had two hundred dollars a month my dad gave me to live on while at Vidal Sassoon. This money had to put gas in my car and pay for my groceries and cover the occasional parking ticket I would get from illegally spending eight hours parked in the two-hours-free mall lot a few blocks away from school. In the ten months I'd spent at the academy, I only got three parking tickets, totaling three hundred dollars. I realized that cars were only ticketed if they parked under covered parking. The top two floors of the garage had no roof, providing no shelter from the sun or the thick Santa Monica fog, and were, arbitrarily, a lawless land of unenforced parking stipulations. Monthly parking in any of the nearby garages cost three hundred dollars per month. Had not this shrewd game of financial chess earned me some extra texts?

It had not, and so one Sunday morning I tried like I did every weekend to find a stolen internet connection on the laptop Sam left behind when he went on tour. It did not work, as it did not work nearly every time I tried, but I saw on his desktop an image labeled "Anna.jpg." I wondered which photo of me he kept visible for easy access. I double-clicked the icon.

A photo appeared on the screen, but it was not me. It was a young woman, around my age, naked, straddling the photographer, who was taking the photo from underneath her. It looked like it had been taken with any average digital camera, similar to the one Sam had. I studied the image of the young woman while my body began to tingle, heat forming in my stomach and chest. Like with the motorcycle accident years earlier, my vision went dark, my ability to hear disappeared. I tried to make sense of what this photograph meant. Had Sam taken this photo? Was he sleeping with other women? Would Sam do that? Who was this woman? But this only led to more questions. How old was she? Why was it labeled with my name?

"Hi." I measured my voice as I spoke into the phone, trying equally to not overreact or vomit. "I need to talk to you about something."

"What's up?" His voice sounded far away, like we were on opposite sides of a door, and I was listening to his words through a glass.

He was overseas, on tour in the UK. I had not seen him in months. I used his house phone to call him so as not to upset my dad with my cell phone charges.

"I was just on your computer, trying to connect to email, and I saw a photo that was labeled with my name, so I opened it and it was a photo of a naked girl, about my age."

"And . . ."

I expected a more fluid excuse, like Brian had given the cop the night we were caught in the parking lot, but it did not come. The indignant laziness of his words made me feel crazy for even mentioning the photo.

"Who is she?"

"I don't know. Probably just some amateur porn girl that Robert sent me."

Robert was the forty-seven-year-old friend I had heard about but never met. Up until this point I had never watched or looked at porn. I did not even know how to find it. It seemed to me something clandestine, not, as Sam made it seem, a thing frequently traded between two grown men. Then again, Sam did not even have internet, so maybe he needed his friends to send him porn.

"Well it looks like it was taken with a digital camera."

"It probably was." He seemed annoyed and was growing impatient.

"So this isn't a girl you slept with? You didn't take this photo?"

"No."

"Well, why was it labeled 'Anna'?"

"I have no idea, okay? Robert probably just sent it to me under whatever the girl's name was. I guess her name was Anna."

"That seems weird."

"Listen, I don't know what to tell you. I don't even know what this photo is. I have to go do a sound check. I don't really have time for this."

We hung up. I closed the photo and then the computer, feeling scared and helpless for the first time in our two-year relationship. Despite his job, one that brought him to different cities every night and offered up adoring fans, I had never considered that Sam would cheat on me. Even though I had met him at a show while he was on tour, I thought of myself as some special anomaly. I had placed my trust in him fully, a bestowal that now felt so stupid and naive. This photo wasn't proof that he was cheating. It was possible he was telling the truth, but doubt had been planted.

I wanted to leave Sam's house, but I could not, because I had nowhere to go. One girl I had become close with at school offered me the couch in her studio apartment, but I knew that was a weekend solution at best. I was too embarrassed to tell my parents that I had found myself in a situation I wanted out of. More than that, I did not believe I could trust them to extricate me from this sad, tiny house in Van Nuys. I worried that if I asked my dad for help, he would tell me he couldn't financially afford to. Then I would always question whether that was the truth.

My final months in Los Angeles.

I missed Sam.

I hated Sam.

I wanted to be in New York, to start college and live with peers my own age.

I wanted to apply to Los Angeles colleges and continue living with Sam.

I kissed a guy who I went to Vidal Sassoon with and did not feel bad.

I sat in my car in the dark of night with one of my teachers, even older than Sam, and politely refused when he invited me into his house after asking me for a ride home. He had a five-year-old daughter who lived in Oklahoma with her twenty-five-year-old mother. They had met when she was his student.

On my nineteenth birthday I opened a card from Sam that had a drawing of a penguin wearing sunglasses and a scarf, with text that read: *You're Eighteen. Coooooool.*

"But I'm not eighteen, I'm nineteen," I said to him.

"I know but, like, you're eighteen, coooool, get it? Like, you're legal now."

"But I'm nineteen."

"It's funny," he said.

I failed my cosmetology state board exam at the end of ten months at the Vidal Sassoon Academy. Sixteen hundred hours of work and a couple thousand in tuition wasted.

I moved to New York City to start the photography program at Parsons School of Design that I had deferred for one year. I promised my parents I would retake the cosmetology state board exams in New York, but never did. Sam was not in LA when I left. He was on tour, like he had been for much of the year. We planned to stay together and be long distance until I could find a way to get back to California. This felt realistic, as we rarely saw each other anyway in the two years we had been together.

"You need to end it," David said to me one night from across the table of a dingy pizza place in Union Square. He had become more responsive since I'd moved back east, and now that we were both in the city, he had agreed to meet up for dinner.

"I know."

A day later I called Sam.

"I'm really sorry," I said, "but being back in New York I just realized, well, I realized I'm not coming back to LA."

"What does *that* mean?" He knew what it meant.

"I'm not coming back to LA. I have to focus on school. And be around people my own age. I don't want to be in a relationship with you anymore. I'm sorry."

"I can't believe this." He was angry, and at the time I felt he was justified. "So you just stay at my place for a year and then you break up with me? I said I'd be with you forever, that I was done looking, and now you're gonna break up with me?"

"Yes. I'm sorry."

"I don't even know what to say to you."

I paused for a beat, unsure if this was an empty threat, but he remained silent.

"I know I left a bunch of things at your house," I said. "I'm sorry. I really thought I would be back. I can tell you're upset, so let's just take a week. At the end of a week I'll call you and we can arrange how to get my stuff back to me. Obviously, I'll pay for it to be shipped." I had no money to cover this expense.

"Fine." He hung up the phone and I felt immediate relief.

Exactly one week later I sat on the edge of my dorm room bed holding my phone, his number highlighted. All I had to do was press the button. I felt sick to my stomach. After two rings his phone went to voicemail.

"Hi. It's me. I said I would call you in a week about getting my stuff shipped from LA. This is that call. I guess, take whatever time you need, and you can call me back when you're ready. Okay, bye."

He never called me back.

Thirteen

My time at the hospital is nearly at its end. Tomorrow, after an outtake meeting, I will leave to return home. The doctors have all suggested I stay longer, but I know I will not. Still, I'm worried about going home.

Last night, around eight p.m., Dr. Philips arrived back at Dalby to speak with me.

"I wanted to come by to discuss the results of the three take-home tests you completed the other day. Would that be okay with you?"

"Yes, that sounds good. Thank you."

"I'll have you look at this page first. These are your answers mapped out."

He holds up a sheet of paper with a line of sharp peaks and valleys. It looks like an EKG.

"The two prominent peaks you see here"—he points with his pen—"show depression and anxiety, while the low valleys mark violence and delusions. So, as you can see, there are no issues with you having delusions. You're obviously clear minded and have a perfect understanding of what is real and what is not. And you have no tendencies toward violence. Does that resonate with you?"

"Yes. Though I'm glad to hear it explicitly."

"What is very concerning is your suicide risk." He points to a peak so high it nearly clears the page. "It's very rare to see suicide risk this high from a person not in in-patient care."

"What does that mean exactly?"

"I mean if someone is this at-risk, they have usually been hospitalized already and they were likely hospitalized precisely due to their suicide risk. You arrived here to participate in an evaluative program. It wasn't communicated by your therapist that you were an acute suicide risk."

"Oh" is all I can say.

"I'd like to ask you, what are some of the things you feel you have to live for at this moment?"

"I guess my dog, Petunia. I love her so much and she loves me. She has a lot of health problems, and I feel a responsibility to take care of her."

"Anything besides Petunia?"

I use the sleeve of my sweatshirt to wipe tears from my eyes.

"Not really. At the moment, no."

"I worry that a dog in precarious health is too unstable a thing to hold on to," he says.

"I do worry about myself if she were to die."

"Yes, I do as well."

We sit in silence for a moment.

Then he says, "We are saving a spot for you in the dialectical behavioral therapy program."

"I've done DBT before," I say.

"Did you find it helpful?"

"I did."

"I think it would really benefit you to stay here."

"I'll think about it," I say, leaving out all the reasons I explained to Beth earlier why this will be impossible. I have already made up my mind to leave.

At ten thirty this morning, after a meeting where I state my goal (to have a good day), I go to the rec center for a class called movement therapy. Caitlyn is there too, and so are a few men from Oscar House whose names I never got. Adam isn't there because he isn't at the hospital anymore, a reminder that time keeps moving forward even though here it's easy to feel like you're on pause. Class is taught by the kooky yoga teacher I met on my second day. I don't think this will be fun, but maybe I'll see the wild turkeys again. Also, I like hanging out with Caitlyn. Much like yoga, movement therapy is a free-form exercise in trying not to get embarrassed. We spin around with our arms stretched wide, we walk aimlessly, we move our faces around, stretching our muscles while making indiscriminate noises. When Caitlyn and I make eye contact between spins, we smile at each other and try not to laugh.

At times I have difficulty following the teacher's stream-of-consciousness speaking style.

"Armsupwiggleyourfingersss. Eyesclosed reachupupup. Envision-yourselfoneyearfromnow. Whatareyoudoing? WHEREareyougoing? WhatandwhoisitYOUwanttobeee? SEEwhoyouareinoneyear. Thank-yourselfforshowingup. Reachyourhandsupupup. Andswingthemdown. Shakeoutyourarms."

I wish she would punctuate with more precision. I see myself in a vintage patchwork dress. I am standing in my yard, bathed in sunlight. Everything feels calm. The teacher tells our future selves to give our current selves a word or phrase that we must hold with us, and instructs us to write it down. I think? When she hands everyone a note card and pencil, I'm positive I heard correctly and write *resilience to survive*.

There is a lot of emphasis on language in the hospital. Putting words to feelings, being able to describe our experiences, expressing our desires and fears—it has the effect of demystifying our traumatic experiences and defanging hard memories. Or so we are told by the doctors.

Class runs late and I have to walk directly to my case conference in the Doctors Office building. There are no turkeys in sight. The case conference is different from the outtake meeting, which is tomorrow. Today, the case conference involves a doctor I have never met, who is nice but is yet again a man, asking me a series of questions. As he does, Dr. Samuels, Dr. Philips, Beth, and my therapist from the outside world, Dr. Karr, watch and listen from a large TV screen. Everyone has been discussing their findings on my mental health prior to my arrival to the conference.

I enter the room, shake the doctor's hand, and direct my attention to the large TV screen. I see Dr. Karr and at once feel very emotional. I have been looking forward to seeing her. It is a face I know so well. I have looked at it for fifty minutes, either one or two times a week, for the past five years. She is sitting in front of the familiar yellow wall she has sat in front of since our sessions went virtual in March 2020. I look at her and smile, but she does not smile back. Her face looks stern. My immediate instinct is that she is mad at me, but I am not sure what I did wrong. I try harder, this time smiling and waving. I say, "Hi, Dr. Karr!" Her face breaks, but only slightly. She still looks incredibly serious. "Hi, Anna," she says, but there is little warmth in her voice. Inwardly, I start to panic.

I make it through the first five or ten minutes of the case conference without crying, but when Dr. Philips begins discussing the findings of my psychological testing, I am unable to keep the tears at bay. I cry through most of the meeting, feeling overwhelmed by some of the questions, despite them being questions I have been asked over and over during the course of my stay.

"Where do you see yourself going from here?"

I have no idea.

"What feels hopeful in your life at the moment?"

Almost nothing.

The conference is short, only twenty minutes. When it ends, I say goodbye to Dr. Karr specifically. She has only been an observer in this meeting.

"It was nice to see you!" I add as enthusiastically as possible. This is my attempt to get an equally enthusiastic response in return, and hopefully absolve myself of any fear that Dr. Karr might be mad at me.

"You too," she says, curt and reserved.

In the evening I walk the grounds with Mary and Caitlyn. We end up at the Labyrinth. The Labyrinth is a mazelike path cut into a field, but unlike an actual maze it is not meant to confuse. It is, instead, a tool of contemplation, prayer, or ritual used as a walking meditation. It is the type of thing you might see at a Native American heritage site, like the Topock Maze in Needles, California, or a thirteenth-century French cathedral, like the one in Chartres. My first meaningful introduction to a walking labyrinth was in an episode of *The Real Housewives of Orange County*. The Housewives walk a labyrinth while clutching sheets of paper scrawled with their hopes and dreams, tossing them into a fire at the maze's center. Later, an enormous fight breaks out when Kelly puts a Tibetan singing bowl over Shannon's head and bangs it with a mallet.

We all walk the Labyrinth at different paces. Quietly, with our heads down, we move into its center and then retrace our steps back out. We inevitably pass one another on the path. When we do, we look up and smile and then return our eyes to the ground directly in front of our shoes. Mary finishes first and waits for Caitlyn and me where we all began.

"I liked that," Caitlyn says.

"Me too," Mary says.

"Do either of you watch *The Real Housewives of Orange County*?" I ask.

"No," they say in unison.

"Never mind."

As we get closer to Dalby, Mary says, "It bothers me that everyone doesn't come to the speaker meetings. We are here to fully engage in this experience, and I think it's important to show up for everything offered to us. Especially the speakers. They're giving their time."

"I agree," I say, and Caitlyn, who's walking next to me, nods.

"Anna," Mary looks at me, "you spoke so eloquently during that AA meeting a few days ago. I really liked listening to you talk a bit about yourself."

"Thank you for saying that, Mary. That's so nice of you."

She smiles at me, and I add, "Really, I mean it."

Before dinner, Dr. Philips comes back to Dalby to discuss the last of my testing results. His consistent openness to explain my results in-depth, coupled with his warm demeanor, is something I have come to appreciate over this past week.

"You do not show any clinical signs of PTSD—flashbacks, violent outbursts—things like that. However, you do show signs of significant attachment trauma beginning in early life. Attachment trauma is usually linked to your primary caregivers. Extreme examples are abuse and neglect, but there can be a variety of adversities relating to primary caregivers that result in trauma—being in an environment where you witness a lot of fighting, caregivers who aren't able to attune to the needs of a child on a consistent basis. Are you okay?"

Of course I'm crying already. I throw up my hands, laugh, and say, "Yes." He smiles and continues.

"When children experience significant relational trauma, it later contributes to an increased risk of feeling insecure in relationships, difficulty with trust, problems managing distress, and vulnerability to anxiety and depression. All of these show up in your test results. In a seemingly intractable dilemma, you feel you can't trust others or yourself. Other people present the potential to dismiss you, betray you, neglect you, or act malevolently toward you. Especially men, it seems."

"Yes, it's hard for me to let people in. And I've grown increasingly angry at men's mere existence."

"It's also clear that you do have a very strong group of female friends who you've had for quite a long time, some ten and twenty years. You trust and love those people deeply. Intimacy and vulnerability might be difficult for you to experience comfortably, and trust is slow to develop, but you obviously have the ability to trust many of the people in your life."

"I do. I'm very lucky to have female friends who love me. I love them back very much."

"I have a lot of hope for you, Anna," he says. "You're open-minded, you're conscientious, you care deeply for other people, for your dog, you're highly self-disciplined. At times you might feel defective, damaged, or unworthy, but these feelings are the result of trauma. You are, in reality, none of those things. I truly feel that with the right therapy you can regain your confidence, become more self-accepting, more self-compassionate, and learn to trust yourself and other people."

"Thank you," I say quietly.

"How do you feel about leaving tomorrow?"

"I feel scared to go back to my house alone and scared to face my life right now."

"I understand that," he says. "I think it's very important that your depression is monitored, and you at the very least participate in our Intensive Outpatient DBT program, to help reduce the frequency and severity of your suicidal thoughts."

"Yes, I agree. Will all of this be relayed to Dr. Karr, so when I'm discharged she has an idea of everyone's thoughts and recommendations?"

"It absolutely will."

There is a moment of silence between us.

"I want to tell you how much I appreciate the way you've gone through all of these results with me," I say to Dr. Philips between tearful, sharp inhales. "I've learned so much and I've gotten so much out of hearing words put to the emotions I've been experiencing throughout the course of my life. I really feel you have a deep understanding of what is happening inside my brain." I wipe a tear from my cheek. "Even though you're a man."

Dr. Philips laughs. I laugh too.

Leaving my meeting with Dr. Philips I hear Shawn practicing violin in her room. She has her door closed, so I sit at the top of the stairs between our two rooms and listen to her play before going to my room to pack. I am going to miss this.

Caitlyn, Mary, Shawn, and I eat dinner in the dining room at Main House. It is nice not to have to grab-and-go on my last night.

"What do you guys do when you're hanging out in your rooms at Dalby?" Mary asks. Her attitude is always perky despite the slight lag in her voice from medication.

"I listen to my iPod," says Caitlyn.

"You get to have an iPod?" Shawn says.

"Yeah, I'm allowed to listen to music for thirty minutes a day. It helps me feel better. After the thirty minutes I have to give it back, though, and it gets locked up."

"Damn. I wish I'd asked for that," Shawn says, looking down at a piece of meatball she's moving around her plate with a fork. "I usually do my DBT worksheets." I'm surprised she doesn't mention practicing her violin.

"I usually read or write," I say.

"Me too! What are you reading?" Mary is excited.

"This is really dumb, but I'm reading *The Secret Garden*. As in the children's book from the early 1900s."

"I don't think that's dumb!" Mary says. "Is it good?"

"It's okay. It's sort of slow and too long, I guess because there wasn't a lot to do back then but read? Honestly, the movie adaptation from the early nineties is better than the book."

"I've never seen it," says Mary.

"Me either," say Caitlyn and Shawn.

"I guess maybe it was a little before your time? 1993," I say.

"I wasn't even born then!" says Caitlyn.

"Me either!" Mary says with her big, full laugh.

"I was just born and not watching movies yet," Shawn says.

I laugh with them.

"What are you reading, Mary?" I ask.

"*Lithium*. It's a book about"—she pauses and laughs again—"lithium!"

Then, making eye contact with no one, Mary adds, "It's a really difficult drug," and we all feel the weight of her words.

At my last wrap-up meeting, I am finally able to verbalize the emotions I have been keeping locked inside. I say how grateful I am for my time at the hospital. I tell the girls how lucky I feel to have met them. After the meeting, the house manager asks if I would like to do a Rock Ceremony. I would, but instead I tell her that I feel I have been too introverted, and I am afraid I would be forcing people to say kind things about me that they may not feel. She tells me she thinks everyone would enjoying giving me encouragement, but I decide I cannot take that risk, even though I want to. Watching people search for compliments and inspiring words would be more hurtful than hearing nothing at all. I ask if I can pick a rock for myself, even if I do not do the ceremony. "*Of course*," she says. I empty all the rocks out of their small, black bag onto the house manager's desk. I choose a rock that reads FREEDOM.

Fourteen

David and I started dating almost immediately after I broke up with Sam. There was no thought of taking time in between relationships to independently sort out what had happened with Sam. I saw no advantage in being alone. I loved David and had probably loved him since I met him three years earlier, so I decided to be with him. He chose me too. I leaned on his companionship heavily. New to New York City, I did not yet have a community. While I was in Los Angeles, Amanda had moved to Chicago to attend Columbia College. It would be two years before she came back to the East Coast, so in the meantime, I folded into David's tight-knit group of friends.

I have a sort of photographic memory for the ways men have asserted their power over me, the ways they have treated me poorly, and the ways I have fought to be equal or conversely sublimated myself to keep peace. My memories of my time with David have none of that. We had bad fights sometimes, yet I never once felt any disrespect or lack of awareness for my emotions, or inclination that he did not deeply care for me. He was the sort of man who was on a constant journey toward betterment. He questioned himself and his thoughts and his behaviors. He always strived to be the best version of himself for the people he loved. In the years since then, I have realized these are very rare qualities for men.

There was the time I got a very bad case of food poisoning and vomited for five straight days. I probably should have gone to the hospital for fluids, but because of how I was raised to view Western medicine, I never considered seeking medical attention. I lived in an apartment with no air-conditioning. For a full day, David followed me from my bedroom to the bathroom with an oscillating fan, pointing it at me while I threw up violently into the toilet. When I was done, I would walk my feeble body, stomach muscles aching, back to bed as he followed behind and set the fan back in place so it was blowing on me. After a day of this he had to go to work, but he returned to my apartment that evening with an AC unit to set up in my window.

I told David about my history with cutting as soon as we started dating, even though it had been a year since I'd cut. I identified deeply with the habit, as if it was a core part of my personality that had to be known by the men who saw me naked. I rarely told female friends. I could speak about my emotions more freely with women, and so this information seemed less relevant to their understanding of me. But with men, I felt they had to know in order to take my emotions seriously. I relied on this attention from men as validation of their feelings for me because I didn't trust I could get their attention any other way. David responded with a mix of concern and fear and an ultimatum that if I did it again, even one more time, he would make me tell my parents and get help.

The threat was enough to keep me from cutting while we were together.

A little more than a year into our relationship, David and I broke up. Like all the other sad or hard things we went through together, the why of it has been surrendered to space and distance, swallowed up by happy memories and affection. At the time, though, I was completely set adrift by the breakup.

I dropped out of Parsons. I was searching for something I loved like I had loved dance, but photography felt empty in comparison, especially within the context of academia.

To save money I moved into a shared studio apartment on Third Avenue with my college roommate. We partitioned off rooms for ourselves by draping fabric from the ceiling, grossly underestimating the way real walls might keep us from violating each other's privacy, which we did constantly.

I took a monthlong course specializing in beauty makeup, but I had no idea how to get jobs doing makeup.

I started working at a salon that was willing to hire me as a shampoo girl with no state board accreditation. Though this was a normal entry-level job for people fresh out of cosmetology school, usually you are also assisting a senior hairstylist with the understanding that you will move up the ranks. With no license, I would be a shampoo girl forever.

Then I started dating another musician, a recovering heroin addict with no job. My attraction to him was based on his resemblance in all ways to Elliott Smith, a man who had two years earlier taken his own life by stabbing himself in the chest. I wasn't looking for romance, I was looking for destruction and heartbreak.

I had just returned from work to my corner of the studio apartment when my phone rang. It was my dad.

"Hi!" he said, his voice chipper. "I'm calling to tell you we set a date for our wedding."

"What?" I said, pacing the edges of my tiny textile-draped room.

"We set a date. For the wedding." He said it plainly, like I knew they were engaged.

"I didn't realize you were getting married."

"I told you I proposed!" he said enthusiastically.

"No. You didn't."

"I'm pretty sure I did, but anyway, we're having it at a really nice restaurant in Brewster. The ceremony will be outside. Beautiful view.

And then the reception will be inside the restaurant. We're really looking forward to it."

"Nice," I said.

"Mark your calendar! October fifth."

"I will," I said. If he sensed my annoyance, he pretended he did not.

My dad had not told me he had proposed. That was absolutely
something I would have remembered. I was shocked, since my parents had not been divorced for even a year, though I suppose they had
been separated for three.

I called my mom a few days later to tell her about the wedding,
walking the same motion around my fabric room as I had when speaking to my dad. My parents had only spoken through lawyers or seen
each other in courtrooms over the past three years, but I knew it would
be hard for my mom to hear that my dad was getting remarried.

She started to cry. "I guess I knew this would happen."

"I'm sorry," I said.

"It's not your fault," she said.

It was a crisp, clear October morning on the day of the wedding. I
was woken up by the sun piercing through my east-facing window.
The sound of the downtown Third Avenue bus that stopped right
outside my second-floor apartment had interrupted my sleep nearly
every hour with the forceful exhale of its breaks releasing. That morning, I left to go get coffee at the corner café for myself and the addict I
had left snoring in my bed. Without having to pay college tuition, and
with my new job as a shampoo girl, I should not have had to worry
about overdrawing my checking account on four-dollar beverages,
but buying the addict dinner, helping him pay to record a demo, and
briefly, but unbeknownst to me, supporting a relapse, I consistently
found myself with no money.

In my poorly lit bathroom I slowly and deliberately applied my makeup for the wedding. The act of getting ready for something was calming, one of the few times my mind went quiet. When I finished, I sat on the toilet and cried everything off. Then I washed my face and started my makeup over again.

"I'll be back around seven tonight, I think. I got you coffee."

"I'll just stay here," the addict said, rolling over and pulling the covers over his head to block out the sun. I never asked my roommate if it was okay for a strange man to stay in our very un-private apartment while I was not there, which was incredibly shitty of me. I broke up with the addict not long after.

I took the 6 train to Grand Central, then the Metro North to Brewster with my brother and cousin. My aunt, my dad's sister, picked us up at the train station and drove us to the wedding venue. Family, both mine and my soon-to-be-stepmom's, had arrived early to do photos before the ceremony. A photographer moved us all around into posed familial formations, projecting the illusion that we all knew one another better than we did. Before the wedding I had only met my stepmom's kids once, more than a decade earlier at a gathering for my dad's work, which was also where my future stepmom worked. They were extremely nice, welcoming people, but at the time I did not know them. Being photographed as though we were any type of blended family felt sad and disingenuous. My dad seemed willfully unaware that this wedding might engender difficult feelings. I wanted my dad to be happy, and it was clear during the ceremony that he was. Yet at twenty, it was a singularly confusing, even enraging experience to watch my father profess his love for a woman who was not my mom.

"This must be a weird day for you. I hope you're hanging in there," one of my dad's longtime friends said to my brother and me at the reception.

"We are just checking to make sure you are okay," my grandmother said, moving to the seat next to me while I picked at a piece of chocolate cake.

"I'm sure this day isn't easy," said a second cousin twice removed, whose name I didn't know and who I had not seen since 1992. He laid his meaty hands on my and my brother's shoulders and leaned in too close to our faces. "Hey! Remember when you guys sang 'Bohemian Rhapsody' at cousin Sara's bat mitzvah?! That was fun!"

I humored him with a small, quiet laugh and tried to back my face away from his.

All I could do was disassociate, which is evident in my nearly nonexistent smile and vacant eyes in the wedding photographs. I wore a pink tulle dress from Urban Outfitters and, even though it was an unseasonably warm day, a black cardigan. I had started cutting again.

Fifteen

I cannot wait to leave the hospital, but I do not want to go. I want to be in my own space where I do not have to ask permission to take tweezers and nail clippers out of a locked cabinet. I want to see Petunia, hug her, and hear her snoring loudly from under my desk as I work. I want to work. I want to watch TV that I want to watch. I do not want to cook for myself. I do not want to be alone all the time. I do not want to face life at all. I hear Caitlyn, Mary, and Shawn discussing movies they might watch after dinner. The familiar feeling of loneliness sets in, heavy and pervasive.

I finish packing my suitcase, making a mental note not to forget my Cuban oregano plant that is sitting on the kitchen table, nestled into a little cluster with the other girls' plants. My goal for the day is to stand up and walk out of the hospital the minute this outtake meeting ends.

It happens over Zoom. Dr. Philips, Dr. Samuels, and Beth are all on the hospital campus but are connecting in from their individual offices. I am in my room at Dalby. Dr. Karr is there too, seated against that yellow wall. Her face is hard and unsmiling.

"Hello, Anna. Hello, everybody. Can everyone hear and see okay?" Dr. Philips asks. We all nod. "Thank you, Dr. Karr, for joining us today."

Dr. Karr gives a quick nod, a half smile, and says, "Sure." She does not address me directly, and this time, unlike yesterday's case conference, I do not address her directly, either. The mood is taut from the outset. I have an intense feeling that she feels wronged, yet I lack all clues as to why. I know the bulk of this outtake meeting has happened before I joined in, with Dr. Philips, Dr. Samuels, and Beth debriefing Dr. Karr on my case and offering feedback on how to best move forward with my care outside the hospital. Has she heard something she does not like, or perhaps does not agree with? I feel I have let Dr. Karr down, or perhaps that I am in trouble. This feeling—that I have fucked up, that I have disappointed someone, that I might be on the verge of getting screamed at—is the one most likely to send me into a state of panic, and Dr. Karr knows this. Her demeanor seems pointedly and purposefully poised to set me off. I don't know why she is doing this. Has she forgotten this whole thing was her idea?

Dr. Philips continues, "Anna, we've been discussing your aftercare. I'm wondering, Dr. Karr, if there is anything that would be helpful for you to discuss with all of us here?"

"Well, Anna," she says, her voice sharp, "you and I need to discuss if we want to move forward working together. You know, perhaps *we* need to get a divorce."

I am stunned and silent, shocked by the nonchalance with which she compares our professional relationship to a crumbling marriage. It is inappropriate and heartless.

She continues, "If we do move forward, we will need a system in place so you and I both understand the boundaries of our relationship."

What system? What does that even mean? We never discussed the possibility that when I left the hospital she would no longer be my therapist. I search the faces of the hospital doctors for signs that what is happening is normal, but their faces are neutral, impossible to read.

"Anna, how are you feeling about what's being discussed so far?" Dr. Philips asks.

I feel it coming before it happens—*implosion*. Now I have the word to identify it. My body is hot, but also shivering. I hide my face completely with sweatshirt-covered hands, believing in that moment, that in such concealment, I will cease to be visible entirely. I devolve into deep, convulsive sobs, the kind that rack your whole body and feel totally out of your control. I am sitting in my chair, facing the computer screen, but I have completely left the room.

Dr. Philips steps in. "Anna, can you describe what is happening for you in this moment, what has brought up this outpouring of emotion?"

I do not answer right away, because I cannot. I'm sobbing to the point that I can't speak, still hiding behind my hands like a child, while everyone sits quietly, waiting.

In too loud a voice, I force out my words. "I feel like I'm getting in trouble!" Then I start sobbing again. A rebound to a normal, calm conversation is impossible for me at this point.

"Anna," says Dr. Philips, "I think it would be helpful if you tried to verbalize what has made you so upset."

"I'm afraid Dr. Karr is deciding she doesn't want to be my therapist anymore. I don't understand why this is happening."

Dr. Karr interrupts me. "Anna, your fear that I will leave is based on nothing." *Based on nothing? It's based on what you just said.* It is impossible not to register her accusatory tone and her contradictions. "Historically, who leaves who more often?" she says.

My mood shifts rapidly, from grief to anger. I want to say to her, "What the fuck are you talking about? I have never left. I never halted our work together, even when my life took me to other states. I have made therapy a priority. I have never missed an appointment in five years. I have never even been late to an appointment." Instead, I just nod.

The meeting ends with no resolution. Dr. Karr and I simply agree we will "continue the conversation" at my next session, once I am out of the hospital. Dr. Samuels tells me I will receive a full report on my time here within a couple of weeks. I thank everyone for their time over the past week. On a virtual platform, this thank-you feels inadequate.

I stand up, grab my bags, and carry them downstairs.

"Are you okay?" the house manager says.

"Yeah," I say, not meeting her eyes. "Are the girls here?"

"No, everyone's at group."

I did not anticipate not seeing Mary, Caitlyn, and Shawn before I left. By forgoing the Rock Ceremony last night, I realize I have missed my opportunity to say any sort of meaningful goodbye. No email addresses or phone numbers were exchanged, as I had watched the girls do with Kristin a few days earlier. We will simply disappear from one another's lives.

"Will you tell them I said bye?"

"Of course."

I walk to where I left my car eight days ago and get into the driver's seat, hitting my head on the sun visor that I left swung to the side, covering the top of the driver's-side window.

"FUCK!" I yell, then check my periphery for anyone who might have heard me. I do not want to be seen or heard screaming at no one in particular the day I am leaving a psych hospital.

It takes me less than one minute to pull my car to the front of Dalby, where I head in to grab my bags from the foyer and use the bathroom in my room. I run up the stairs two at a time. When I turn the knob to my bedroom it has already been locked by the house manager. "Fuck," I say, more quietly this time.

There is a knock at the front door. I descend the stairs as rapidly as I went up them, propelled by an impatient intensity to leave the hospital.

"Hi, Anna." It is Dr. Philips. "Can we chat for a moment about the outtake meeting?"

"I'm just getting ready to leave." My words come out as a hard statement unrelated to Dr. Philips's question, a mere narration of my actions, a pure reflex of anxiety.

"This won't take long. I just wanted to mention a few things."

"Sorry, I didn't mean— Yes, I can talk."

"How did you feel about the meeting?"

"Not great." I laugh, then gather myself. "I was severely caught off guard by what Dr. Karr had to say. It was deeply upsetting."

He nods. "I want to be respectful of your relationship with Dr. Karr and I don't want to impede your work together. However, I also want to tell you that it is clear to me that you possess a very strong intuition. That intuition should be listened to. If you are feeling at all unsure about your dynamic with Dr. Karr, I would urge you to pay attention to that."

Dr. Philips, a person who seems to understand me at a core level, is telling me to trust my intuition, to listen to myself, to believe that if I feel something is off, it's because it likely is. This is the first time in the last few months I don't feel crazy.

"Thank you for everything," I say.

"I'm wishing the best for you."

My intuition tells me he means it. He leaves, I toss my bag into the trunk, and I drive off the hospital grounds.

Five minutes into the drive, I advance into a sharp turn with way too much speed. I hit my breaks hard and avoid hitting a rocky embankment by swerving my car into the oncoming lane. I lay on my horn to alert traffic that might be coming in my direction. My purse flies forward from the passenger seat, hits the dashboard, and falls to the floor, its contents spilling everywhere. Loose coins and ChapStick clang together and roll back under the seat; my wallet smacks the floor with such force, credits cards go flying. I hear the grating scratch of my suitcase against the plastic floor of my trunk before it slams the back seat so hard I feel it in the driver's seat.

"FUCK!" I yell as loud as I can; no one can hear me now. I keep driving.

Am I going to need to find a new therapist? How will I start over with someone new right now? What the fuck did Dr. Karr mean by "Historically, who leaves who more often?" Was she trying to sow seeds of doubt in my competence in the other doctors—make me look flighty, or unreliable, or worse, erratic? I should have challenged her. Why didn't I challenge her? What exactly am I going home to? What's left in my life? Should I be driving right now? Fuck, I forgot my Cuban oregano plant.

A recent memory with Dr. Karr bleeds into focus, one that has been sitting right below the surface for months now, one I have not told anyone about, not even the doctors at the hospital. While living and working in Washington, DC, I admitted to Dr. Karr that I was feeling hopeless, that ideations of suicide had returned, and that I had begun to cut myself again. She was mad and she did not try to hide it. She told me I never should have left New York to take the DC job in that mental state. I explained that it had nothing to do with taking the job. The job made me feel good; it made me feel like I was building a career of my own. It was bolstering my self-confidence. Yet from my perspective, she did not seem interested in hearing this.

"You're sick," she said, her voice harsh. "You need to come back to New York tomorrow to meet me. In person. This is nonnegotiable."

"I have work tomorrow," I said.

"I don't care. Figure it out, but come to my office tomorrow to speak. Come at noon and I will clear two hours for you so we have time to discuss what's going on."

I agreed, calling my boss in DC to ask if I could take the following day off. The next day I spent three hours on Amtrak to Penn Station. I rode the C train downtown to Dr. Karr's office and arrived precisely at 11:55 a.m. She seemed mad at me the entire time, reiterating that I was "sick" and needed serious help.

At 12:50 she said, "Okay, that's it for today. We'll plan to see each other over Zoom at the normal time on Wednesday."

"I thought you said you were clearing two hours for us to talk?"

"You're right," she said, her tone matter-of-fact. "I did say that. And I forgot. I'm sorry." But there was no sign in her demeanor that she was actually sorry.

"Oh," I said. "Oh, you're serious."

"Yep." She stood up and opened the door. "I forgot, I apologize, but that's all the time I have for today. I'll see you Wednesday."

I walked out of her office and spent the three-hour train ride back to DC weighing whether she had truly forgotten what she had told me less than eighteen hours earlier—mistakes happen, after all—or if she had insisted I miss work and travel six hours to and from DC to purposefully excuse me from her office only fifty minutes after I arrived. It was an answer I would never get, and I knew that, so I decided to pretend it had never happened.

Back in the car I'm crying; my insides feel disorganized, like they are breaking apart. I start looking for a place to pull over, but the narrow, wooded roads force me to drive another two miles ahead. At a four-way stop I see an old white church with a tall steeple, a familiar New England sight. The parking lot is empty, and I pull in and turn my car off. I take a few deep breaths before gathering the contents of my wallet from the passenger floor. I pick up the business card Dr. Philips gave me at the close of our testing session, dialing the number before I can talk myself out of it.

"Hello?" Dr. Philips answers.

"Hi, Dr. Philips. I'm so sorry, this is Anna." My voice easily exposes my distress. It is obvious I am crying. "That meeting was really disturbing."

"Yes, it was disturbing. Everyone on your team has discussed it and we agree with you and were also concerned by what we saw and heard."

"I shouldn't have left so quickly; I should have talked to someone about it. I don't know why I did that." I look around for a tissue but cannot find one and resort to using my sleeve to wipe the tears and snot from my face. The convulsing sobs start again.

"I think you should take a few minutes to collect yourself, and then you should drive back to the hospital. You can come right to the building where my office is. I'll wait for you outside and then we can go discuss the meeting."

"Is that okay?" I ask.

"Yes, of course. It's no problem at all. I'm very happy you called and reached out for help instead of going home. It was the right thing to do."

I turn my car around and drive back to the hospital.

When I arrive, Dr. Philips is standing in the parking lot with Beth, my social worker. They look like they are having an intense conversation. I park and walk up to them.

"I'm very happy you came back," Beth says to me. "I know I look upset right now. I am upset right now. I just want you to know that we all saw that, and whatever happened in that meeting wasn't about you."

I nod and follow Dr. Philips to his office.

"I saw some very concerning dynamics play out between you and

Dr. Karr. Everyone in the meeting did. I was taken aback by many of her comments."

I start to cry, hard.

"Can you explain the emotions coming up for you right now?"

"I feel relieved mostly, that everyone else thought it was disturbing too. I've just felt crazy all year. I don't even know if I can trust myself."

"From what I've seen of you this week, you can absolutely trust yourself. I'd like to recommend that you stay the weekend. Beth checked and you can go right back into your room in Dalby. I'll meet with you again. The other doctors will meet with you again, and we can all come up with a better, more concrete plan for your aftercare."

I step outside to call my mom, who is expecting me to show up at her house to collect Petunia at any minute.

"Hi, Mom."

"Anna." She sounds surprised.

"Something happened when I was leaving. Something with my therapist from the outside. I don't really want to explain right now. The doctors here are asking me to stay at least until Monday. Can you keep watching Petunia?"

She doesn't answer immediately, but then says, "Um, yeah, I can do that."

I can tell by her tone of voice that she's caught off guard by the request. Maybe she doesn't really want to say yes, but feels she has to. I get it, Petunia isn't the easiest dog to take care of. I add, "I would really appreciate it, thank you," before she can change her mind.

"I think Petunia is going to be disappointed not to see you. I told her you'd be coming home today. She's been waiting by the door," my mom says.

"I'm sorry. I think she'll be okay though."

"I'll have to go to your house to get more dog food. And I already cooked food for you to have when you get home."

"Can you put it in the freezer?"

"I guess I can just put it in the freezer."

"I really appreciate it and I will update you later on what happened. Right now I need to go tell them I'm able to stay. Thank you. And I love you."

"Okay," she says.

I hang up the phone and breathe. In for three. Out for six.

The hospital makes it incredibly easy for me to check back in. I have to meet briefly with Dr. Samuels, the psychiatrist, to explain what happened and where exactly I went in the time between checking out and driving back. When it's clear I only drove four miles and was gone for about twenty minutes total, they allow me back into Dalby without searching my bags.

"I'm really proud of you for coming back," the house manager says, carrying my suitcase up the stairs. "I don't think many people would have done that. The girls will be happy to see you."

When Mary, Caitlyn, and Shawn walk into Dalby that afternoon, I'm sitting on the couch.

"I'm back." I throw my arms into the air and smile as big as I can. Making light of the situation is the best way I know how to deal with it.

Caitlyn runs over to the couch and sits down next to me, smiling. "I wasn't ready for you to leave!"

"I wasn't ready to leave you guys, either."

Keeping in line with unwritten hospital code, no one asks me what happened. No one pries. No one oversteps. In here, you don't need to know backstory, you just accept what is in the moment and move forward from that point.

We do grab-and-go dinner and ask the house manager if we can have the wrap-up meeting early so we can watch a movie. The routine is comforting and familiar. I acknowledge that I failed my morning goal—to leave the hospital immediately after my outtake meeting— and I feel grateful to Dr. Philips for telling me to trust my instinct about Dr. Karr; I don't need the color-coded feelings card to tell me that if it wasn't for that conversation, I never would have come back when I started to panic. Before moving on, I add that I'm grateful to be spending my Friday night with Mary, Caitlyn, and Shawn. Each of them adds to their gratitude statement that they are grateful I'm back as well.

Flipping through Netflix, Mary stops on *Catch Me If You Can*.

"I love this movie," she says.

Caitlyn puts her hand to her forehead, pretending to faint. "Oh, Leo!"

"I agree," I say. "One of his all-time best eras. Not as good as *Titanic*-Leo."

"Or *Romeo + Juliet*–Leo," Caitlyn adds.

"But still very good," I say.

"Let's watch it," says Shawn.

"Everyone agree?" Mary's thumb hovers over the play button.

"Agree," we all answer.

The four of us are spread out on the couches, covered by blankets, eating gluten-free chocolate chip cookies like it is any normal Friday night with friends. The further we progress into January, the more we are aware that our small group will soon be infiltrated by new house-mates. People whose New Year's resolutions are to stop drinking, stop using, stop self-harming will fill the rooms of Dalby. Our quiet balance will be demolished; we are, after all, four living in a house built for sixteen. For now, though, it is just us, four women ages eighteen to thirty-five, all trying to face ourselves, all coping the best way we can, all agreeing that Leonardo DiCaprio is undeniably hot, no matter what year you were born.

Sixteen

I got two tickets to the Death Cab for Cutie show at Webster Hall. Do you want to go with me?

The text was from David. We were still broken up but were now communicating sporadically.

I missed David immensely, but that was only one of the reasons I agreed to go to the concert. The other was that I trusted him to make good on his promise of forcing me to get help if he found out I was cutting again. The past two years—my relationship with Sam, failing my cosmetology state board exams, dropping out of school, my parents' divorce, my dad's remarriage—left me in a state of anguish, depression, and anxiety that I simply did not have the tools to deal with healthily. I did not know how to ask for help, either. In preparation for the concert, I did what I thought would be the best chance for getting it: I cut myself from my elbow to my wrist bone, left the cut unbandaged, and then wore a three-quarter-sleeved shirt so David would see the cut. I didn't mean for the cut to be so big, but once I started it felt impossible to stop. The pain was comforting and more so was what I thought I deserved.

David and I stood close in the crowd, taking in the songs we had often listened to together. I danced to the up-tempo ones, knowing that eventually David would see my arm. When he did, he was immediately angry. David turned from me and walked toward the exit. I followed him, not quite expecting this reaction.

"I told you you would have to tell your parents if you did it again," David said outside Webster Hall, the bass of the music still audible.

"Okay, fine!" I said, trying to sound like I was giving him what he wanted, when really I was getting what I wanted. "You can tell them."

"No, I'm not telling them. *You* are telling them. I will go with you to talk to them, and I will be there to reiterate how serious the situation is, but you have to be the one to tell them."

A week later I was in the living room of the house where I grew up, sitting on the futon sofa. It was the same futon Ethan had pinned me to six years earlier, still covered in a tartan fabric of burgundies, blacks, and tans. My mom had sewn the slipcover herself, just like she had sewn all the curtains in the house. I picked at a raised thread in the fabric's weave. To my left was the small, black-and-white-checked pillow I had sewn through my finger making in home economics class; to my right was David, just as he said he would be. My parents sat across from us on intricately woven sisal chairs that they'd bought before I was born. This was the first time they had seen each other in years. I knew they didn't want to sit in a room together, but I was not willing to have this conversation twice.

"I'm really struggling," I started. "I feel very depressed. I've felt very depressed since I was a teenager."

My parents watched, fearfully, as I spoke. David sat nearly motionless except for his eyes, which moved between me and the floor in front of him.

"Since freshman year of high school, I've been cutting myself. I'm really good at hiding it, so don't feel bad for not noticing. I recognize that it's very destructive, and it's not something I want to keep doing. I want to stop, but I think I need help stopping."

My mom's eyes filled with tears. She placed her hand gently to her mouth.

"Well, I'm surprised," my dad said. "What do you feel you want to do about it?"

"I guess therapy?" I didn't know the right answer. He was the school psychologist, I figured he would know what to do.

"If you think that would be helpful, then definitely you should go to therapy," my mom said.

"I can't afford therapy on my own," I said.

"That's going to be expensive," my dad said.

"I think it's really important that Anna gets some help," David said. It was the first thing he said since entering the house and saying hello to my parents. "I know Anna well. I've known her well for a long time. She is really struggling. And she's been doing this for as long as I've known her, and it's not good."

"We can pay for you to go to therapy," my mom said.

"I obviously don't want you to be so distressed that you are resorting to this behavior," my dad said. "I love you and I want you to be okay. But this will be a significant expense."

"I understand and I appreciate the help," I said.

My mom turned her attention to David, whom she had always liked. She had been so disappointed when we broke up. "Thank you, David, for always looking out for Anna."

"Of course," he said. "I love her."

The talk was not long, maybe an hour total. I had no desire to belabor the conversation, nor did I want my parents in the same room for longer than needed. Afterward I borrowed my mom's car to drive David to the train station so he could go back to the city. I planned to stay at my mom's house for a few days.

"Thank you for being here," I said.

"Of course."

We sat quietly and watched his train approach the station.

"I can take the next one," he said.

Very little work was done by either of my parents to find me an appropriate therapist. They sent me to the therapist my mom saw, who was the same therapist my parents had seen for couples' therapy. I had seen him once before when we had a family therapy session during my parents' divorce. My experience with him was unnotable, except for the time he told me my mom was "a difficult woman," exemplifying precisely why two people in the same family should not see the same therapist—especially when that therapist was also your parents' couples' therapist. We did not unpack in any meaningful way why I was cutting or what led to my cutting, but I was at an age where I did not yet understand how to unpack that. Perhaps that had to come later. I saw the therapist for about six months, a time during which I did not cut, and then I stopped going. I am not exactly sure why I stopped, but likely I saw the brief lapse in self-harm as evidence that the habit was dropped.

David and I got back together not long after the talk with my parents, but broke up a year later, right after my twenty-first birthday. The weight of everything we had gone through was too heavy for us to outrun or work through. It was sad to give up someone with whom I had so much fun, laughed so hard, and with whom I felt entirely myself. It was, however, the right thing for both of us to walk away. With love and respect for the time we spent so closely entwined, we parted ways, this time for good.

Seventeen

I wake up with my period. It is six days early and I am supposed to be home by now. When I go downstairs for our morning meeting, I learn the other girls either have theirs as well, or just had it. Our cycles have synced up from communal living. The house manager helps me cobble together a stash of tampons to get me through the day, then puts in an order to the pharmacy off campus for a full box.

I attend a meditation group at one p.m. at the rec center. Shawn is there, as well as five of the men from Oscar House. Sitting upright in a plastic chair, my hands resting palms up on my thighs, a growing discomfort in my left ovary erupts into intense pain. It becomes harder and harder to breathe. I remain seated, placing my hands to my womb, positive I can breathe through it. In for three. Out for six. Lifting one eyelid, I check the time on a big, round clock on the wall, the kind they have in school classrooms. There are still fifteen minutes left in the meditation. As the pain mounts, tunnel vision and hearing loss set in. I'm surprised tunnel vision can be felt even with closed eyes. It's clear I'm not going to breathe through it; I'm going to faint.

I stand up from my chair, leaving the room as quickly as I can. My goal is to make it to the couches in the building foyer before I fall over. When exiting a room quickly during group, it usually signals you've become so overwhelmed with emotion, so triggered, you have no choice but to step out. This is a preferable alternative to the Oscar men seeing me faint, especially from my period. I get to the couches and sit with my head between my legs.

I know what's happening, or at least I have a pretty good idea. I have a history of benign cysts forming on my ovaries and rupturing at the outset of my period. The first time it happened I thought I was dying. It was 2016 and I was living in Los Angeles, where I had relocated for my husband's job. I was home alone when I woke up at six a.m. with my period and normal cramps, but within twenty minutes the pain in my ovaries was so unbearable, I fainted. When I came to, I was in the most intense pain I had ever experienced in my life. I lay on my bathroom floor, phone in hand, weighing whether to call 911 or to power through it. Writhing in agony, I remembered an article I'd read years earlier in the *New York Times*, which reported that more women die in emergencies than men because women are more inclined to downplay a situation's severity and less inclined to call 911. We put ourselves in danger due to an asinine narrative that we are too dramatic, while men have been recorded dialing emergency services because they've run out of toilet paper. *I will not be that woman*, I said to myself.

Once connected to the dispatcher, I couldn't speak. She kept saying, "Ma'am? Ma'am? I need you to speak, ma'am."

Finally: "I'm at home. I need help. I'm in so much pain."

"Are you alone?"

"Yes."

"Can you tell me why you're in pain?"

"It's my ovaries."

"Might you be pregnant?"

"No."

"I've dispatched an ambulance. In the meantime, can you get near a door to let them in?"

"Yes." I hung up the phone.

I didn't know if I could get to the door, which was down a flight of stairs. I army crawled out of the bathroom, through the hall, and slid down the stairs like a mermaid might. I lay on the floor right by my front door, looking pitifully at Petunia, who, still in her crate from the night before, met my gaze with a look that said, *At what point do you let me out of here?*

I heard the sirens from down the block. Apparently, emergency services dispatches a fire truck before sending an ambulance. I did not know this and started to regret calling. A fire truck is so big and embarrassing. I realized very soon I'd meet a gaggle of uniformed men to whom I'd have to explain that I had my period and that my ovaries hurt really bad. There was a knock on my door, and from the floor I opened it to see perhaps the three hottest men I had ever seen in my life.

I always thought the "hot fireman" trope was just that, a trope. It is not. They were built, strong, masculine—the stereotypical fireman. I couldn't dismiss or overlook their unbelievable hotness.

The hottest one spoke first, with the authority of a hot person. "Ma'am, you're safe! Can you try to sit up and tell me what's happening?"

I sat up, really wishing everyone would stop calling me "ma'am." I was thirty-one, basically still a "miss"!

"I'm having intense pain in my ovaries. I fainted from the pain. I didn't know what to do. Maybe it's a cyst rupture?" I said.

"I'm going to take your blood pressure," he said, already wrapping the monitor around my upper arm. "Could you be pregnant?"

"No." I paused, delaying the inevitable. "I am getting my period."

"Got it." He was all business. "Your blood pressure is very low."

"It's always low," I said.

"This is the unsafe kind of low. Are you still in as much pain as you were in before?"

"No, actually, I'm not." Part of me hated to admit this because I feared it would only support the narrative that I'm a weak woman who can't handle a little period pain. "I think I might be okay now and you guys can go."

"Ma'am, you're alone here?"

"I am."

"We can't actually leave you alone with blood pressure this low, legally speaking. We have to take you to the hospital."

"I really don't want to go to the hospital."

"How about this— Let's sit here for five minutes, then I'm going to have you stand up. If your blood pressure stays in normal range when you stand, we will leave and you can stay here. But, if you stand and it drops, we contact the ambulance and take you to the hospital."

"Sounds good."

We sat quietly at first, the hot fireman looking around, taking in my house from his spot on the floor next to me. "The interior design of your house is very nice."

"Thanks," I said. "I did it myself."

"Wow, great eye for design."

I definitely sold this man short based on his appearance—a hot fireman couldn't possibly appreciate turn-of-the-century-era interior design, I'd thought, but I was wrong.

"Alright," he said, checking his watch. "Try to stand up."

When I did, my vision went dark, and my blood pressure plummeted.

"Call the ambulance," he said to one of the other firemen.

The ambulance arrived and two new men (EMTs, not hot) helped me onto a gurney. Being wheeled into the ambulance, my fireman could tell I was in distress.

"What's wrong?" he said.

"I never walked my dog. She's still in her crate from overnight. I don't know how long I'll be gone."

"Hold the bus," he said, smacking the side of the vehicle. Then he turned to me said, "Let me have your keys. I'll walk your dog, lock your house up, and give you back your keys. What's your dog's name?"

"Petunia. Her harness isn't on. It's on top of her crate; so is her leash. Can you put her back in the crate when you're done?"

"You got it."

I watched hot fireman open my door, help Petunia into her harness, walk her to the curb to pee, then bring her back into my house, usher her into her crate, and relock my door behind him. It was the hottest thing I'd ever witnessed.

"Thank you so much," I said to him as he dropped my keys back into my purse beside me—not even into my hand, into my purse, *where they belonged.*

"You're off! Good luck!" he said, closing the ambulance door.

The ride to Kaiser Permanente's emergency room on Sunset Boulevard in Los Feliz was quick. The EMTs talked the entire way.

"Where's the pain?"

"My ovaries."

"Could you be pregnant?"

"No." Jesus Christ, didn't these people talk to each other? "I have my period."

"Oh"—he looked across my supine body at the other EMT—"it's just your period?"

"I don't know if it's *just my period*," I said, mocking him, but I also worried maybe it was just my period.

"You're as white as this sheet wrapped around you. You look like you need to put on some lipstick."

"Ew," I said to him, and was wheeled into an exam room at the ER.

I did have a cyst rupture that day, and as I sit with my head between my legs outside the meditation room, I worry it might be a repeat occurrence. When the group is over, Shawn walks me back to Dalby. We walk slowly and she keeps her hand near me, but not on me, in case I faint. She updates the house manager, who calls a nurse, while I lie on the couch in the fetal position, my teeth clenched.

The nurse stands over me. "Do you know why you might be experiencing such intense pain?"

"I get cysts . . . sometimes . . . they rupture . . ." The pain makes my words fall in stilted statements.

"That's a serious medical condition that requires hospitalization. Do you need to go to the hospital?" the nurse says.

"No. Never mind. I just need Advil. I can't talk anymore." I close my eyes, willing the nurse to leave me alone.

Protocol says the Advil has to be approved by my psychiatrist, so it takes about ten minutes before I get it. Eventually the pain subsides enough for me to walk upstairs to my room, and also enough for me to register my extreme embarrassment. I'm ashamed that my ovaries can bring me to my knees in pain and I'm ashamed that I'm ashamed of that. Why are women so fucking ashamed of ourselves? I blame men.

Within an hour of taking the Advil I feel weak but fine, so I decide to attend a spirituality group led by the chaplain in the building across the street from Dalby. Shawn and Mary are there, as well as the men from Oscar House. I obscure my embarrassment from this morning by soft-focusing my eyes; this way I can't tell if anyone is looking at me. Then I pick up the sheet of paper that has been placed on the chair I'm about to sit in and concentrate on it like it's the most important thing I've ever read. The topic of today's group is loss. The paper is printed with a list of thirty-four losses and check boxes beside them. We are to check the ones we have experienced. Some of them are big, concrete losses—divorce, death of a parent or child, termination from a job. Others are more enigmatic and ambiguous—mental illness, death of a personal dream. I check fifteen of the thirty-four losses.

My eyes never rid themselves of tears through the forty-five-minute session. We are all seated in a circle, and the guy sitting directly across from me is watching me intently. Too intently. His name is Henry. I think. He arrived at the hospital the day after I did. My first introduction to him was on the bus from the houses to grab-and-go dinner, and I immediately did not like him. On the sixty-second bus ride he managed to mention three things that revealed his affluence. The first, his preferred brand of high, both the kind and the amount. Second, the town he was from. And third, that he worked in administration for a real estate contracting business his dad owned. I imagined one day he would gain access to a trust that would easily support him for the rest of his life. This was conjecture, of course, but I built his world real enough in my mind to make me resentful.

My early twenties brought with them my first interaction with truly rich men. I quickly realized these were perhaps the worst sect of people. Not only did they believe their wealth and wealth-adjacent power made them better, smarter, and more interesting than those with less, they also moved through life with unassailability. They accepted without question the reality of an existence where every inconvenience could be paid to go away. They were also entitled. This was how I saw Henry, based on nothing but his zip code, attitude, and the knowledge that he worked for his dad's company. Now he is watching me cry in a small room with linoleum floors and a popcorn ceiling.

People in the group share lessons they have gleaned from their own moments of loss, but I have nothing to contribute. I still feel stuck in its dense forest, lessons unlearned. I do not know when I will reach the edge of the trees, or if the trees even end.

Henry tells a story about losing a sports career due to an injury in college. I feel sad when he recounts this because I know intimately from dance what this type of loss feels like. It is disorienting to feel compassion for a person I have decided not to like. I want to put my

167

hands on his shoulders, look him in the eye, and say, "I'm *so* sorry," but I am not sure what I want to apologize for—never speaking to him? Being myself a person he does not want to speak to? His sports injury? Finding him annoying? Assuming that his life is somehow easier than mine because he was possibly born wealthy? I do not say anything, instead I focus on his words and giving him my full attention. When the group ends, a bunch of people hang back outside to smoke. I think this might be a good opportunity to be social with the other patients, or maybe to say something meaningful to Henry, perhaps offer a word of support or solidarity. Instead, I grab two hot chocolate packets and walk back to Dalby to cry alone in my room.

In the evening there's a new house manager I've never met before.

"This one literally never comes out of the office," Mary tells me.

We test our luck with the TV, all agreeing to watch the Ted Bundy movie where Zac Efron plays Ted Bundy.

"Was Ted Bundy this hot?" Caitlyn asks. At eighteen, she's too young to have entered into the fascination-with-serial-killers phase of adulthood.

"Not *this* hot, but he was quite good-looking. Unfortunately. It's one of the reasons no one suspected him," I say.

"Wow," Caitlyn says. "Fucked-up."

We likely wouldn't be allowed to watch this were we to ask permission, but luckily none of us find a bludgeoning serial killer who fucked corpses and kept severed heads in his freezer triggering.

Eighteen

By 2007, Amanda had moved back to New York from Chicago and we were living in a three-bedroom apartment in Astoria, Queens, with a rotating cast of third roommates. Amanda got a job at a tech company that made comedy videos for the internet, while I was still working at the salon—though after a year and a half as a shampoo girl they kindly moved me to working the front desk. Every day Amanda and I came home to watch *Arrested Development* or *Gilmore Girls* on DVDs rented from Netflix. We lived on Trader Joe's vegetable gyozas, steamed green beans, and weed.

I was making eight dollars an hour at the salon, doing makeup jobs on the side, and taking classes toward an art education degree at Queens College, yet another weird diversion that amounted to nothing, when I met Amanda's boss, Theo, at a party in his Chelsea apartment. Theo had recently made multimillions from the sale of his website, one he still ran. After the party, he asked Amanda if he could have my email address, which she happily gave, and he emailed me to go on a date.

Theo's appeal lay couched in all the ways he was not like David. Where David exuded an alternative, effortless cool, Theo was preppy and goofy. Where David was intense and emotional, Theo was light and uncomplicated. David and I read the same books—*The Wind-Up Bird Chronicle*, *Henry and June*, *The Hotel New Hampshire*—and would discuss them, dissecting the things we loved or loathed, and how they made us feel. With Theo, conversation was superficial and easy, if not confusing, with him often posing ridiculous hypotheticals.

"Would you rather give up sex or give up cheese?!" he asked one night at dinner.

"Huh? I don't know. I guess cheese?"

"What?! Cheese is delicious!" he said, laughing hysterically. "What about this! Would you rather have sex with a dolphin or let a dolphin have sex with you?"

"Neither," I said.

"You *have* to pick one!"

"Do I?"

Theo was not particularly funny, but he was fun. He planned activities, like going apple picking or skydiving. He threw dance parties and took me to restaurants I could never afford on my own.

Theo was nice and he was generous, never making me feel bad for the things we did that he paid for. Our financial disparity scared me, which I communicated to him, though Theo urged it would not be an issue.

"I like you because you don't care about fancy things! You're down-to-earth, but you know how to rise to the occasion. Like, you're the perfect person to take to a party: attractive, well-dressed without needing expensive clothes, and you know how to make conversation. Actually, you'd make a great beard!"

"Thanks. I think?"

I had never known someone with millions of dollars. Wealth was merely an abstract thought. My impression of having money meant driving Ferraris and wearing Louis Vuitton. It can, of course, mean that, but mostly being rich means having power, and that was not something I understood until I witnessed it up close.

The power wealth engenders is not always overt, it can be wrapped in a facade of generosity. That generosity can even be genuine and well-meaning. Having money (power) means you get to make a lot of the decisions that other people with less money (less power) simply have to go along with, even if they don't want to. *I didn't pay for it, who am I to complain.* This inequality might begin as innocent, but eventually it coalesces into an insidious dynamic where the person with less remains submissive and pliable to the will of the one with more. They become mentally imprisoned by their debt. Theo and I were young when we met, twenty-six and twenty-one respectively, and so just as I could not anticipate how money might affect our footing, he likely couldn't, either. I don't believe Theo was malicious, or mean, or that he wanted me to feel subordinate to his power. I just think he did not consider it. Like men since the dawn of time, like so many men who have passed through my life, he simply did not consider it.

"He doesn't really want to be dating someone who works in a hair salon."

"WHAT?" I leaned toward a pretty brunette named Rachel, one of Theo's friends and a writer-sometimes-actor who had adopted him into the New York media elite as soon as he made money. Theo was throwing a party in his apartment, which took up an entire floor of the building. I had to yell over the insanely loud electronic trills of LCD Soundsystem. The song "All My Friends" was what newly rich people and finance bros listened to when they wanted to feel cool and alternative. There was a DJ, an open bar, and lots of people on very high-grade Molly. "CAN YOU REPEAT THAT? I DIDN'T HEAR YOU," I said.

"Theo isn't at a point in his life where he wants to be dating someone who works in a hair salon and lives in *Queens*."

"I don't think he really cares that I work in a salon," I said back to her, but before it even left my mouth, I knew it was a lie.

Mean girls circled Theo, many of them disregarding my existence entirely. A few months into our relationship I was at his apartment doing schoolwork when he went into work and left his computer open. His email was visible on the screen. I watched email after email pop up between him and Rachel. They were making plans to drive upstate together for a day that weekend to visit the Storm King Art Center, a sculpture park in a huge outdoor field. The emails were flirty, not excessively so, but definitely not the kind of conversation you want to see your boyfriend having with another woman. It was clear that she liked him and he was indulging it.

"What are you up to this weekend?" I said over dinner that night.

"I'm not sure yet. What are you up to?"

"No plans," I said. "Want to hang out?"

"Let me see. I might want this weekend to myself, but I'll let you know."

Theo never let me know, and I did not see him that weekend. I did not immediately speak up about the emails or about not hearing from him because I did not want to be seen as difficult or demanding, but eventually I could not remain silent.

"I'm sort of sick of Rachel's attitude," I said to him while sitting in a Tribeca restaurant we frequented. "She either ignores me or she says shitty things, insinuating that you deserve someone 'better.' It's pretty fucking elitist. Also, she clearly has a crush on you and wants me out of the way. Did you guys used to date or something?"

"What?!" He laughed. "That's literally crazy. She does not have a crush on me. We never dated, and she doesn't hate you."

"I didn't say she hated me, I said she treats me like I'm below her and below you. I think you're actively choosing to be blind to the crush because you like the attention."

"You're overreacting, we're just friends. She knows that," he said. He was now shoving french fries into his mouth.

"But you watch her treat me like shit. Why would you want to be so close with someone who treats me like that?"

He looked down at his meal, shaking his head. "This conversation is ridiculous."

I realized I could not convince him, so I let it go.

"Oh, but re: the salon . . ." He was the type of person who used "re:" in conversation. Theo looked at me with wide and mischievous eyes. "I've been thinking you could make more money if you started your own business. You don't have to stop cutting hair, just, like, go out on your own."

"I'm not sure I even want to be cutting hair."

"Cutting hair is cool. But you need to be the boss."

"I've thought about trying to transfer from Queens to the New School. I don't want to be an art teacher. I have literally no idea why I'm in an art education program. I want to write or study psychology or something."

"Oh! Great! Here's what you do: Quit the salon. It's annoying you have to work on Saturdays anyway. Plus, once the summer comes, I want you to be able to come to the Hamptons when I invite you. So quit the salon, apply to the New School, but on the side come to my office and cut the guys' hair."

"How am I going to convince the guys in your office to let me cut their hair?"

"I'll have you cut my hair in the office one day. Then everyone will see you cutting my hair. I guarantee you they will want their hair cut too. You're tapping into a market—young guys who are willing to pay forty dollars for a good haircut and not have to go to a salon or a barber. You go to them!" He reached over to my plate and grabbed three of my fries.

"That could work. I'm willing to try it out."

"Now you can be like, 'I own my own business,' so you don't have to say you work in a salon."

A friendly waiter approached our table. "Can I box up these leftovers for you guys?" he asked, motioning to our half-eaten fifteen-dollar burgers and barely touched sides of sautéed broccoli, crispy brussels sprouts, and spicy corn off the cob.

"Nah, that's okay," Theo said.

The waiter stacked the plates on top of one another, crushing the leftover food.

"Why don't you take food to go when you don't finish it?" I asked Theo.

Theo shrugged, pulling a heavy, silver American Express Business card from his wallet and tossing it onto the table with an audible thud. "What's the point? Food is cheap."

I withdrew from Queens College and started the bachelor's program, a course of study at the New School specifically designed for working adults who wanted a degree but also had a full-time job. I could make my own curriculum, and classes took place in the evening. I focused my areas of study on psychology, literature, writing, and art. I quit working in the salon, but on evenings I did not have class, I still cut hair. Theo had been correct, when guys saw me cutting his hair, they too wanted their hair cut. Soon I had a steady clientele of twentysomething men from Theo's office.

On the weekends Theo and I went to the Hamptons. Theo and his friends—some couples, some singles—rented a big house. The house was never quiet or as relaxing as you might assume "the beach" would be. There were constantly people around. My relationship to the Hamptons was confusing. I hated it, but I feared that if I stopped going, Theo would break up with me, and I didn't want that to happen. Not because I loved him so much, or thought we were such a good match, but because I felt that if he broke up with me or I with him, the interpretation would be that I could not hack it in his world, a world I wanted no part of, a world that made me feel bad about myself. It was a strange psychological paradox whereby I both wanted to be there—a way to say, "Try to make me feel small, but you will not run me out of town"—yet simultaneously fantasized about walking into a party and screaming, "OH YEAH?! WELL, I THINK YOU GUYS ARE FUCKING LAME WANNABES WHO DON'T KNOW THE MEANING OF COOL!!" I could not see how little either mindset served me. It was a test of my will. No matter how unhappy I was, I would not back down or bow out. Instead, I kept coming back for more. Being with Theo and surviving the Hamptons became a petty, masochistic game, one I was determined to win.

The only time I looked forward to the Hamptons were the few weekends a group of friendly women, one of them named Sarah, another named Carmel, rented the cots in the shitty, unfinished basement of the house. They paid significantly less money to be relegated to this area. Sarah and Carmel seemed like normal people who didn't so much give a shit about being in the Hamptons but wanted an occasional weekend outside their small apartments during New York's oppressively hot months. Sarah often made sure I had lunch, a meal Theo never ate and never offered to me. She and Carmel invited me to join afternoon Scrabble games when they saw me sitting alone by the pool, and they would hang out with me at parties when they noticed Theo wasn't.

The second summer in the Hamptons I was offered a job at the Donna Karan store in Southampton. When the manager told me I would have to pay out of my paycheck for Donna Karan clothing to wear to work, I declined. I called Theo that afternoon to say that I might have to stay in the city that summer to work.

"What about this! Would you be willing to clean the rental house at the end of each weekend? All of us renting the house can pay you to clean!" he said.

"I guess I would do that?" That summer we had upgraded to a six-bedroom, seven-bathroom mansion with two kitchens and an indoor squash court. His basic lack of consideration had many facets. First, he was suggesting work be taken away from actual professionals and given to his twenty-two-year-old girlfriend. It was a basic undervaluing of work he assumed took no skill. Second, it took me out of my position of girlfriend and made me into a paid employee. When Theo asked the homeowners if I could do the cleaning instead of the people who had been working there for years, they said no.

Rachel was not part of our house share. She did, however, rent a house not far away and seemed to be everywhere Theo and I went. When he forced me to dinners with Rachel, I was as friendly as possible. When Rachel asked me to cut her hair, which I did, and then didn't offer to pay me, Theo just laughed it off. "That's Rachel!"

Theo was undoubtedly generous with his money. One summer we took a two-week vacation to Japan. We woke up at dawn to see the tuna auction at Tsukiji Market in Tokyo, rode bikes through Gion in Kyoto, even caught a rare glimpse of a maiko walking from one house to another. The trip was not particularly lavish, especially for a millionaire—we flew economy both ways and stayed in nice-but-not-luxurious hotels—yet at my age even this would have been highly unaffordable. I got to see Japan because Theo was happily willing to take me for free.

In the Narita Airport on our way back home, I sat next to him with my head resting on his shoulder. He answered emails on his laptop. I glanced at the computer and saw an email from Rachel. She's a gold digger . . . When you and I were hanging out, I insisted on paying for everything myself, even though I didn't have the money . . . She's taking advantage of you . . . You're blind to who she actually is . . . She will leave you broke and alone.

I sat up and Theo quickly closed the window to his email.

"What. The. FUCK. Was. That?" I said to him.

"What?"

"Are you kidding me? I saw that email."

He said nothing. There was no way he could defend himself.

"For the past year you have been looking me in the eye and telling me I'm crazy, I'm ridiculous, I'm creating something where there is nothing, making me out to be a paranoid, jealous girlfriend, when in fact I was fucking right about Rachel." I was yelling now.

"I'm sorry," he said sheepishly. "You know I don't think those things about you. That's just her opinion, and it's wrong."

"I don't give a shit that you don't think those things about me. I know they're not true, you know they're not true. I just can't believe that you have refused to stand up for me, you have repeatedly told me I'm overreacting, you have continuously put me in social situations with this woman, you pretended you didn't have a previous relationship. Not a single time have you considered my feelings. You were only worried about protecting yourself and not losing her attention." I turned and started walking away from him, to where I had no idea, but turned around and screamed as loud as I could, "Also, you are a FUCKING LIAR!" An entire section of the airport looked at me.

Here is the thing about men lying to women while telling them they are crazy or overreacting. The lying, the underplaying on their side, makes us doubt our intuition and intelligence, so eventually when suspicions are confirmed, when we find out we have been correct all along, we do go batshit fucking crazy. And it is warranted.

Theo and I sat next to each other for the fourteen-hour plane ride from Tokyo to New York City in total silence. I was too angry to even look at him. Rachel was planning to join that summer's Hamptons house. I asked Theo to ask her to drop out. How was I supposed to share a house with her after reading that email? He would not agree to this and instead decided he and I would only go on the weekends she was not there. Though this compromise in no way made me feel my boyfriend had my back, it did successfully keep Rachel and me apart.

Come fall, Theo and I were back in the city full-time and I decided to take a special-effects makeup class. I thought perhaps special-effects skills would allow me to work more interesting jobs in film and TV. I was searching for something creatively fulfilling that would also allow me financial stability. I had no idea if this would be it, but I had to try something. Basic beauty makeup was boring, and I did not want to be dependent on Theo to do even simple things like go out for dinner. To get to that place I still needed Theo's help. He generously offered to split the cost of the class with me, which was close to four thousand dollars. Two thousand dollars was nothing to him, but it was a lot to me. I felt extremely grateful for his help but also guilty, given he had paid for nearly everything over the course of our relationship.

We broke up not long after I completed the class. I finally realized that fitting into his world meant nothing to me and that by continuing to play his game, I was sacrificing myself. That was not me, it was not what I cared about, it was not what I wanted.

"I should pay you back for half of the makeup class," I said to him. He was a multimillionaire. No part of me expected he would agree to the repayment.

"Great, I'd appreciate that," he said.

"Oh."

There was an uncomfortable pause.

"I don't have two thousand dollars I can give you right now," I said.

"That's no problem!" He was using his chipper, businessman voice, like the one he used when he suggested I quit the salon. "We'll do sort of a payment plan. How about you continue to cut my hair for free, and I'll keep track of when it has added up to two thousand dollars."

"I guess that's okay."

"Perfect! Let's do a haircut next week. I'll get in touch about day and time."

For the next eight months I cut Theo's hair every five weeks. He was always friendly, talking to me about work, or that week's episode of *The Bachelor*. When I finished the haircut, he would pull a slip of paper from his desk with my name at the top and *$2000* scrawled in blue pen. Each time he would write *–$40*, and place the paper back in his desk. It was humiliating but also, I supposed, fair.

At the urging of every single one of my friends, I finally called him to end the arrangement, citing our comically unparalleled financial situations.

"I have a hard time feeling you need this money as much as I do," I said.

He did not protest.

Nineteen

My goal for the day, as communicated in morning meeting, is to not obsessively ruminate on what will happen in the coming days and months—I want, instead, to be present in the now. I decide that for the rest of my time here I will participate in all activities available to me, so at two p.m. I find myself at Hope & Healing, a meeting led by the chaplain in a small wooden chapel built to accurately appear as if it were raised during colonial times. The service is nondenominational. Mary, Caitlyn, and I all sit in different pews, but the chapel is so small we're no further than three feet from one another.

Mention of God makes me uncomfortable. No one in my family ever talked about God when I was growing up, except to say we didn't believe in him; our Judaism was only cultural. I attended a private Episcopalian school from kindergarten through third grade, but at my parents' request I was excused from all Religious Knowledge classes. These classes, taught twice a week, were Bible teachings distilled and made palatable for elementary-age children—basically Sunday school, but during the week. I spent those periods in the art room alongside Miss Violet, a woman with butt-length silver hair who wore chunky metal jewelry she'd made herself. Her oversized batiked pants and gauzy tops contrasted with the students' plain dress code, which allowed us only solid-colored slacks or skirts in khaki, navy, or burgundy. She spoke with an accent, but at that age I was unable to identify its country of origin. If asked at the time, I might have guessed her age to be around ninety years old, but in reality she was likely closer sixty. Together, Miss Violet and I made collages from old *National Geographic* magazines and sculpted rudimentary bowls from clay. Once, the weight of an enormous, amoeba-shaped silver earring proved too heavy for her small ears and ripped clean through her lobe. Running toward the nurse's office, she waved her hands, joyously yelling, "Keep creating!" while leaving me at the large wooden art table alone with my scissors and glue stick. My classmates seemed unfazed that I didn't have to participate in Religious Knowledge.

In addition to Religious Knowledge, there was mandatory chapel period. I had the option to skip this too, but chose to participate because it gave me thirty minutes to fully retreat into my own thoughts amid the beauty of stained-glass windows. I utilized chapel to map out stories I would later write down; one of these was my own sequel to The Chronicles of Narnia, a series whose religious allegory eluded me until embarrassingly late in life. When a high school classmate told me Aslan was a proxy for Jesus, I was shocked. "They pull a *thorn* out of his paw," she said to me, thinking this would immediately clear my confusion, but it still took me a minute to draw the connection. I suppose that's what I get for making abstract clay sculptures with Miss Violet.

I've always felt embarrassed when people talk of God as if he is a real person, especially one who has any control over the chaos of life. Seated in the hospital chapel today, listening to the chaplain, is no exception. I know this isn't nice. I tell myself to be less judgmental of religion, but I can't help it. I can understand how God, as a concept, is extremely comforting. I am, I admit, even a little envious of that comfort. I don't believe heaven is a place we go when we die, but if it were, it sounds amazing. I sometimes wonder how different, and perhaps more optimistically, I would view life if I thought every dead person or animal I ever loved was in a utopia waiting for me. Though unable to palpably feel it, I can summon the idea of peace that comes with believing in a great benevolent force watching out for us, who even has a plan for us.

This isn't to say I believe in nothing, however. I believe in a spirit world, populated by healing guides and ancestors. I believe that people can get stuck in the liminal space between life and death. I believe in reincarnation and feel wholeheartedly there are people I've encountered in this life who I've also met in others. In this sense, I suppose you could call me spiritual, but I even wear this label with discomfort.

"Epiphanies are phenomena common to people who are overcoming addiction or mental health issues," the chaplain says from a very small pulpit. "Perhaps it was an epiphany that led you here or maybe you've had an epiphany regarding your recovery while you've been here. Epiphanies are divine messages from God."

Silently, in my mind, I correct her. "Actually, according to the psychologist Mihaly Csikszentmihalyi, epiphanies generate from hard, unconscious work the mind is doing while we are at rest. Rest creates space for unconscious thought to reach the surface of consciousness. All of a sudden (or so it seems) we have a great idea. It's not God, it's a confluence of so many factors—hard work, rest, necessity, intelligence, time, to name a few."

I focus my attention away from critique and back to listening. I know my inner voice is insufferable. *Just take this for what it is*, I tell myself. *Stop being so self-righteous, you chose to come to this chapel.*

"God can be whatever or whoever you want God to be," the chaplain continues. "God is energy. God is the divine spirit. God is the force within you that says 'It's time to make a change.'"

I have no idea if God is sitting in this chapel with Caitlyn, Mary, and me. The light is beautiful, though, brightly filtered through stained glass, throwing colorful shapes on the walls. The sun's rays illuminate dust particles that I watch float in the air. I know this is a once-in-a-lifetime moment, not because it is particularly novel or exciting, but more simply because I will never again sit in this place with these women who I have come to care for deeply. With hard work I hope to never sit in this place again at all. I suppose that is my epiphany—I will do what I need to do to never come back here.

I look over at Mary, who is seated with her eyes closed. She looks so peaceful.

Mary, Caitlyn, Shawn, and I gather at the kitchen table before Laurie, the lady with ten thousand beads, has even made it through the front door. It doesn't matter that we will likely never wear this jewelry, it's so fun to make. I have my too-big bracelet from last time with me.

"Laurie, I was wondering if you could help make this clasp smaller for me?"

"Yes, of course! Give it here." She stretches her arm across the table, and I drop the bracelet into her hand.

This time around I go straight to the letter beads; I don't even do the charade of looking at other options. What to spell? I plan to make a necklace this time, so I've got more real estate to work with. However, it's going to be a choker, so concision is still necessary. I think about spelling out my favorite line from my favorite book: "Keep passing the open windows," from *The Hotel New Hampshire* by John Irving. I have this line tattooed on me, and every time someone asks me what it means and I say, "Don't jump out the window," I get a nervous laugh. I count out the letters—twenty-five not including the spacer beads I'd need in between each word so they're individually legible. Too long; besides, I think once is enough times to corporally advertise this senti- ment. The more I signal to keep passing the open windows, the more people might worry I'm about to exit from the top floor.

Instead, I spell out "extraordinary machine," which is also the title song from Fiona Apple's 2005 album. Hard at work with our beads, we are interrupted by Dalby's front door opening. A woman in her late forties or early fifties walks through wearing a giant red Norma Kamali Sleeping Bag Coat. The woman looks frazzled and annoyed. She's carrying a suitcase, which means she's our new housemate, but the coat gave her away before the bags did. I could recognize that phenomenon of 1970s fashion anywhere—a staple garment of the fashion elite and monied counterculture in New York City. If you were wearing a Sleeping Bag Coat in the '70s or '80s, chances are you were *living*, and by living I mean doing drugs at Studio 54. We all look at her and then back at our in-progress jewelry projects. None of us speak, but to me the immediate change in the house feels seismic. It's no longer just the four of us. The equilibrium has died.

At the end of jewelry making, Laurie hands me back my New Year bracelet. This time it fits perfectly.

I walk to the rec center building. There are small rooms in this building that have been set up for appointments we are able to pay for, like massages and acupuncture. I schedule an acupuncture appointment hoping to mitigate my ongoing, general anxiety. I walk into a small room outfitted with a massage table, a small speaker, and a desk where the acupuncturist's materials are all laid out.

"Welcome," she says. "Have you ever had acupuncture before?"

"I have, yes."

"Is there anything in particular you'd like to address today?"

"I have anxiety. All the time. It makes me dizzy, it gives me headaches. I want to not feel constant anxiety," I say.

"We can work on some of that. I'll do points for anxiety and headaches. Your anxiety isn't going to suddenly go away, but maybe you'll feel a little calmer and the headache will dissipate. I'll step out, you can undress and lie under the sheet face up."

I realize this is the first time someone other than the intake nurse will see the cuts and scars on my arms and legs. I wrestle with whether I should warn her, or just assume by working at a psych hospital this is something she's encountered many times before.

"I have a lot of cuts and scarring," I say the second the acupuncturist reenters the room.

"Thanks for letting me know," she says, giving a soft smile. She inserts ten needles, turns on Native American flute music, and leaves the room.

I recognize the song immediately. It's by a Navajo and Ute flutist named R. Carlos Nakai. My parents bought me a CD of his when I was eight years old while on a monthlong road trip through the American Southwest. I listened to that CD every night for the next three years while I was falling asleep. That vacation was amazing and terrible all at once. My memories of it are mostly populated with fights between my parents while my brother and I played Go Fish in the back seat. A majority of these fights were about money—what we could and couldn't afford to spend. We made our way through Arizona, Utah, Colorado, and New Mexico, all four of us cramming into one room at seedy Super 8 motels desperately in need of fresh paint and a deep clean. My mom enraged that our accommodations were unsafe and unhygienic, my dad responding that this was all we could afford, reminding my mom that she didn't bring in any money and if she did, perhaps we could stay somewhere nicer. It was impossible to tell if we actually couldn't afford something nicer or if this was just the one power move my dad had to counter my mom's anger. We stayed for a few nights in a small town in New Mexico teeming with stray dogs. I played with them happily for an entire evening. I had always wanted a dog and begged my mom constantly for one. She said it was too much responsibility. The next morning, tacked to a public bulletin board, was a notice warning about recent outbreaks of bubonic plague.

"What's bubonic plague?" I asked my mom.

"You don't want to know. But it's not good," she said.

"It's when all your skin turns black and falls off your bones!" said my brother.

"Don't tell her that," my mom said, but he already had, and I spent the rest of the trip obsessively checking my body for blackened, dead patches of skin whenever I got a moment alone.

There was a swimming pool at a motel in Utah where my brother and I raced each other doing the backstroke. I only used my legs, while my arms dangled by my sides. Without my arms to clear my path, I slammed my head into the concrete side of the pool and immediately started crying.

"Why would you do that!" my mom screamed at me. "That's how people drown! Do you want to drown?!"

I didn't want to drown. I apologized, accepting I had done something bad. At eight years old I didn't yet understand what I would come to realize later, that my mom's anger was often a secondary consequence of a primary emotion—fear.

While lying on the massage table, needles gently housed within my skin, my mind is quick to recall the series of calamities that colored that arduous road trip through the desert. Yet sitting just adjacent are memories less fraught, even joyful. The towering spires of Bryce Canyon National Park; the beautiful alien-hued earth of the Painted Desert; my brother and I convincing each other we could feel the energy vortexes in Sedona, Arizona; using my mom's camera to photograph the prehistoric cliff dwellings built by the Ancestral Pueblo people in Colorado; the morning we all woke up at four a.m. to watch the sun rise over the Grand Canyon. These images are alive too, brought forth by the song I recognize from my past.

I'm no less anxious when the session ends, but my headache is gone.

* * *

At wrap-up meeting that night, we do a Rock Ceremony for Mary. To-morrow she will leave the hospital and transfer to sober living. She tells us how grateful she is to have met us and how grateful she is for everyone who works at the hospital who has helped her find a new path. She says that after sober living she looks forward to studying for the LSATs so that she can go to law school and become a lawyer. The new woman is sitting with us and she's still wearing her Norma Kamali coat. She doesn't know what to say to Mary because she only just met her. I think back to my first Rock Ceremony with Kristin. I hope Kristin is doing okay. When it's my turn to speak, I tell Mary how special she is—kind, determined, optimistic. I tell her that I believe she will be okay—no, better than okay; she will be great. I tell her I have no doubt that she will become a lawyer.

"Guys! You're making me cry!" she says after we've all shared.

The following morning as Mary is leaving, she approaches me with a question.

"I am not allowed to bring anything except my luggage to sober living," she says. "Will you take my Cuban oregano plant? I don't want it to just sit here and die."

"I would love to. I promise to take very good care of it. It will thrive," I say.

With that, Mary heads into the outside world, a place where we will likely never meet again.

Twenty

Hello Anna Marie, the email started. I am reaching out to see your availability for grooming for a Men's Italian Vogue shoot this coming Thursday.

I spent my early and mid-twenties bumbling through a makeup and hair career that felt neither fulfilling nor upwardly mobile. After working on the videos for Theo's comedy website, which I did even after we broke up, I realized I hated being on set. Waking up at five a.m. to spend twelve hours for essentially one hour of meaningful work—when the actors first sat in the makeup chair; everything else was touch-ups—became soul-crushingly boring. I thought maybe it was just those specific sets I did not like, so I tried working on some TV shows and short films. Also boring. Occasionally I would do hair and makeup for weddings, but I hated this too. I found interacting with strangers in these high-pressure, one-off situations incredibly anxiety-inducing. I had trouble making small talk and I was in a constant state of panic that I would ruin their day with bad hair or makeup, the one thing I was being hired to do well.

Yes, I responded. I am available. Is there anything pertinent to the shoot styling that I should know ahead of time? If the creative director can pass along any notes, that would be much appreciated.

No notes! This is just basic men's grooming.

I arrived at a SoHo apartment with my grooming kit—haircutting scissors, an array of hair products, a blow-dryer, a flat iron, foundation, powder. I even threw in some of my beauty makeup—eyeshadow, blush, lipstick—just in case. The artistic director did not appear to see me when I walked in the door. She and two assistants were all huddled together staring silently at her phone.

"Hi, I'm Anna, the groomer. I'll set up at the table." I motioned to a wooden dining table and waited for some acknowledgment.

"See what I mean," the director said, coiling her hand through a striking mane of jet-black hair that hung past her butt. "Everyone is trying to copy me; everyone is trying to rip me off. They know I'm the best."

"Excuse me?" I said, before realizing she was not talking to me. I went to the table and set up my kit.

The shoot was for a short profile of a young, up-and-coming French Canadian actor and filmmaker. He sat in my chair and I did basic men's grooming: I styled his wavy hair with some product, applied light foundation and powder, and I assumed my work was done.

"I want to do something crazy with the hair. Don't you think it would be just amazing to do something crazy with the hair?" The director was addressing the actor, not me. "I want a crazy, long wig, like this." The director, to whom I was now suddenly visible, pushed a torn-out page from a magazine in my face of a male model with long curly hair. He resembled a high-fashion "Weird Al" Yankovic.

"I'm sorry," I said, beginning to internally panic, but trying to remain composed. "I asked the producer if there was any special styling I needed to be aware of ahead of the shoot. I don't normally carry wigs or hair extensions with me for basic male grooming. For something like that I would have needed to be alerted ahead of time so I could shop for the correct products."

This was not okay. The director crouched down in front of the small suitcase where I kept my products and began pulling things out and throwing them on the floor, assuming if she looked hard

enough, eventually she might find a wig or extensions. I really had
no idea.

"You call yourself a groomer!" she yelled. "How can I realize my vision, how can the world see what I see if you show up unprepared???"

If I had not felt so humiliated in the moment, I would have found
this very funny. I find it very funny now.

"I'm sorry," I said. "There's a beauty supply store right up the
street. I can walk there and see what they have for extensions. I just
want to mention ahead of time that the extensions will be synthetic,
not made from real hair. Synthetic hair is not heat stylable, so I can
grab a few options, but I will not be able to style them with a flat iron
or curling iron."

"You are a sorry excuse for a professional! You have ruined this
entire shoot! You will never get a job again!" she yelled, pointing to
the door.

I knew I was about to cry. "I'm very sorry for this misunderstand-
ing. I can be back in twenty minutes with extensions."

"GO!" she screamed.

I ran down the stairs and up Broadway toward the beauty supply store on Mercer Street. Why did the producer tell me this was
just basic grooming? Maybe she did tell me I needed to bring wig options? No, she definitely did not. I cannot believe I fucked this up.
No, I did not fuck this up, they fucked this up. That woman is a nightmare. What if I really cannot work again? Do I even want to work
again? What if I just do not go back to the shoot? Just go home and
disappear. Not answer emails asking where I am. I don't have to work
for Men's Italian *Vogue* again if I don't want to. But my kit is at the
shoot. I can't just leave my kit. Or can I? Maybe I can. How much
money's worth of product would I be losing if I just left my kit there
and did not go back for it?

I was in front of a wall of synthetic hair extensions. There was a wavy option and a straight option and thankfully there were options that looked close to the actor's dark brown hair color. I grabbed some, paid, and returned to the shoot.

"DID YOU NOT SEE THIS PHOTO I SHOWED YOU?! CURLY! I WANT CURLY! YOU ARE A MORON!"

Fuck, I should have just left my kit.

"I'm sorry, these were the options. I think the wavy extensions could work."

"You have a curling iron! Curl them!"

"This is synthetic hair. It's made of plastic. If I put heat to it the hair will burn."

"Do it anyway!"

I plugged in my curling iron and waited for it to heat up. This felt like two hours. I very lightly curled the synthetic hair around the barrel of the iron, hoping a small amount of heat might give it a slight curl without singeing the hair.

"Give me that!" The director pushed me out of the way with the force of her body and grabbed the curling iron out of my hand. She wrapped a piece of the hair around the iron as tightly as she could. The hair smoked, then burned, then fell to the floor.

"Fine! We will have to do wavy. You ruined this shoot!"

I silently clipped the extensions into the actor's hair, giving him a long front bang that covered his face and ended at his shoulder blade. Aside from the extension being the exact color and texture of his natural hair, it looked ridiculous.

"Perfect," the director said. "I'm a genius. Do you see this?" she addressed the two assistants. "I'm a fucking genius."

I left the shoot that day resolute that I would never step on any set as a makeup artist or a hairstylist ever again.

* * *

I had no idea what to do. I eventually started a makeup blog on Tumblr. The menial success of which prompted talent agents to reach out to me.

"I think you should be doing on-air beauty content!" was the collective refrain. I was not passionate about the beauty space, but lacking any sense of direction, I agreed to audition for some female-led shows looking for a "beauty expert." All these auditions went the same.

"Great!" the casting agent would say. "Now, can you do it again with a bit more energy?"

I would do it again with what I interpreted as a bit more energy.

"Let's see it one more time; this time you're excited about it."

I would do it again with a slightly different vocal inflection.

"Better, now really sell it to me! We want people to see this and want to be your best friend."

I would do it again, exactly the same.

I never got any of these jobs. Forced effervescence, especially about something I did not care about, was impossible to muster. I realized people saw my social media and filled in the blanks about who I was. They were expecting loud, bubbly, extroverted, and über-friendly, when I was not any of those things. I was, as I am still, quiet around strangers, guarded except with close friends, and not the type of girl who is going to sell you anything.

These opportunities were exhausted, save for a web series I did about makeup and ghosts (yes, correct) for the website Amy Poehler's Smart Girls. This series worked because I was allowed to lean into who I was. No one was asking me to be a bubbly saleswoman. I simply got to show a weekly guest how to do one makeup trick and asked them to share a ghost story or paranormal encounter. When the web series aired, it was met with backlash from women, mostly moms, who insisted that a show about makeup was antithetical to the very ethos the website touted—that girls are smart—and the decision was made to stop making episodes. May we never forget that females cannot be intellectual and aesthetically minded at the same time.

I was utterly lost. I felt like a failure who could not choose a direction for her life. I watched as all my friends built careers they appeared to love. I felt life was passing me by.

To fill the time, and to distract myself from my worthlessness, I bought an instructional DVD off Etsy, recorded from a VHS made in 1992, on hand-making Victorian lampshades. Putting my hands to work with something creative always made me feel productive. Why not pick up a very weird hobby?

The first lampshade I made was fit only to be placed in the garbage, but the second shade looked pretty good. The third shade looked kind of amazing. It had lush velvet fabric printed with illustrated peacocks, chocolate-brown trim, and gold, beaded fringe along the bottom. When illuminated, the light sparkled through the gold glass beads, refracting onto a nearby wall.

Huh, I thought. *I wonder if other people would like these?*

Twenty-One

Six new women arrive at Dalby over the course of the morning. I walk into the living room to find them watching reruns of *Grey's Anatomy*. *Goliath* has been abandoned now that Mary is gone and a bunch of strangers have commandeered the TV. Most of the women are young, early to mid-twenties, but one woman appears to be in her late sixties. She is not happy to be here and is making this clear by near-constant scoffs, audible exhales, and eye rolls.

"Well, *I* don't want to watch this," she says quietly, but loud enough to be heard. The statement is directed at no one in particular, thereby making it directed at everyone. The girls around her exchange glances but ignore her. Scoff. Eye roll. More glances exchanged. Laughs stifled.

"Then I guess I'll just go to my room," she says. Again, everyone ignores her as she gets up from the couch and walks into the kitchen.

I'm making tea in the kitchen when one of the new young women walks in wearing shorts and a tank top. The older woman squints her eyes and says, "Put on a bra. Where do you think you are, the beach?" The young woman raises her eyebrows and walks out of the kitchen.

I make a point to say hello to everyone as they arrive, but I largely keep my distance in order to avoid interactions like these. I've gotten so used to my little group, now just me, Caitlyn, and Shawn, that branching out feels intimidating. Besides, all three of us are leaving tomorrow; what's the point of trying to make friends?

I and my hospital team have decided that tomorrow morning, before I check out, I will end my care with Dr. Karr.

"Listen, if my own daughter was in this situation, I would tell her to leave her therapist," Dr. Samuels said.

Dr. Karr will get that divorce she was so quick to suggest, but first I must be set up with proper support ahead of my discharge.

For the next six months, Beth, my social worker, will work as my case manager. She will help monitor my suicidal ideation and self-harm urges, while also providing support on follow-through of behavioral changes I want to make. She enrolls me in the hospital's Intensive Outpatient Program, or IOP, where I will participate in three-hour, virtual DBT meetings three times a week for three months. Both Beth and Dr. Philips will help me find a new full-time therapist to see weekly. I realize the foreseeable future will be monopolized by therapy, but I'm okay with that, remembering my chapel epiphany—to do what I need to do to never come back here.

In the afternoon, Caitlyn, Shawn, and I go to the gym to play basketball and volleyball. I'm terrible at both. The basketball feels unwieldy in my small hands and the volleyball stings when it smacks against my forearms. I watch Caitlyn bump a volleyball up and down sixty times without letting it drop. Shawn and I count in unison as she goes, excitement building with every factor of ten. I think of Caitlyn's Cuban oregano pot, scrawled with the words "LOOK UP."

At dinner I can tell something sneaky is going on. The men from Oscar and the women from Dalby are talking more than usual, and in hushed voices. I only hear small clips of information.

". . . after wrap-up . . ."

". . . say 'the gazebo to smoke' . . ."

". . . Labyrinth . . ."

I am curious about what's going on, but I'm also aware no one is filling me in and that feels purposeful. I'm not sure why.

Before wrap-up, the house manager finds Caitlyn, Shawn, and me and asks if we want to pick rocks for our Rock Ceremony. This time I'm going to participate.

"I already picked a rock last week," I remind her. "I'll grab it before the meeting."

"I don't want to pick a rock," Shawn says.

"Why?" I ask.

"Because I don't know what to pick. It feels dumb to pick a word for myself."

"How about I pick one for you?"

"Yeah, okay, I guess so," she says.

"I'll keep it a secret until we've all spoken, then I'll give it to you," I say.

Shawn agrees.

I sift through the rocks with care; it's important to me to choose the right one. Shawn is special to me, and I want the word to resonate with her. I want her to look at the rock and know that I understand the slice of herself she's made vulnerable over the past eleven days. I'll miss her the most of all the girls. I know this because I can see myself in her the most. I know she'll think "hope" is cheesy, and she didn't come with us to the chapel yesterday, so I think "faith" will be meaningless. Finally, I close my fingers around a rock and place it in my pocket.

Our ceremony is filled with platitudes and diverted eye contact from the new people who don't know us. This isn't their fault; what are you supposed to say to someone you've only known for a day besides "Wish you luck out there!" When Shawn and I speak, we look directly at each other.

"Shawn," I say. She tries to fight a smile but the smile wins. "I'm so grateful we were here at the same time. You remind me a lot of myself. We can both be skeptical, guarded, angry." Shawn nods. "You're really cool. And you're really, really interesting. I don't think you realized this, but whenever I heard you practicing violin, I would go to my room and lie on my bed and listen through the walls."

When I say this, tears fill Shawn's eyes. I continue. "You're so good. I loved listening to you play, even when you were just repeating scales. I picked this rock because this is what I hope for you. This is what you deserve, and this is what I believe you will find." I place the rock I picked for her in her cupped hands, which she has extended in front of me. She reads it: PEACE. We both wipe tears from our faces.

At around nine thirty p.m. I notice a bunch of the girls putting on their coats and heading toward the sliding glass door that leads to Dalby's back porch, and beyond that the smoking gazebo.

"We're going outside to smoke," someone says to the house manager.

I follow them outside, knowing this is my answer to the murmuring at dinner. They blow right past the gazebo.

"Where are you going?" I say to no one in particular.

"On a walk," says Caitlyn. "You wanna come?"

"Sure," I say, following them.

They are walking in the direction of the Labyrinth. It's through a set of woods that is not illuminated at night.

About a hundred yards from Dalby I say, "Wait, where are you really going?"

"We are meeting the Oscar guys in the Labyrinth to smoke," someone says. I don't know her name.

I stop walking but say nothing. I just stand there, watching the girls moving away from me, an amorphous mass, undulating in the dark. No one even realizes I'm no longer there. I don't remember if walking the property at dark or socializing with the men for nighttime smoke breaks has been explicitly forbidden, but I can't imagine it's encouraged. An entire childhood of being yelled at for minor offenses—accidentally spilling food on a nice sweater, hitting my head in a pool because I wasn't using my arms in a backstroke—have shaped me into a person who doesn't take risks when it comes to following rules. I'm not about to change that now. No momentary burst of fun is worth the shame of getting in trouble. I wonder if the girls sensed this about me and this is why I wasn't looped in—they thought I'd ruin their fun with words of caution, or worse, rat them out. I turn around and walk back to Dalby alone, the frigid January air biting at my cheeks.

"Where are the others?" the house manager says to me when I enter the door.

"I think they're smoking at the gazebo," I say back to her, and ascend the staircase to my bedroom without ever making eye contact.

Twenty-Two

After making a few lampshades for myself, I posted photos on social media to the immediate requests by strangers, friends, and acquaintances who wanted to pay me to make lampshades for them as well. Making lampshades was tedious, time-consuming work for which the hours spent did not always result in monetary payoff. I rarely made more than fifteen to twenty dollars an hour for a shade, but I loved doing it. Keeping my hands busy meant my brain could momentarily relax. Luxuriating in this quiet peace for a while would have been good for my nervous system. Instead of doing this, I got a puppy.

Petunia, a twelve-week-old French bulldog, was placed in my arms on June 20, 2013. I had already named her before she was mine. I knew French bulldogs were notorious for their health issues, but I assumed a Frenchie from a reputable breeder would be healthier due to closer genetic oversight. Even when I spoke with the breeder, she was careful to go through the list of complications common for the breed—breathing issues, allergies, spinal disc problems, ear infections, heart murmurs. "I completely understand the risks," I said confidently to the breeder, thinking my dog would be different. I thought maybe Petunia would have one of these things, but she had them all.

From the moment I saw her I knew I had never loved anything as much as I loved her. Holding her against my chest, feeling her warm body and her strong heartbeat, I felt a mixture of pure love and panic. I was terrified because it was now my job to protect her and care for her. I was also terrified by the love. Concurrent with the excitement for this adorable new puppy, something I had wanted since I was a kid, was the near immediate realization that one day Petunia would die; that I would be present for her death and that to love her was to one day be without her. My brain did not allow me one day to not consider her mortality.

Her first night with me I felt racked with guilt that I had separated her from her mom and brothers. *She must be so confused*, I thought. *She must be so scared*. I prepared a crate with soft blankets for her to sleep in. I positioned it on the floor near my bed.

"It's time to go to sleep now, Petunia," I said to the little face staring back at me. "I'm going to be right here in the bed."

I got in bed and turned off the light. Almost immediately Petunia began to whimper.

"I'm right here, Petunia. It's okay. You're safe."

She continued to cry.

I turned on my bedside lamp and retrieved a chair from the living room. I placed the chair so it was facing the bed and put Petunia's crate on top of the seat, making her level with the bed. Now we could see each other.

"Don't be sad, Petunia. I promise to take such good care of you."

She looked at me and then threw her head back and howled like a wolf would howl at the moon. It was the only time in her whole life I saw her do that. I opened the crate, took her tiny body in my hands, and placed her in my lap. She went quiet and licked my thigh. I kissed the top of her head. "I'm your mom now, P. I love you and I'll always love you." I pet her until she fell asleep and then gently put her back in the crate, careful to make sure she was positioned so if she woke up she could see my face.

* * *

Petunia had an undeniably adorable face, but she was not what you would call "a good dog." She was, in fact, very, very naughty. Petunia inherited one of the worst terrier traits: resource guarding. Resource guarding happens when a dog is so protective over something, they will become aggressive when you attempt to take it away from them. Many dogs resource guard their toys. Petunia didn't do this, but she did guard literally every single thing on the floor that she deemed belonged to her—which were most things.

You dropped a tube of ChapStick? Forget about it, that's Petunia's now. A sock didn't make it into the laundry hamper and Petunia found it? That's now Petunia's sock. You *dared* to accidentally spill coffee on the floor and want to clean it up? I'm sorry, don't even consider getting near that area with a paper towel. Not only does that spilled coffee belong to Petunia, the floor below it does as well. Should Petunia's ultrasonic bat ears, or her saucer eyes, detect an ill-fated human accident that landed an item on the ground, she was poised at any moment to rush toward it at full speed, growl rumbling, bark sounding. It was terrifying. It was also extremely funny.

I never left anything on the floor; shoes always went on a table, to the confusion of anyone who entered my home. For many years I could not leave remotes on the coffee table—she would jump on the table and steal them. In those occurrences, when I did drop something and she got to it before me, there was an entire protocol I followed to get that item back.

"Petunia, leave it," I would say in a firm voice, which she completely ignored. "Do you want a treat?" I really hit the word "treat," my voice scaling a full octave.

She would look at me, unimpressed. She would look back at the stolen item (let's call it a pen). She would look back at me; a woman who carefully weighs her options.

"Petunia, go to bed." I would point to the bed. She knew that if she went to bed and let me pick up the pen, her reward would be the treat, but she didn't yet know if it was worth the trade. We would engage in a three-minute eye-to-eye stare down that ended with her not going to her bed but instead lying on the floor right where she was, with her muzzle on top of the pen.

"Petunia," I would say. "Go. To. Bed."

Two more minutes would pass.

Reluctantly Petunia would get up, walk over to her bed, and sit.

"Good girl! Stay." I would put my hand up, the signal she and I agreed on for "stay." I would move toward the pen. So would she.

"Petunia . . . STAY." I would sound like a mom who means business now. I would walk over and pick up the pen while Petunia glared at me like she wished me a slow death.

"Good girl! You're such a good girl! GOOD STAY!" Then Petunia would get her treat and immediately forget that she was ever guarding anything. She would turn back into a sweet, affectionate dog who wanted kisses and attention, and who would lovingly headbutt you if you stopped petting her. This was our life, over and over and over.

I once contacted an animal communicator in hopes that Petunia would be able to tell me things about herself to better my understanding of her. In turn, I would be able to ask her to maybe stop guarding everything. The animal communicator was very clear in her directives— during the session, which was over the phone, all I needed to do was have Petunia in the room and make sure she didn't fall asleep. She explained to me that Petunia might appear to go into a sleepy trance (she absolutely did), but as long as she wasn't asleep, the communicator would be able to speak with her and translate back to me.

"Animals have their own personalities and free will, so just because

I ask something of Petunia, does not guarantee Petunia will listen," she forewarned.

Now, please know I am a woman who owns five tarot decks; a woman who burned a Death candle to break the psychic bond with her past life; a woman who collects the bones of dead animals, cleans them, and puts them on her altars. Yes, "altars" is plural. I never once questioned if the communicator was for real, but when she described some of Petunia's behavior and correctly connected it to the specific layout of my house at the time, I was totally sold.

"Sometimes your mom drops something or puts something on the floor and needs to pick it up," the communicator explained to Petunia. There was about a fifteen-second pause and then the woman said, "Hmm, Petunia is saying that yes, it's true, she does guard things and sometimes she goes upstairs to your closet and steals things she is not supposed to have. But Petunia would like to point out that she has never destroyed anything."

The communicator then broke from communication with Petunia and asked me directly, "Is that true?"

Yes. It was true. In all her years of stealing socks, shoes, pens, ChapStick, remotes, hats, the list goes on, she never even one time destroyed anything. She would simply lie with her head on top of the stolen item, growling at anyone who dared approach her. Petunia's objective was not to chew, rip, or destroy; her objective was merely to have a little treasure of her own.

Petunia also believed she should be included in everything a person might do, and acted out when she sensed she wouldn't be included. Let's say it's evening, I've been home all day wearing jeans and a T-shirt, but now I have to get ready for a dinner with friends. Watching me change into nicer clothes would prompt a hunt for something she could steal. She would then bring that item back to me, so ensuring my lengthy dance to retrieve it from her. If she could find nothing to steal, she plopped against the front door, her twenty-one-pound body obstructing my exit.

"I'm telling Petunia that sometimes you need to go out," the animal communicator said, followed by a pause. "Right, Petunia is saying that's fine, she can come too."

Then, speaking to me, she said, "I think I'll rephrase this for her." She continued, "Now I'm telling Petunia that maybe Mom might take Petunia out with her, but when you arrive at your destination, there might be a sign that says 'no dogs allowed.'"

Another brief pause. "Well. Petunia says if she can't go inside too, then you can both go home together."

Eventually the communicator said, "Petunia thinks she is a star and a queen, so I'm not sure she is going to respond to anything about her being left out simply because she's a dog."

I already knew this to be true about Petunia. I'm not sure why I thought an animal communicator could convince her otherwise.

Petunia became my constant companion, my de facto daughter. I had trouble being away from her and she rarely let me out of her sight. She came into my life during a time when I felt no purpose or direction, and so I made my purpose to care for her. Petunia's health was precarious from the start. When she was spayed at five months, she came home with pneumonia. This illness, beyond being heartbreaking to watch, weakened her. She became susceptible to more bouts of pneumonia, which she fought through three times before the age of six. For years I would make lampshades from home while Petunia chewed a bone, or guarded fabric I dropped, or slept in the slice of sun that spread from my office window across the floor. The familiar feeling of boredom eventually saturated my lampshade making, as it had with everything that came before, but at least doing this I never had to leave

Petunia. My anxiety mounted, fearing some health calamity would strike when I was not around, and she would die without me there. I thought if she was always with me, under my desk while I sewed my fingers raw making maximalist lampshades for a community of aesthetes willing to spend the money on my work, I could keep her safe.

Twenty-Three

Zoom connects on the hospital iPad I've propped against a windowsill in my room. I see Dr. Karr sitting in front of the yellow wall. She gives me a tentative smile and says hello like she already knows what's coming. I plan to keep this short and tidy. I'd rather not discuss the whys of it all, just say, "Thank you for your time. I appreciate everything you've done for me over the past five years," and end things on a pleasant note.

"How's everything going there?" she asks me. I had emailed her when I checked back in to let her know I had extended my stay.

"It's okay. I feel okay," I say, but I don't really feel okay. I feel very scared.

"So, what's up?" Dr. Karr's voice is soft and kind. This is more like the Dr. Karr I knew for so many years, before whatever happened between us happened.

"I feel sad to say this," I begin. "I think it's time for me to move on from our work together."

"I had a feeling this might happen," she says, as if she didn't suggest "the divorce." Then she adds, "I'm sad too."

I believe that Dr. Karr is sad. I think she and I both presumed we would work together for many more years. Our first four years together had a good dynamic. I felt safe with her and I learned so much about myself while in her care. I felt she understood me. Dr. Karr was the person who suggested I start medication for my anxiety; this changed my entire life for the better. She believed I was a strong, capable, intelligent woman, and helped me recognize those qualities within myself. "Anna," she said to me during those panic attacks my first month of grad school, "you can't possibly do all the reading. No one does *all* the reading, trust me. Pick a few of the readings, read them closely, and then participate when discussing those readings. You don't have to be perfect. Sometimes the best we can do is good enough." This advice saved me.

I don't know what happened over the last year. Maybe it was all my fault—my depression caused me to act out in ways that caused the riff. Maybe my return to cutting scared her and she didn't know how to deal with it. Maybe the pandemic—being cooped up in our homes with infrequent respite to the outside world—made us both a little crazy.

"I really appreciated our time together," I say to Dr. Karr. "It helped me enormously and I'm extremely grateful to you."

"I, too, appreciated our time together," she says, "and I will miss you."

"I'll miss you too."

This feels more like a breakup between two friends than a doctor and a patient, and perhaps, I realize in this moment, this is why it needs to end. I feel good about this conversation. I also feel surprised at how easy and how nice it is. I am about to wrap up our meeting when Dr. Karr begins to speak.

"I must tell you, Anna," she says, her tone now sarcastic. "You really had those men wrapped around your finger in that outtake meeting the other day. I gotta hand it to you."

My brain begins rapidly calibrating her words and my emotions. I see two scenarios laid before me. One—push back, say exactly what I want to say to her: "Excuse me? What in the actual fuck are you insinuating?" Two—say nothing, recognize that this is the last time we will ever speak, that ultimately what I might want to say in this moment doesn't matter. Recognize that she has said this to make me mad, or to make me question my perception of myself, but don't give her the satisfaction of knowing she has done either. She has, however, done both.

In the seconds it takes for me to weigh my options, Dr. Karr adds, "I was like, 'Damn! She really knows how to work a room of men.'"

Now I'm furious, so angry my whole body feels hot, and I can tell I'm about to cry. Should I point out that there was a female social worker in that meeting who had the exact same reaction—perhaps a stronger reaction—than the male doctors? Should I yell at her, unleash my rage? Should I let her see me cry? Should I make her explain herself?

I think back to my first conversation about the hospital with Dr. Karr, how I hated knowing I would see mostly male doctors and how she told me to give them a chance. *They're professionals*, she'd said. Now, she either thinks they're not so professional—easily deceived by a guileful female patient—or, she thinks my propensity for manipulation is so cunning, I've swayed doctors of psychology to run to my aid, when perhaps I don't need help at all. Either option is bad and puts me at blame for what happened during the outtake meeting. It leaves no room for my emotional implosion to be honest. It questions my motives. It strips me of all power in asking for help. She has made me into a one-dimensional Jungian archetype of a woman whose influence on men would be considered destructive and bewitching.

That I am manipulative—but specifically manipulative of men—is not something that has ever been suggested by Dr. Karr in our five years together, even as I recounted my strained, confusing, and outright maddening relationships with Ethan, Julian, Brian, Sam, and Theo. I will likely hear these words—*You really had those men wrapped around your finger*—replay in my mind over and over, long after this meeting ends. Worst of all, no matter how untrue I feel this to be, there is now a small voice saying, *But what if she's right?*

I decide not to react, keeping my face as neutral as possible. As of thirty seconds ago, Dr. Karr is no longer my therapist and has no right to my thoughts or emotions. I'll process this with whoever comes next.

"I have to go now," I say. "Thank you again."

"Take care, Anna," she says.

I turn off the iPad.

I walk into the living room to find a bunch of the girls sitting on the couch. Everyone looks tense. I probably look tense too.

"What's up?" I ask Shawn.

"We're all being piss tested." She pauses, registering my look of confusion. "Because of last night."

"Even you guys?" I look at Shawn and Caitlyn. They nod. "You're leaving today, what does it even matter?"

Caitlyn shrugs.

"All we were doing was smoking cigs at the Labyrinth. It was literally no big deal," says a girl whose name I don't know.

"We think someone in Forest House snitched on us," Shawn says, rolling her eyes.

Fear hits me—I hope no one thinks I snitched on them.

"That sucks," I say. "But you don't have to do anything besides a drug test?"

"Nope," Shawn says. "Everything's gonna come back clean anyway."

All the tests do.

I have individual meetings with Dr. Philips and Dr. Samuels to process my breakup with Dr. Karr. I recount exactly what happened, only this time I cry and project my voice with anger.

"I just don't understand why she said that to me. What was the point to throw that in at the very last second?"

"Why do *you* think she said it?"

Unfortunately, it's a question without an answer. No matter how much I, or the doctors, hypothesize, the result is only theory. No one knows except Dr. Karr. If I had asked her why she said it, I'd have trouble believing anything short of *I wanted to make you feel bad.*

"I'm very sorry it happened that way," Dr. Philips says to me. "That must have been disappointing. I know you wanted to end things positively."

I ask Dr. Philips, Dr. Samuels, and Beth if they have found me manipulative, and they all have the same answer: no. Dr. Philips and Dr. Samuels both add that Dr. Karr's statement suggests offensive intimations about them—that they are unable to assess a female patient objectively, without enacting something sexual or custodial. I actually do wonder if male doctors are wholly capable of assessing female patients objectively—but not necessarily for the reasons they've suggested. From my view, the field of psychology was developed by white men using white men as the baseline standard for behavior and sanity. Centuries of conditioning has taught them, and us as a society, that when a woman expresses anger, paranoia, fear, anxiety, depression, or even intuition, they might be crazy. Years of my own experiences with men have taught me they struggle to see women as autonomous creatures with complicated, interesting, rich inner lives. Usually, they see us only in relation to themselves. How can a person with such limited scope of another objectively analyze them?

I only truly care about Beth's experience of me. Since Beth is the only woman on my team, part of my brain tells me her no is the only no I can trust. For some reason, Dr. Karr being a woman has not undermined Beth's authority. If I have wrapped the male doctors around my finger, as Dr. Karr suggested, then how would they be able to objectively tell me I'm not manipulative? By that logic they are acutely in the midst of my manipulation.

"I find you to be a kind, honest, extremely conscientious woman who is in crisis. I know I have only known you for nine days, so this assessment might mean less to you than Dr. Karr's comment. If you would like, as we continue to see each other weekly over the next six months for outpatient care, I can pay attention to my experience of you and be upfront about what I find. However," Beth adds, "the doctors on your team are some of the best I've worked with, and I truly believe if manipulation was part of your personality, it would not have evaded two psychologists with PhDs working at a psychiatric hospital."

I nod. By Beth's assessment the men were rightly insulted by Dr. Karr's comment and not merely responding to an ego wound. Perhaps I shouldn't be so quick to pathologize everything men do as merely a failing of being male—though men do make it difficult not to.

"Thank you. I appreciate hearing this. And yes, if in the future you experience me as manipulative, I want to know. That's not the type of person I want to be," I say.

"It's a deal," Beth says.

When I return to Dalby to pack my things, I learn Caitlyn has already left. I'm sad I didn't get to say goodbye. In the kitchen I realize she has left the Cuban oregano and the jade plant she potted before I arrived. I decide to take Caitlyn's plants along with Mary's and my own. The thought of leaving them to wither on the kitchen table or to be thrown out when no one claims them makes me deeply sad. Besides, I want something to help me remember Caitlyn.

Packing my car feels familiar, but this time I won't turn back. I can't. My mom is meeting me at the hospital to hand off Petunia. Instead of going back to my house, I will immediately drive into New York City, for an appointment with a dermatologist vet. Life does not pause long for a mental health crisis, especially when a French bulldog with chronic ear infections is involved.

"I wish I could meet Petunia," Shawn says to me. We are both standing outside Dalby. My car is packed; I'm just waiting for my mom. Shawn's ride is here and it's time for her to go. We exchange phone numbers, writing them down in the little blue notebooks we got at check-in when they took our phones away. It's the only time I have written in this notebook.

"Keep in touch," I say. "You're gonna do really well. I know it."

I don't know it, but I hope by saying it I can sway the future. We give each other a hug, she gets into a black sedan, and it disappears quickly into the bends of the winding country road. Tears roll down my cheeks. I wish I had a plant to help me remember Shawn too.

Within ten minutes my mom arrives with Petunia, who practically leaps out of her crate in the back seat and into my arms. I am so happy to see her, to feel her soft fur, and to hear her grunting breaths. My little reason for living. I hold her, rocking her back and forth like she's my baby, because she is.

"How are you doing?" my mom asks, giving me a big hug. It's nice to see her too. Whenever I haven't seen my mom for a stretch of time and then I do, I am struck by how beautiful she is. Her long, silver hair, her high cheekbones, her big eyes. Seeing her as a beautiful woman, rather than just my mom, strikes a gnawing, physical type of sadness. I remember she is a whole person, one whose fears, whose joys, and whose disappointments developed long before I materialized into her life. There is a whole history before me and a life she thought she'd have—child-free, working in fashion, living in New York City. Instead, she ended up a stay-at-home mom who cooked dinner every night and carted her children to their activities. She never held that against me; instead she made her whole life about my brother and me. For the first time I can appreciate how much the depression I've been wearing like a dress—face drawn, body withering, evidence of cutting strategically hidden—must have been terrifying for her to witness.

"I feel okay, I think. I'm ready to leave, much more ready than before."

"I'm glad. I made you a bunch of food and put some in your fridge and some in your freezer. Just let me know when you're running low and I'll make you more. Text me when you get home from the city," she says.

I thank her and give her another hug. I can see in her face she's deeply worried about me, probably afraid of me being alone in my house.

"I'm going to be fine. After living with so many people, I'm happy to be going to my own space where it's just me, my things, and Petunia." It's a half truth, but it's what she needs to hear. I promise to text her as soon as I get home. She pulls out of the parking lot.

The house manager comes outside to pet Petunia, who jumps all over her, trying to kiss her face.

"So, this is the famous Petunia who you love so much," the house manager says, knees on the ground, now at Petunia's level. "You take good care of your mom."

I thank her for everything. I have probably said the words "thank you" at least thirty times before noon, but I wish there was something bigger than "thank you" that I could say to everyone here.

Alone in front of Dalby, I pick up Petunia, kiss her head, and put her into the crate in the back seat.

"Okay, girl," I say, petting her head through the thin metal bars. "Now it's your turn to see a doctor. Different type of doctor though." She licks my hands.

I look in my rearview mirror and see Petunia looking back at me.

"Time to do it, P."

I pull out of the driveway and press play on the only song that feels appropriate to play me out of this moment in time. *Be kind to me, or treat me mean,* Fiona Apple sings. *I'll make the most of it, I'm an extraordinary machine.*

Twenty-Four

Petunia's vet is not allowing pet owners inside the exam room during appointments, due to Covid. Instead, we wait in the freezing cold and speak to the vet via phone. I take a photo of myself sitting on a plastic folding chair set up on a New York City side street, bundled in a black coat, red hat, and scarf.

Crazy lady out of hospital and officially on the loose! I write, texting the photo to Amanda, Carmel, and Sarah. The replies come immediately.

Clear the streets!
She's back and better than ever!
Yay! We missed you!

Now if only there wasn't a global pandemic and we could actually see each other, I type.

I smile looking at the text bubbles. I have not seen any of them in person for ten months, but they are still right there with me.

After an hour a young vet tech brings Petunia out to me along with a small paper bag stuffed with medication for her ear infection. I will have to do an antifungal ear flush and administer ear drops twice a day for the next six weeks, at which time I will bring her back for a recheck. I can look forward to Petunia trying to bite me every day, twice a day, for a month and a half. I pick her up, hug her tightly, and put her in the crate for a ninety-minute drive home to Connecticut.

Stepping into my house after nearly two weeks in the hospital gives the eerie feeling no time has passed at all. It is like returning from a vacation where everything at home is so as it was, you wonder if the trip had been a dream. I bring in the three Cuban oregano plants and Caitlyn's jade plant from where I had carefully tucked them with a blanket in the passenger footwell of my car. I put them in the middle of my kitchen table so I can look at them every morning while I drink coffee. I open my fridge to find the food my mom cooked for me—soup, lentils with vegetables, half a chicken, banana bread. There is more in the freezer.

I walk around, Petunia at my heels, reacquainting myself with the house. I circumnavigate each room, touching the furniture, bed linens, and walls. This house that will now hold me, containing my continued recovery, is beautiful and calming in its aesthetic delights. It is my greatest artwork to date. It is just what I need.

For dinner I heat up my food and take it into my dining room, one of the best rooms in the house, also the one I touched the least. It is entirely paneled in dark English oak. The ceiling, which is vaulted, is thirty feet high. There is a fireplace with a mantel and a stone hearth. The room appears not of this time, which is why I love it. It is decorated with wooden furniture that was once in my grandparents' dining room—a large table, chairs still upholstered in their 1950s floral fabric, a china cabinet, and a small buffet side table. On the wall sits a cuckoo clock that once hung in my great-grandparents' house. I light a fire, then light all the candles in the room. There are too many to be technically safe. While eating dinner I talk to Petunia, who is lying down under my chair at my feet, just waiting for me to drop something—a piece of food, my napkin, a fork, anything.

I look into her huge brown eyes. "The fire is nice, huh, P?" She relaxes her head, half closing her eyes.

I decide I will eat every dinner like this, a whole production with the fire going and all the candles lit. Even if I am wearing sweatpants and microwaving precooked food, I can make dinner feel like a special occasion, not something sad I have to do alone. There is comfort and happiness in beauty if I am willing to relish it.

The following Monday at nine a.m. I begin my Intensive Outpatient DBT group. The classes are ongoing, with new people joining at the start of each new module and staying until they have cycled through back to where they began. When I join, we are starting the Mindfulness module. I connect via Zoom, where six other people and the teacher wait. One of them is Shawn.

Oh my god! Shawn! I text her.

She looks away from her camera. I can tell she has picked up her phone and is typing.

Shawn: Yo Anna! I feel like I JUST saw you!

Anna: Hahaha I'm so glad you're in this group too. Is the sober living place ok?

Shawn: Me too ☺ Yeah it's ok, kinda weird, but overall fine. Better than going back to an apartment alone where I can get into trouble.

Anna: Totally. I'm glad you decided to do sober living. Ok, I guess we should pay attention to the group.

Shawn: lol, yeah.

The group starts with an icebreaker. The teacher, Rebecca, tells us to say our names and our favorite movie. An older woman in her late sixties says *Casablanca*, an attractive man in his early forties says *Goodfellas*. The answers are so cliché and predictable, I find them endearing. A young man who looks fresh out of high school says his favorite movie is *Titanic*, which I think is very funny. I would never expect a teenage boy to love that movie.

"What do you like so much about *Titanic*?" Rebecca asks.

"I like that once the ship hits the iceberg, we see it sink in real time. That makes it feel more real and that's cool. And Leonardo DiCaprio is a really good actor," he says.

Appreciation for Leo really does span generations.

Next it is my turn. "I also love *Titanic*," I say, "and I agree, the ship sinking in real time is very cool." I pause because I can see people laughing. "Wait, what's going on?"

"It sounds like there is a large man sleeping right next to your computer."

I laugh. I am so used to Petunia's loud snoring I forget it is there. This same exact thing happened every time I unmuted my computer microphone to speak during grad school Zooms.

"That's my dog, Petunia." I move the computer camera so everyone can see her. "She's extremely loud." Everyone laughs too.

"She's very cute. I love when people's pets make appearances on camera. Petunia seems like a very nice companion for you. Alright, back to your favorite movie," Rebecca says.

I continue, "My favorite movie is *The Royal Tenenbaums*."

"And what makes that your favorite movie?"

"I guess it was the first movie I saw that really spoke to my personal sensibility. It was sad but also very funny, funny in a quiet way. I had just never seen anything like it before, and it made me feel there were other people like me out in the world beyond my small town."

After the icebreaker, each person shares something that happened over the weekend and how they used a DBT skill to deal with it. The attractive man in his forties, whose name I have now learned is Eric, starts. As soon as he speaks, it is apparent he is on eleven.

"Well, *of course*, my bitch ex-wife—"

"Eric," Rebecca interrupts him. "I'm going to ask you to start again, and this time use more constructive language."

"Right. Fine. Whatever. My horrible, *very* challenging ex-wife is making my life literally miserable again. I'm currently in Wyoming, in the middle of nowhere bumblefuck—"

"Eric . . ."

"Sorry. I'm in the middle of nowhere. On a frozen tundra with absolutely nothing around. I'm trying to see my kid. She told me I could see my kid if I came here. Well, I'm here. It's awful. And now she's saying she might not let me see my kid. I'm so mad. She's literally an insane person. She—"

"Eric, I'm going to jump in. That all sounds very stressful and disappointing. I can understand why you are so upset. In what ways have you been able to use DBT to mitigate your stress?"

"You can't use DBT to reason with a crazy woman," he says, laughing with condescension.

"I understand, but maybe, taking her out of it, what's something you personally can do for yourself to relieve your anger? Perhaps something we discussed from the Distress Tolerance module. Look on page 155 of the book."

Eric looks down, sighing audibly, and opens his book. We all wait in silence.

His voice is quiet as he says, "I guess I can go to the gym."

"Great! The hotel you're staying in has a gym?" Rebecca says.

"Yeah."

"I know you've said in the past that working out helps to relax you, so I think going to the gym sounds like a really good way to channel some of the anger you're feeling."

"Well, I wish it would make my ex less terrible."

I hate Eric.

* * *

In the second week of the Mindfulness module, Rebecca asks us if anything has happened recently that may have reminded us to be mindful. I share first.

"I came across a poem this week. It's a poem I first read many years ago, but I had forgotten about it. Then I randomly saw it online. It's by the thirteenth-century Islamic poet Rumi, and it's called "The Guest House." The poem is about letting in emotions, honoring them, but then letting them go. I wondered if I might read part of it? It feels very applicable for all of us who wrestle with big emotions."

"Please, go ahead," says Rebecca.

I read:

This being human is a guest house.
Every morning a new arrival.

A joy, a depression, a meanness,
some momentary awareness comes
as an unexpected visitor.

Welcome and entertain them all!
Even if they're a crowd of sorrows,
who violently sweep your house
empty of its furniture,
still, treat each guest honorably.
He may be clearing you out
for some new delight.

"That is beautiful. Thank you for sharing," Rebecca says to me.

"Yes, I really liked that," says the older woman who loves *Casablanca*.

The boy who loves *Titanic* asks if I can provide a link to the poem in the Zoom chat.

"I'll go next," Eric's voice booms through the microphone. "I guess I'm not smart enough for your poetry, but I do follow the words of New Jersey poet Jon Bon Jovi, and he says, 'Shot through the heart and you're to blame . . . you give love a bad name.'"

I stare at Eric through my computer camera, trying to eliminate all expression from my face.

"Eric, can you say a bit more about how that relates to mindfulness for you?" Rebecca says.

"I guess it doesn't. But it does relate to my ex who is making my life a living hell."

"Let's get started with today's skills," Rebecca says. "I'll share my screen and everyone turn to page 201 in your book."

While Rebecca lectures, my brain is completely subsumed by my dislike of Eric. It is neither helpful nor is it mindful. I fantasize about turning on my microphone and confronting him.

"Sorry to interrupt," I would say. "Eric, what the fuck is your beef with me? Do I remind you of your ex? Is it my fault you can't see your kid? Does belittling me make you feel like more of a man?"

In my fantasy he would immediately back down and apologize. He would miraculously see all the ways he is living out the stereotype of misogyny and would vow to make a change. But I know in real life that is not what would happen. If I challenge Eric, he would just become more combative, and I would have given him concrete evidence that *I'm* a bitch, or crazy. He could stop projecting a fuzzy image of his ex-wife onto me and instead hate me for me in sharp focus. I choose not to afford him that luxury, so I stay quiet.

* * *

In a meeting with Beth, I voice my concern over Eric.

"I'm just not sure I can be in the group with him. He feels like the embodiment of everything that's maddening about men."

"I hear you and I understand why that is so frustrating to you right now. I'm wondering if perhaps being in the group with Eric could be its own DBT practice—how can you cope with the distress and anger he causes?"

"I guess I can't avoid men for the rest of my life. Maybe this is exposure therapy?"

Beth and I laugh.

"When you feel yourself getting angry at him, what are some things you can do?" Beth says.

"I can certainly check the facts," I say, "and remind myself that my time with him is finite. Nine hours a week for twelve weeks is nothing."

"That's very true, a good way to reframe things. Anything else?"

"I can acknowledge that I don't know Eric's whole story. I actually know very little and therefore can't really pass judgment on why he's so mad at his ex. Also it's none of my business. I can have more compassion for his situation. I'm sure it is very hard to fly to the-middle-of-nowhere-Wyoming to see your kid and then be told you can't see your kid."

"I'm sure it is," Beth says.

"Ultimately I do believe that when someone belittles something you've shared, it usually means you've hit one of their sensitivities or insecurities. I don't know why the poem made him feel the need to undercut me, but it likely has very little to do with me."

"That is usually the case, isn't it?"

I laugh.

"Let me know if anything else concerning happens, but for now, do you feel okay going forward in the group?" asks Beth.

"Yes, completely. I think it's important for me to stick things out with this group."

* * *

Later that day I walk the aisles of a grocery store, aimlessly putting items into my cart, which I think, but am not positive, will summate to some edible meals. The shelves are sparse because a snowstorm is coming. My life is so mundane, so empty at the moment that a snowstorm feels like a fucking soiree. At the checkout I place my items on the conveyor belt; the cashier slides them one by one past the barcode reader. A head of broccoli. *Beep*. Two potatoes. *Beep*. Butter. *Beep*. A box of penne pasta. *Beep*. Eggs. *Beep*. Cheerios. *Beep*. I won't realize until I am home that I forgot tomato sauce and milk. *Beep*.

The next morning I wake up and immediately get out of bed to look outside. Everything is white. The snow is falling hard and fast. Every so often gusts of wind blow the snow up from the ground into swirls in the sky. It's beautiful but also angry.

I go downstairs to my kitchen, grabbing Petunia's ear flush and drops. I sit down in front of her and pet her once so she wakes up and is not startled. I have figured out if I do this first thing in the morning she is less likely to react. I squirt the antifungal liquid into both ears and massage them. She does not look happy. I let go, allowing her to stand up and shake the liquid out of her ears. I grab her right ear and put three drops of medicine in it. As fast as I can, I grab the other ear, but while I am putting in the drops Petunia snaps at me, nearly biting my hand. I have no idea if the medicine made it in her ear. She watches me put the medication back up on the counter.

"Look, see? It's gone. No more. All done." I put my hands up in front of me, flipping them back and forth so she can see I am not holding anything. Petunia shakes her whole body like she's shaking off a bad vibe and runs over to me, snorting and burying her head into my legs. I squat down; she jumps into my arms.

I hold her tight and she nuzzles into my neck, breathing loudly.

Her food is prepackaged and specially made for her allergies, but I do not get to simply put it in a bowl and place it on the floor for her. Petunia will not eat out of a bowl. She has not in years. Instead, she will only eat if I roll the food into tiny meatballs and hand feed them to her one by one. It is incredibly tedious. Sometimes for no reason she decides she does not like the food anymore, and when I reach out to give it to her, she snarls and lunges at me. Sometimes it's scary when she does this. As soon as I put the food away, she returns to her happy, affectionate self. Petunia seems to understand her job—to take care of me. Aside from food aggression and hoarding the occasional errant sock, she has stopped resource guarding.

I make myself coffee, slice a piece of my mom's banana bread, and sit in silence at my kitchen table watching the snow. I begin to envision myself sitting in the snow, it all swirling around me. I look quiet and lonely, but also peaceful. The landscape of my yard is vast around me. I look at my blue jacket hanging on the chair next to me. The back of it has a rainbow sunburst that would really pop against the snow. Now in the image I am wearing the jacket, looking at myself from the back. That could be an interesting photograph, I think.

I finish breakfast and go upstairs, pulling out my camera, my wide-angle lens, and my tripod. I put on long underwear, a pair of burgundy corduroy pants, and a red, white, and blue knit hat with a yarn pom-pom on top. I head back downstairs and aim my camera outside to calibrate the ISO speed and exposure before latching it onto the tripod. I put on the jacket and zip it all the way up.

As I move toward the door, tripod and camera in hand, Petunia follows me.

"I don't think you're going to want to go out in this, my friend, but you have to at least pee."

She looks up at me.

The door opens, letting a blast of cold air into the kitchen. Petunia jumps, running away from the door. A bunch of snowflakes fly inside. I put down the tripod, pick up Petunia, and put her outside. She runs to the closest patch of snow, pees, and runs back inside.

"I know," I say to her. "Not fun, but unfortunately a necessity." She snorts at me, walks to her bed, and lies down with her head up and her paws crossed. "What a lady," I say to her, picking up my tripod and going out into the storm.

I get the shot I envisioned on the first try, but I take twenty more, just in case. I was correct, it is an interesting photograph.

When the snow finally stops falling, there are eighteen inches on the ground.

At the next DBT meeting Eric makes an announcement that he has to leave the group early to deal with the custody issues concerning his kid. He tells us he will rejoin a DBT group at a later time when things have settled. I feel sad for him. I really hope he follows through on that promise. At the end of class, when the teacher has signed off, he puts his phone number in the chat and tells us anyone can feel free to stay in touch or to reach out if they need someone to talk to. It is a kind gesture and one that can mean a lot to people who have been hospitalized. We are the select few who have shared in the experience.

I wish him well. I tell him good luck and that it was nice to meet him, even though the latter is not totally truthful. I thank him for sharing a small, private part of his life with us. I say I really hope he gets to see his son. Both of those I mean. I wave goodbye and sign off Zoom. I do not write down his number.

Twenty-Five

"They said you're crazy. They also said your comment was a godless and soulless thing to say. I agree with them."

"Excuse me?" Rage is bubbling up inside me. I can feel it in my solar plexus, hot, acrid, burning; quickly diffusing throughout my entire body. I press my fingertips into my palms.

He shrugs as if to say, *You heard what I said.*

I hate men. I hate them so much. Men are the cause of all my problems. Men are the cause of *everyone's* problems. They are stupid and they are arrogant. They think everything they say is true and right. I hate them so fucking much I don't even know if I can fuck them anymore. Men are argumentative. Or they are avoidant. The argumentative ones, like the one sitting in front of me now, are the kind of men who google things you say to verify if they are correct. If you disagree with them, or present an alternative point of view, they claim you are attacking them, which in turn makes *you* apologize to *them*. What are you apologizing for? You aren't actually sorry for anything; you simply recognize this as the path of least resistance to ending the conversation. The avoidant ones tell you what you want to hear while privately living an alternate reality that eventually surfaces as resentment and hatred and deceit. Either way, there is no winning. Men are the worst. They are the goddamn fucking worst.

I sit quietly for a few moments, allowing the words "godless" and "soulless" to sink deep into me, marinating my anger. Right now,

Reece and I are sitting down for breakfast at a Brooklyn restaurant, but the argument that precipitated this current conversation began days earlier in my kitchen, when I expressed my desire to have female children over male children, should I ever have children.

"I just feel like raising boys would be difficult for me," I said. "I know I would love whatever child I had, but I have so many negative feelings about men at the moment. I'm afraid it would color my ability to parent well. How do you even raise a boy without ingrained misogyny and patriarchal views of the world? You can try to do it at home, but as soon as they are in school or consuming any type of media, you're fucked."

"That's misandry," he said.

I picked up my phone and googled the definition of misandry. "First of all, misandry isn't a real thing," I said. "It's like claiming 're-verse racism.' It doesn't exist. Second, I feel strongly that if you spoke with many women in their thirties about this, you would find an echoing of my sentiments."

"That's an innocent child you're talking about. And I think you're wrong."

"This is a hypothetical. It's not like I have two sons I just said I hated. Also, sometimes mothers dislike their children. Women, even mothers, have a whole inner life with a complex range of emotions that change and fluctuate by the hour. It's entirely possible for a woman to see the ways in which, for example, her son is afforded certain social luxuries that her daughter isn't. Maybe she watches people speak to her children differently based on their sex. That might infuriate her. That might make her say, 'God, my son has it easier. He has a seemingly innate sense of confidence that my daughter lacks. That makes me mad.' I'm not saying she doesn't overwhelmingly love her son, but she might feel complicated emotions watching these gender dynamics play out. *I* would have complicated emotions watching these gender dynamics play out. And for that reason it would perhaps be easier for me to know what to do with a female child. That's all I'm saying."

"No. If you raise a boy to be nice and to be kind to others and to think for himself, then you will raise a person who understands the ways they might be problematic."

"This doesn't have anything to do with being nice and kind. Plenty of nice and kind men have deeply misogynistic points of view. And that's exactly the problem. You think just being nice and kind solves the problem of gender inequality? It isn't a matter of thinking for yourself. We live in a world steeped in misogyny. It's pervasive. This conversation we're having, your point of view, is misogynistic. You are refusing to listen to the thoughts and experiences of a woman right now. I'm telling you that I have complicated feelings about men, and you are telling me it's misandry."

I could feel myself becoming more and more exasperated. A state that once entered, no woman can win. It is the hysterical state. The angry state. The state that men cannot tolerate and therefore twist back in your direction as evidence of your unfounded lunacy.

"You don't have to attack me."

"I'm not attacking you!!" I yelled. I suppose yelling could be evidence of me attacking him, but also, no.

Now, sitting across from Reece over breakfast on one of the last warm days of fall, I don't know where to channel my rage. With a sense of artificial calm, I reach into my purse, place fifty dollars on the table (enough to pay the whole check and then some), take one last sip of my iced coffee, and silently but purposefully walk away from the table, leaving him to deal with the hopefully ripe embarrassment of turning a waiter with two plates of food back to the kitchen because regrettably his companion has walked out on him. I walk half a block to my car, get in, and sob.

* * *

Reece is the first relationship I've been in since leaving the hospital nine months ago. The first since my divorce began. In the time between I focused solely on my mental health and finishing my master's thesis, which I was able to do with only a month extension. Through DBT I gradually learned how to substitute constructive behaviors for destructive ones. I noticed that even in my most emotional moments, taking photographs never failed to intercept my worst thoughts and change my brain's direction. After that first portrait in the snow, I continued taking self-portraits as a means of survival. I needed to remind myself that I still existed. I built a body of work I was surprised to find I could sell as a way to support myself. I was invited to The Other Art Fair as their guest artist in Los Angeles and New York and became their highest-grossing artist in the history of the fair. With my career moving in a direction I liked, I decided to start dating.

Right before my thirty-sixth birthday I downloaded all the apps I'd previously had the luxury of never needing. I set my location to New York City, even though I lived in Connecticut now. I figured I'd be pulling from a more desirable pool with my location set to the city, and it was easy enough for me to drive in and out of New York for dates. I could even make a night of it and treat myself to a hotel sometimes. I thought, *This will be fun, dating will be fun*. It was not fun. Instead, what ensued was a series of unfortunate dates and romantic encounters that only reinforced my aversion to men.

There was the man who, on our one and only date, told me his favorite movie was a nine-hour French film, who drank from my straw without asking permission, and with whom I never exchanged a single message after our cold, hug-less goodbye. A year later he attempted to rematch with me after clearly forgetting we had already met up.

There was the man who kept his dog in a crate in his bedroom while we had sex. The dog had separation anxiety and would whine if kept behind a closed door. He put a towel over the crate for privacy, but the dog and I shared an unfortunate moment when, during sex, I changed positions and saw a single eyeball peering at me in desperation from under the shroud.

There was the man who texted "Don't sass me" in response to a joke I made while on my way to the date. My brain told me to keep walking when I reached the bar, but I took two deep breaths and went in anyway. After a painful hour of arrogance on his end and a bad attitude on mine, the date ended. Our final correspondence went like this:

Him: It was good to meet you, I had a nice time on our date. Let me know when you're coming back into the city so we can meet up again.

Me: It was nice to meet you too. I don't think we are the right fit for each other, so I don't think I need to do another meetup.

Him: Are you serious?

There was the man who I met in person only after months of sporadic texting. He was nice and handsome and good at conversation. After a ninety-minute drink at a hotel bar we never met again, but he did text and call with updates about a house he was buying in Massachusetts.

Him: So there's a creek nearby and some water damage.

Me: Not a great sign.

Him: I don't know what I should do. Bid lower?

Me: I honestly don't know what to tell you.

Me: So are we going on another date?

Him: Why you gotta kill the vibe?

There was the man who used a slur in our second conversation, and after pressing send on a message that read "It is 2021 and you absolutely cannot use that word," I unmatched him.

Because of all this, I insisted on FaceTiming with Reece before deciding if I wanted to meet in person. Happy to oblige, Reece set the day and the time and even followed up the day of the scheduled talk to make sure it still worked for me.

My attraction to him on the call was overwhelming. He was conventionally handsome—short hair somewhere between dark blond and light brown, an angular face with short stubble speckling his strong jaw—but it was not so much his appearance as it was his energy that captivated me. Even through my laptop screen I felt his presence.

"I thought you'd be different," he said toward the end of our call.

"What do you mean?"

"You're more smiley than I anticipated," he said. "Lighter."

"So what you're saying is, you looked at my artwork and thought I'd be morose."

Reece laughed. "Yeah, maybe. A little."

"I'm never what men think I am or what they want me to be. It's actually quite annoying."

"Well, I'm slightly smitten," he said.

"I'd like to meet in person," I said.

I wore the same outfit for every date I went on that summer—Levi's jean shorts and a lightweight button-down shirt with an abstract cactus print. I had to keep my arms covered on first dates because of bad scarring, and I wanted to mask my extreme thinness. I recycled the loose, gauzy shirt over and over. It was my only long-sleeved garment thin enough to wear in the middle of summer and not seem insane.

On a humid evening five days after the call, Reece and I sat across from each other at Ernesto's on the Lower East Side.

We briefly discussed the menu, what looked good, and what we would be ordering.

Then I said, "So I was in a psych hospital for disordered eating and self-harm and suicidal thoughts like six months ago due to a very difficult time in my life. The pandemic has basically been my worst nightmare because I'm a germaphobe, but actually things were better for me once everything was locked down. Now that stuff is more open, it's pretty anxiety-inducing because everyone is just playing by their own rules and I'm not really sure what's safe and what's not. This is the first time I've eaten indoors since the pandemic started. Everything is a calculated risk. Anyway, I'm in the middle of a divorce."

An absolute slam dunk.

"No problem," he said. "We all have things we are dealing with. I certainly have my own things I've struggled with. I've also been hospitalized."

I was surprised but comforted to hear this. "Thank you for telling me."

We shared a bit of our hospital experiences with each other, and after a moderately long explanation of anxiety and how it affects the human body, he said to me, "Not to mansplain anxiety to you. You obviously know what anxiety feels like."

I laughed.

When we left the restaurant two hours later it was pouring. We hurried through the rain and into the back of a cab. He slid next to me and I put my leg on top of his.

Reece lived in a fifth-floor walk-up in the East Village. His apartment was small, but all New York City apartments are small unless you are a multimillionaire. His furniture was mismatched, but I found it endearing. In his bedroom, stacks of books were piled on the wood floor as if he was a bohemian poet, no bookshelf in sight.

I took a seat on the couch, expecting him to follow me, but he grabbed a chair from his desk, placing it in front of a window he opened.

"I like this couch," I said, running my hand against the grain of its maroon velvet, making stripes in the fabric with my fingers. It was a Federalist-era reproduction, similar to the couch I'd sat on while waiting for my psych test at the hospital.

"I got it off the street," he said, grabbing a pack of Marlboro Lights off the windowsill.

"Did you have it cleaned?"

"Nah." He shrugged.

I got off the couch, grabbed another chair, and pulled it up next to his.

"Do you want to make out?" I said, leaning toward him.

"I'm gonna smoke this cigarette."

"Oh." I leaned back in my chair. "I guess I'll have one too."

We sat next to each other, silently smoking out of his living room window. After a few drags he grabbed the back of my head and kissed me. I would have loved for that to have happened before the cigarettes.

Reece moved me from my chair to his chair so I was straddling him, and then stood up in one confident movement while holding me.

"Couch or bed?" he said.

"Bed," I said.

He lay on the bed with me sitting on top of him, legs on either side of his torso. He tried to remove my shirt, but I held it down.

"I have sort of a lot of scarring on my arms," I said.

"It doesn't bother me," he said.

I unbuttoned the long-sleeved shirt. "And I don't want to have sex. Of any kind. This is a make-out only."

"That's totally fine with me. Making out is perfect."

In between making out we would pause to have little conversations. When we talked, he would run his fingers up and down my ribs. We did this for hours.

"What made you move to the East Village?" I said, still straddling him, our hands intertwined.

"I'd been in Bed-Stuy before, but I really wanted to be in Manhattan. I would ride my bike here during lockdown and I thought it seemed so quiet. When my lease was up, I decided to move here, but then lockdown ended and I realized it's not quiet here at all."

I laughed. "No, the East Village is absolutely not known to be one of New York's quiet neighborhoods."

"Well, it was during lockdown." His voice had an edge.

"Yeah, but everywhere was quiet during lockdown. The East Village is literally one of New York's busiest neighborhoods, especially on weekend nights."

"It *was* quiet. But then all the college kids came back. Because there's NYU housing here, and all the classes went back to in-person. And it's, like, overrun with college students."

I could tell he was getting annoyed, but I wasn't sure why. I decided to lighten the mood with a callback from earlier in the night.

"I've lived here since 2004. Are you *mansplaining* how New York City works to me?"

"Don't do that," he said. I assumed he was participating in the joke.

I leaned closer to his face, smiled coyly, and repeated myself: "Are you mansplaining New York City neighborhoods to me?"

"Stop. Don't do that." He picked me up swiftly and moved me off him. "That's not funny."

"Are you serious?" I said.

He got off the bed and walked into the living room. "I don't like that. I said stop. So don't do that."

I sat for a beat on his bed, still trying to sort out if he was kidding or serious. When he sat in the chair facing the window with his back to me and reached for a cigarette, I realized he was serious.

I followed Reece into the living room and sat on the chair next to him. "Are you actually mad at me right now?"

He didn't answer me, he just stared straight out the window, exhaling a massive plume of smoke into the air.

"I'm sorry," I said. I wanted Reece to like me, not be mad at me. "I was just joking around because of the 'mansplaining the hospital' thing you said to me at dinner. It wasn't meant to offend you."

He didn't respond, he just nodded. I checked my phone. It was after two a.m. I hadn't had any water since we left the restaurant. I felt dizzy from a combination of dehydration, nicotine, and the Klonopin I'd taken to ease my nerves just before the date began.

"Can I have another cigarette?" I said.

"Sure." He handed me the pack and I removed a cigarette and lit it.

"I had a really good time with you," I said.

He kissed me—a good, hard kiss.

"I wish it was the beginning of the date," I said, ashing my cigarette out the window.

"Why?" Reece said.

"Because then we'd still have the whole night ahead of us."

"That's so fucking sweet," he said, looking me in the eye for the first time since we reentered the living room.

I called an Uber to take me back to the hotel where I was staying. Lying on the bed, fully clothed, I felt pathetic sleeping in hotels after meeting strangers from an app. The emotional labor of dating, sifting through the made-up rules men expected me to follow was exhausting. I picked up the free bottle of water from the bedside table and ripped off a tag from its cap, which read "Welcome back, Ms. Tendler," and which I could only digest as mockery. None of this felt welcome. I chugged the water, a lot of it missing my mouth. I was crying and my face was wet anyway. I didn't care. I ate a whole bag of Doritos from the minibar without ever breaking focus on its foil-lined interior. They weren't even Cool Ranch, they were Nacho Cheesier, the kind I didn't like. I caught myself in the mirrored wall adjacent to the bed, mascara running, fingertips orange from the chips, water dribbles staining my shirt.

"How the fuck did I get here?" I said to my reflection.

The second date was in Los Angeles, where I was staying for the month of July.

"There's the Griffith Observatory," I said to him on FaceTime, showing the white Art Deco dome perched high on a mountain ridge.

"I wish I was with you," he said.

"Then come here."

"Are you being serious?"

"Yeah, why not," I said. "Life is short."

Five days later we were lying together, limbs entwined in the bed of a Silverlake hotel.

"You're so hot," Reece said to me.

"Really? I feel old," I said. Reece was seven years younger.

"Nope. You look amazing. I'm so attracted to you."

These words meant something important to me. I had felt so unattractive, so unsexy for a long time. I felt broken and crazy. I felt I had ruined my body with cuts and scars. Reece made me feel beautiful, and that was a gift.

During our relationship we argued often, usually about gender dynamics, political issues, and my overwhelming feeling that all men are some version of problematic.

"I don't believe in bringing larger social issues into personal relationships," he once said to me.

"That's an impossible way to live unless you are a financially stable, straight, white man," I said back. "For most of us, social issues are inextricable from the individual experience."

Reece didn't like my photography. He told me it was "performative." When I let him read my master's thesis on injectable plastic surgery, his only comment was, "The second half is stronger than the first."

"Well the first half is a history of injectables, so maybe history isn't as dynamic a read to you, but that doesn't mean it's not strong or very well written."

"I just thought the writing was stronger in the second half," he said.

"I disagree with you. Also, I wasn't asking for feedback. I just thought you'd find it interesting."

Even as it was happening, I couldn't understand why I was defending myself to a twenty-eight-year-old man who had no idea what it took to research and write an academic thesis. I knew at the root of my insecurity his comments triggered a need to qualify my achievements, my work, and my intelligence, something I had been doing my whole life. That realization, however, couldn't override my instinct to engage. There were so many moments like that with Reece, moments that if they were told to me secondhand I would have said, *Don't deal with that, break things off immediately.* Yet normalizing and withstanding this type of behavior from men is exactly what it means to be a woman. I didn't break things off because my value had always been tied to what men thought of me; because I didn't want to seem reactive, or difficult, or mean; and because acts of defiance toward men are easier said than done, even on the smallest scale. Despite how difficult I found Reece, I also loved him. He was the first man I let into my life after my divorce, and I had to give him credit for boldly stepping into that role. He took my emotions seriously and for the most part treated me with care. He was the type of person who said, "It's okay to cry," and would hold me in his arms as I did.

But being called *soulless* and *godless* before ten thirty a.m. isn't for me, and leaving Reece at the table is an act of rebellion unlike any I have ever mustered. Yet from inside my car, his accusations feel more powerful than my unwillingness to withstand them. Tears still rolling down my face, I call my friend Carmel and recount what just happened.

"Anna, you're not crazy, or soulless, or godless. You're allowed to have complicated feelings about men. It's 2021, we're all having complicated feelings about men. Also, why is he reporting unflattering things his female friends are saying about you back *to you*? It's so immature. And frankly, it's mean."

"Thank you," I say between sniffs. "It felt unnecessarily mean, but I don't know, maybe I'm awful."

"You're definitely not awful," Carmel says.

"I'm sorry you've had to take so many crying phone calls over the past few months," I say.

"It's totally fine, of course. I love you."

"I love you too."

I sit for a second, collecting myself. I flip the sun visor down and wipe last night's mascara from under my eyes. Exiting my car I can see that Reece has left, so I walk back to the restaurant and order an iced coffee to go for my drive home.

The next day I get a text from Reece asking if I want to talk about what happened.

I drive into Manhattan, figuring a quick exit, if necessary, is better than possibly having to drive him to a train back to the city should we get into a fight at my house in the middle of the woods. The air in his building stairwell is hot and stuffy, even though it's October. When he opens the door to his apartment he gives me a hug.

"I'm sorry," he says.

"Thank you," I say. "Telling someone they're godless and soulless is pretty fucked-up."

"I agree and I'm sorry."

"I understand that you need and want to talk to your friends about our relationship, but I don't need to hear what women in their twenties think of my life choices and opinions," I say.

"They didn't say that you were crazy or that you were godless and soulless," Reece says.

"What?"

"They didn't use those words. They said it was harsh, but yeah, they didn't use those words."

"So you just made that up?"

"Yes. I'm sorry."

"Wow."

I sit in silence for a moment, wrestling with what to say next. Accept his apology and move on? Or dig in further to make my point?

"This is a perfect example of why men are problematic. You can't just tell women they are crazy because you don't agree with their opinion. Or tell them that other people said they were 'soulless and godless,' whatever the fuck that means, when no one actually said that."

"Yes, I get that it was wrong to lie about that and I'm sorry I did that. I'm not proud I did that. I still have a problem with your ideas about men, but I admit what I did was not nice."

I can tell he is truly sorry, but he still cannot take in a broad critique of male power from a woman. We decide to put it behind us and go eat Indian food at one of the last Indian restaurants still left on Sixth Street.

* * *

"I feel stifled by your level of need for communication during the day," Reece says to me two months later. I get what he's saying. I feel less and less that he wants to talk or text, and the more I feel him pull away, the closer I try to move toward him. I want to convince him I'm worthy of his time and attention. I want him to see how special I am and I want him to choose me. I want him to want to text me, but if he doesn't want it, I'm pretty sure I can persuade him to want it.

"You're upset that I want to talk to you?" I say.

"I'm not upset you want to talk to me," he says, "but I feel like you're always checking in on me, like to keep tabs on what I'm doing, not necessarily because you want to talk. Also, I just generally don't like texting."

"So what are you proposing instead?" I'm defensive and annoyed.

"If it were up to me, we wouldn't text at all and we would just do a phone check-in at the end of the day."

"I don't think that's a sustainable way to have a relationship. What time are you willing to speak to me?"

"Maybe six p.m."

I laugh out loud. "I think if we do this our relationship will fall apart, but I'm willing to try this out so you can see if the experiment works." I agree to his terms, arrogantly thinking I'm about to teach him a lesson.

The following week is Christmas, and Reece returns home to spend the holiday with his family. We haven't been talking much, but now that he's home, we're talking even less. I thought he was going to decide he missed talking to me, to acknowledge he was wrong about my communication style and beg me to start texting with more frequency. That never happens.

"Are you enjoying *The White Album*?" I ask him one evening while FaceTiming him from the bathtub. I'm wearing a ridiculous terry-cloth headband with a bow to keep my hair from getting wet.

Before he went home, I made him watch a documentary about Joan Didion after he revealed to me that he didn't know who she was.

"You have to expose yourself to female authors and female points of view," I had said to him critically.

He read a couple of essays and loved them. While at home for Christmas he decided to read *The White Album*.

"I love it," he says about the book. "It's amazing. It's actually surprising to me that you like her so much?"

"Why? She's an amazing writer," I say.

"Yeah, but she's an anti-feminist," he says.

"I wouldn't say she's an anti-feminist. She's a cultural critic and has a strong critique of the second-wave feminist movement, but I would say what she did with her career and her life was pretty feminist from a present-day view."

"I mean, she basically calls feminists stupid."

"I know what essay you're referring to and I'm not saying she was a textbook feminist, but she brought a very female perspective to a world that was largely dominated by men. I'm not sure why we are arguing about Joan Didion right now. We haven't spoken in, like, two days."

Reece shrugs, annoyed. I change the subject.

"So you're going to come to Sarah's New Year's Eve party with me? It should be fun."

"Yeah, I guess."

"Do you have something else you want to do instead?" I say, sensing his hesitation.

"No."

Reece looks away from the screen.

"You don't seem like you want to be dating anymore," I say. "If you don't want to, just break up with me."

Reece looks surprised, not because I've suggested he doesn't want to be with me, but because he wasn't planning on having this conversation right now.

"I'm sorry I started in with the thing about Joan Didion. That was pointless. I don't think this is working for me anymore," he says guiltily.

"Then I guess we should break up," I say, fighting back tears.

"I'm sorry."

"You don't have to apologize. It's the right decision. If you're not happy, then we shouldn't keep dating."

In this moment it's impossible for me to admit to Reece and to myself that I also am not happy and haven't been happy. My feelings of mutuality are obscured by those of rejection. I'm convinced the breakup is his fault and the result of everything he did wrong. However, in the months to come I'll realize what I did to contribute to our unworkable dynamic. I wasn't willing to meet him where he was ideologically or even to overlook how our ideologies were discordant. And that's fine. I don't need to share ideology or overlook what I disagree with if it feels wrong for me to do so. But I stayed with Reece because I wanted to change him, I thought I *could* change him. And that was a mistake.

"I don't know what to do now," Reece says.

"I think we hang up."

Twenty-Six

"So, yeah, it's a fairly easy process," she says to me. "After we are done here, I'll send along the videos on how to do the injections. Email your nurse coordinator if you have any questions!"

I stare through my laptop at the woman wearing a white lab coat who is sitting opposite me.

"Wait, I'm sorry," I say. "No one walks me through how to mix the hormones or inject them?"

"The videos do," she says.

"Right, but I mean an actual person?"

"No, but you don't need it. It's all very easy. You'll see once you watch the videos. And of course if you have any questions at all, just email the nurse."

"Sure," I say tentatively. "A couple more questions, sorry. Once I start injecting the hormones and I come to the office to do morning blood work and ultrasounds, you'll be the doctor seeing me?"

"No, not necessarily. It will be the doctor who is on duty."

"Oh, all right," I say, a little surprised. "But when it's time for the egg retrieval, you'll be the doctor who does that procedure?"

"Not necessarily. That will also be done by the doctor on duty that day, and unfortunately we can't predict exactly what day the retrieval will happen. That all depends on how you respond to the hormones."

I'm incredibly confused. For the twelve-thousand-dollar price tag, I didn't think freezing my eggs would entail learning how to mix and inject hormones from glorified YouTube videos with relatively no oversight from a health professional. For a twelve-thousand-dollar price tag, I also didn't think I'd be spreading my legs for any old doctor on duty.

"I assure you, all of the doctors are very good. Everyone has access to your file and all your information. No matter who you have doing the retrieval, you'll be in excellent hands. And you know, if we are not able to get the desired number of eggs, we can discuss tweaking the medication and doing another round. The second round is two thousand dollars less expensive than the first round."

Oh, how generous. "Let's maximize this one," I say.

I didn't realize having children was a choice until I was in my early twenties. It seemed like something everyone had to do at a certain point, a natural progression of life stages. No particular moment catalyzed the choice. I simply remember thinking one day, *Oh wait, I don't* have *to be a mom.* From that day forward I never really wanted to be one. My reservations about motherhood have been shaped by my feelings about men, their general incompetence, their propensity toward selfishness, and their inability to empathize with the female experience. My obsession with equality in relationships restricts me from balancing the weight of what men put into child-rearing versus what women do. I wonder if it can ever be equal. I feel instinctually it can't, while also recognizing that instinct might be wrong.

My reservations are not only tied to men, however. They're also shaped by the particular ways I want my life and my time to be my own. I've never woken up at eight a.m. on a Saturday and thought, *God, I'd love to take a kid to soccer practice right now.*

In my twenties and early thirties, the concept of life without motherhood was easy to maintain. I still had "so much time," followed by a "pretty good amount of time" to make the decision. It's not that in the far reaches of my brain I wanted to be a mother and was just waiting to feel ready. But it's easy to be resolute when you know you have the luxury to change course. Now, at thirty-six, I have not much time at all.

I'm often preoccupied by thoughts of what my life will look like without children. Will I be sad when all my friends have kids but me? Will I have regrets?? Will I feel left out??? Will the bonds of shared experience draw those friends closer to one another while pushing me to the outside???? Will everyone have a group chat that I'm not on????? These feelings have compounded since I had to move out of New York City, where they all still live. I'm afraid I don't matter anymore.

I know mothers feel excluded from life too. I guess that's the paradox of being a woman: no matter what path you choose, chances are you'll feel invisible.

At least for right now I have Petunia.

A large box arrives via FedEx to my front door. I open it and am immediately overwhelmed by the amount of medication, glass vials, alcohol wipes, and syringes. I take out the inventory sheet and double-check that I have received everything just as my nurse coordinator has recommended. Some of the medication needs to be refrigerated. I'm positive I will leave it out of the fridge at some point, most likely after an evening injection. I line up all the vials and meds on my bathroom counter. I set a thick plastic Sharps container next to the bags of syringes. The container is a color best described as "danger red."

The instruction videos for mixing and administering are confusing. You have to suck air into the syringes and then pump air out of them to create pressure. You have to pull medication out of multiple different vials and then mix them all in an empty vial. Once everything is mixed you have to change the needle on the syringe from a pulling needle to an administering needle. The vials in the videos all have gray rubber tops. When I look at the medication vials I've received, some look exactly the same as the videos, but on others the rubber tops are covered by thick foil. I guess I have to take that foil off?

I call Carmel the morning after I receive the box of medication. "I can't believe they just give us needles and a bunch of drugs and we are supposed to do this on our own." I'm crying onto a piece of my mom's banana bread.

"I know," she says. "It does seem crazy to trust civilians with this type of medical protocol. But I promise you by day three you'll be mixing the meds and injecting yourself while half watching *Real Housewives*."

"I'm terrified I won't get all the air out of the syringe and will inadvertently kill myself. It would be so annoying to have gone to a psych hospital and done Intensive Outpatient only to inadvertently end my life doing IVF."

"They are subdermal injections, not intravenous injections. The worst thing that will happen if there's air in the syringe is you get a tiny air pocket under your skin."

"Right." I wipe my cheeks with my sleeve.

There is no way I will remember all the steps when it's time to inject, so I bring my laptop upstairs and watch the videos while I mix the medications. Next to my computer I have a sheet of paper with a list of the hormones and the exact milliliters I have to inject in the morning and at night. The injections have to be done exactly twelve hours apart. I pull the liquid drugs into a syringe and accidentally squirt it toward the bathroom mirror.

"Why am I doing this?" I say to Petunia, who has followed me upstairs.

Once all the hormones are mixed in one of the previously empty vials, I suck them all up with a large needle into a fat syringe. Then I change the needle to a thinner needle. Without ceremony or hesitation, I grab a small piece of flesh with my thumb and pointer finger, right below my belly button, and jab the needle all the way into my skin. I press the syringe plunger until the liquid disappears under my skin. I wonder if self-harm prepared me for that to be so easy.

Three days after I start doing injections, I drive to the clinic for my first morning appointment. My blood is drawn by a nurse who has the lightest touch I have ever experienced. I barely feel the needle go in. I tell her this. When she's finished, she brings me to an exam room with an ultrasound machine and tells me to undress from the waist down. She hands me a disposable paper sheet to cover myself with.

A doctor enters the room. This is a different doctor than the one I Zoomed with—a male doctor. He is accompanied by a female nurse.

"How are you this morning?" he asks me, while pulling up a stool and taking a seat.

"I'm good, thanks. Also—" I point to the ultrasound wand that is about to end up inside my vagina. It has a condom stretched over it. "I'm allergic to latex."

The doctor sighs a little too audibly for my taste. He moves away from the ultrasound machine and the nurse jumps in, removing the latex condom and fitting the wand with a non-latex one.

"Next time, please tell the nurse who shows you to the room about the latex allergy so she can change the condom before we come for the exam," he says.

"Sorry," I say. I had forgotten to mention it because I only recently learned I had a latex allergy. Through a complete fluke, Reece had used a non-latex condom the third time we had sex. It was the first time in my entire life that sex wasn't painful. As an experiment, we tried using a latex condom the next time, and once again I was in pain.

I was so conditioned to believe pleasurable sex wasn't for women, that for twenty years I did not even think to complain or question the pain. Turns out it wasn't a me problem. It was a latex problem. And a patriarchal problem.

The doctor inserts the ultrasound wand inside me. I watch on the monitor, but it is difficult to discern what I'm looking at. He tells me I have ten follicles that will hopefully develop into mature eggs. I don't know if that's good news, bad news, or neutral news, and I don't ask because I feel bad for taking up his time with the condom swap. He tells me to continue the medication as directed and come back in two days for blood work and another ultrasound.

The next morning I begin using a new vial of medication, one that has foil wrapped around the rubber cap. A small, circular section of foil pops off easily from the top, where I will insert the needle to draw up the liquid. It seems like that's all I need to do in terms of foil removal, but I can't be sure. In the videos, none of the vials have any foil. I like to follow rules exactly, and I decide to remove all the foil so my vial looks like the vials in the video. I figure if these videos are created purely for the purpose of instruction, I should replicate them exactly. The foil is very stiff and hard to peel off. There are no perforations or areas to cut. This should be my indication that this part of the foils stays put, but instead I take cuticle scissors from my bathroom drawer and start mutilating the cap. As I am pulling on a tiny piece of foil I've managed to cut free, the whole rubber top pops off. The vial goes flying out of my hand and lands in the sink. I watch all the medication run down the drain.

I try to remain calm, using a DBT skill called "check the facts," which is meant to help parse out the reality of a situation from the brain's anxiety doom spiral. The facts are that I can at least still administer one of the hormones. Then I can call the clinic and find out my options for replacing the spilled meds. I walk downstairs to my kitchen and open the fridge door. The medication isn't there. I look to the left of the fridge and the bottle is sitting on the counter in front of my toaster oven. The big red sticker that reads KEEP REFRIGERATED is mocking me.

"East Coast Fertility Clinic, how may I help you?" The voice on the other end of the line says.

"Hi, this is Anna Tendler. I'm in the middle of IVF. Two questions. First is I left some medication out of the fridge. How bad is that? Second, I had a malfunction with one of my other medications and I need a new bottle."

"The medication out of the fridge shouldn't be too much of an issue," she says.

"Shouldn't be an issue or isn't an issue?"

"Shouldn't be."

"Would you recommend I replace the medication?" I ask.

"No, it should be fine."

"Okay . . ."

"What do you mean by malfunction with the other med?" she asks me.

"The whole cap fell off and all the hormones went down the drain."

"The *whole cap* came off?"

"Yes, the whole cap."

"Was it not enclosed in foil? The foil keeps the rubber cap from moving."

Shit.

"It came off when I was trying to remove the foil," I say.

"That's really weird. The small circle on the top should peel off very easily."

"No, I know. So weird."

"It sounds like you got a defective bottle."

"I'm not sure. Is there a way for me to buy more?"

"Well, if it's defective you shouldn't have to pay for more. That's the manufacturer's mistake, not your fault. So we can contact the pharmacy and explain the issue."

"That's fine! I don't mind." As I try and fail to sound very chill about replacing very expensive medication out-of-pocket, I picture myself hacking at the foil with cuticle scissors. "It was probably my fault!" I add.

"Really though, the cap shouldn't come off. If it did, your bottle was defective. The pharmacy shouldn't charge you to replace it."

"Is this a hormone you keep at the clinic? Might I be able to buy it directly from you? I'll pay!"

"Unfortunately, we don't keep this hormone on hand. You will need to pick this up from the pharmacy." There's a pause and then she adds, "In Brooklyn. I'm sorry. We'll call it in for you right now."

"Thanks," I say, resting my forehead on the kitchen counter next to a warm bottle of hormones that is supposed to be cold.

At nine a.m. I log into Intensive Outpatient. The vibe is much less aggressive without Eric present, but it's hard for me to focus knowing I have to drive from Connecticut to downtown Brooklyn and back again because of my idiotic mistake. I have no idea how long it will take me to run this errand because for sure I will get stuck in rush-hour traffic coming home. I can't leave Petunia because she will need to be walked. I hate bringing her in the car because I'm so afraid she will vomit, aspirate, and then get pneumonia. During IOP break, I give Petunia a treat with anti-nausea medication slipped inside.

"Sorry, P," I say, scratching her head. She immediately starts snorting, which she does whenever she's happy. "We have to go on a little field trip this afternoon." I stop petting her. She headbutts me as if to say, "Don't stop." As always, I listen.

I talk to Petunia almost nonstop throughout each day, but she can't hear me. Due to chronic ear infections she is now completely deaf. It took me a while to realize it. She'd always had selective hearing, depending on what she did and did not want to do, but one day she was across a room with her back to me and as I called her name, she made no acknowledgment of my voice. I approached her while saying her name; she continued to have no reaction. I bent down to pet her back, and when I did, she startled. She hadn't seen me coming, but it was clear she hadn't heard me, either. It occurred to me that she was making much more eye contact with me than she had before. She was reading my face for cues. Now she stays in close proximity to me always, and in the absence of sound, we have become even more attuned.

IOP is now in the Distress Tolerance module of DBT, where we learn coping skills for acute distress and panic. They are not meant to be long-term methods of dealing, but rather actions usable in the midst of direct chaos, instead of turning to unhealthy habits. For me, Distress Tolerance coping skills should divert my desire away from wanting to cut myself.

My favorite and most effective way for diverting panic is to stick my face in a bowl of ice water, which sounds ridiculous, but it works. Before the hospital, during my first stint in DBT, my personal DBT therapist taught me how to do this during a moment of intense unraveling. I called her, hyperventilating. I had already begun psychically going to pieces.

"Go get a large bowl," she said. "Fill it with the coldest tap water possible. Tell me when you're done."

I followed her instructions. "Got it." My face was burning and fainting felt imminent.

"Do you have ice?"

"Yes."

"Put a bunch of ice in the bowl, as much as you can without over-flowing the water."

"The ice is in."

"You're going to take a deep breath, fully submerge your face in the ice water, and leave it there until you can't hold your breath any longer."

"What?"

"You heard me." She was firm but kind. "Put your phone on speaker, set it next to the bowl, and stay on the line with me. Dunk your face in the water and try to stay there as long as you can."

I went face-first into the ice bath. It was unbelievably cold, and it was hard to hold my breath leaning forward over the bowl. It felt like I was drowning, which was the point.

When I lifted out of the water, my DBT therapist said, "Now do the same thing again."

I learned forward and submerged my face in the ice bath again. This time I held it there for a few seconds longer than I had the first time.

"You're going to do this three more times."

I did.

"Now," she said, "do you still feel like you're going to faint?"

I took a couple of seconds to scan my body. "No. Actually, I don't."

"Do you feel in control of your body?"

"I do."

"Is there a friend or friends you can call to come be with you?"

"I think so," I said.

"We are going to hang up, you're going to text your friends, and you're going to ask them to come over. Tell them you are in crisis and it's important at least one of them shows up. Then text me and let me know your plan, okay?"

"Okay," I said.

I texted the group chat exactly what the therapist had directed, and within forty minutes my girlfriends were at my apartment, Doritos and cookies in hand.

When I arrive in Brooklyn I park and walk Petunia. She squats her slim hips down to the pavement and pees off a curb on Atlantic Avenue. I love her so much. I put her back in her crate and drape a blanket over it while I run into the pharmacy.

"Picking up for Tendler," I say.

A woman goes to the back and reemerges with a small brown bag in her hand. "The clinic said something about a defective vial, but unfortunately we are going to have to charge you for the medication. It's packaged off-site, so it would be a manufacturing issue."

"No problem, I understand." I know this is my fault, but I still think the videos are partially to blame. If the foil is supposed to stay on the cap, then please in the videos use vials with goddamn foil on the cap.

The woman slides the brown bag across the counter to me. "That will be one thousand two hundred seventy-five dollars and eighty-five cents."

Ten days into hormone injections I go back to the clinic for a morning appointment. The doctor, a different man, says my eggs are ready for retrieval.

"How many are there?" I ask him.

"We can't be sure until we go in, but I'd say ten to twelve."

I sit with two nurses I've never met, and they explain how to do the "trigger shot," a high dosage of hormone exactly twelve hours before the procedure.

"It is imperative that you do the trigger *exactly* twelve hours before the retrieval."

"Got it," I say. "Will do." I love this sort of exact direction.

"We are able to schedule you in for one thirty p.m., so that means you will have to do the trigger at one thirty a.m. Sorry about that."

I set an alarm for one fifteen a.m., but don't end up needing it because I never fall asleep. I am so afraid of sleeping through my alarm, my body doesn't let me relax. To pass the time I watch the moon throw tree-shaped shadows onto the wallpaper in my bedroom.

Finally it's time for me to do the trigger shot, which I do at one thirty a.m. on the dot.

"How do you feel?" my mom asks as we drive to the clinic the next day. A stipulation of the procedure is that someone must drive you home afterward. I wanted to ask either Amanda or Carmel to do this. I pictured feeling empowered, sitting in the passenger seat of my car as a friend chauffeured me to and from one of my most adult experiences to date. But this ask would have required them to come to Connecticut and take a day off work. I didn't want to make that imposition, so I asked my mom, who also lives in Connecticut and is basically retired. Now, instead of feeling empowered, I'm sitting in the passenger seat of her car feeling infantilized and sad.

"Bloated," I say. "My stomach hurts."

"Do you feel any different emotionally?"

"I honestly can't tell. I felt depressed and anxious before the hormones; I feel depressed and anxious on the hormones."

"Maybe that's an upside to doing this now."

I laugh because she's right. "It very well may be."

An hour passes with me sitting in the waiting room. It's now one p.m. I don't see how this retrieval will happen in exactly twelve hours from the trigger shot.

"Hi," I say to the woman at the front desk. "My procedure is supposed to be at one thirty."

"They're just a bit backed up. It won't be long," she says.

"Okay, but they made a big deal about the procedure happening exactly twelve hours after the trigger shot."

"It won't be a problem."

I return to my seat.

Forty-five minutes later I'm taken back to a hospital bed in a row of bays partitioned with fabric curtains. It is quiet, but I can hear the breathing and shuffling around of people on either side of me, waiting their turn to undergo the same procedure. I answer some standard health questions for the anesthesiologist and am wheeled into a room where I assume the vulnerable position of legs up and spread in foot stirrups. The room is very dark except for one spotlight positioned to shine between my legs. A thin sheet is draped over me. A man's voice comes from a head I cannot see; he introduces me to the surgeon, who is also a man and who is pulling on surgical gloves. I guess it was the female doctor's day off.

The voice informs me he will now administer the anesthesia.

"Count backward from ten," he says.

"Ten . . . nine . . . eight . . ."

I wake up in the same bay I'd started in. A nurse tells me it's over and when I feel ready I can get dressed. As I pull on my clothes, she hands me a small white card.

"That's how many eggs they retrieved," she says quietly. "The doctor will call you tomorrow to let you know how many were mature enough to freeze."

I squint, holding the card close to my face. I haven't yet put on my glasses.

"Eight," she says in an even more hushed tone. She leaves the bay.

I put on my glasses and look at the card, now able to read it. There is an underlined space where the number eight has been manually filled in with blue pen. Under the number is a block of text that reads: PLEASE REFRAIN FROM SAYING THIS NUMBER OUT LOUD. WE ASK THAT YOU BE MINDFUL OF THOSE WHO MAY NOT BE RECEIVING THEIR DESIRED OUTCOME TODAY.

My eyes fill with tears and I can no longer read the card. It doesn't matter that my glasses are on. Eight is how many eggs were retrieved, but the number of eggs mature enough to freeze can drop by half, or more. I never considered I might not get many eggs. Most of my friends who have also gone through this process froze double digits. I just assumed I would follow suit. I feel like a failure—like one of the sad women you must be mindful not to say your number out loud around.

You have to come in to sign me out, I text my mom, who is waiting in her car.

She asks me how many eggs they retrieved, even before we exit the building.

"It didn't go great," I say. "Not terrible either, I guess."

"Do you want anything to eat?"

"Yes. McDonald's."

"McDonald's???" She almost never let us eat fast food when I was a kid, but now I'm an adult and I can do whatever I want. So there.

I order a ten-piece chicken nugget, medium fries, and a Sprite. I don't eat anything on the ride home. I wait until I'm back at my house, even though I know by then it will be cold.

"Do you want me to come in?" my mom asks.

"No. I'll be fine. I just want to be alone."

"I'm going to text you later to see how you're doing."

I sit at my kitchen table eating room-temperature chicken nuggets. Then I spend the rest of the day in bed watching an entire season of *Selling Sunset*. I cry when Chrishell buys her first house after getting divorced.

I find out only four eggs were mature enough to freeze, and the doctor—the woman I haven't seen since that first Zoom meeting—suggests I do another round of IVF. I waffle on this decision for a year, but in August 2022 I start the process all over again—meeting with the doctor, eight days of birth control, a routine appointment for hormone levels, and the vaginal ultrasound to make sure everything looks good to start injections the following day.

"Hmm," says the doctor, a man I haven't met before, while moving the ultrasound wand around my vagina. "You have a rather large cyst sitting on your right ovary."

"What?" I say, rattled.

"It's nothing to worry about. These are benign. Do you know if you have a history of cysts?"

"I do, actually." I picture the hot fireman walking Petunia and placing my house keys in my purse. I'm momentarily aroused by the memory of a man properly doing a chore.

"I don't recommend going forward with the IVF process until this cyst has gone away. Likely it will disappear with your next period."

"So I just stop and start all over another time?"

"Unfortunately, yes. With the cyst present you'll get suboptimal results. I'm sorry to give you that news." He removes the wand and it makes a squishing sound as it exits me.

* * *

A few days after the news of the cyst I decide to take myself to the beach. It's hot out, but not humid. There are no clouds and the sky is an almost artificial shade of blue. I lay out my blanket on the coarse Connecticut sand and erect an umbrella to lie under. I listen to the small, lapping waves and the sounds of people playing in the water, which have been carried to shore with unusual clarity by the light breeze. I pick up my phone, open the group chat, and send a text.

Me: We need to take another trip. It feels like we went to Miami forever ago.

Sarah: Yes I agree! Always looking for an excuse to get away from work.

Amanda: Where should we go?

Me: Well we've been talking about going to Puerto Rico for Carmel's 40th birthday. Carm, should we plan that?

Carmel: Guys, I love that you all want to spend my 40th birthday with me, but there has been a slight hitch in plans in regards to travel.

A few seconds pass and then Carmel texts again. I am . . . with child.

The chat erupts in a flurry of congratulations. Carmel has been trying to have a baby, so I don't know why I'm surprised, but the news still catches me. So far I have been the last one in the group to find out when someone is pregnant. I worry this is because my friends are afraid I will be mad at them for having a baby or sad for myself for being left out. I don't want them to feel this way. I want them to know I am happy for them, that I will celebrate all the phases of their pregnancy and impending motherhood. I am excited to watch them embark on this miraculous and, at times, very difficult journey, one that I am too afraid to do myself. I am also a little mad at them for having a baby and sad for myself for being left out.

I am momentarily relieved that we are all finding out at the same time about Carmel's pregnancy, but then she tells us that Sarah has known since mid-June. She guessed Carmel was pregnant when she didn't eat salami at a party. We all know Carmel loves salami.

I think back to late June when Carmel and I had a picnic lunch in Prospect Park. As we ate sandwiches on the grass, we laughed at a group of men throwing a football around. At least three out of five throws were missed or dropped by the receiver. They were completely oblivious to a woman trying to breastfeed her baby twenty feet away from them. This woman was there first. One of the guys missed a pass and the football nearly hit the baby. The woman stretched out one arm to block the ball as she cradled the baby to her breast with the other. She smiled at them. Only then did they move.

"God, what absolute fucking idiots," I said.

"It's as if that woman and her baby don't even exist," Carmel added.

I told Carmel that afternoon that ever since being in the hospital, the idea of death has never felt far from my thoughts.

"Every time something bad happens or I get broken up with by some guy I met on a dating app who I honestly don't like that much, I just think, 'I would be okay if this all ended.' I know now I'll never act on it, but what if the thoughts never go away?"

She comforted me and told me that she understood, which I knew from nearly fifteen years of friendship she did. She told me that when she was single, the small breakups often felt worse than the big ones because the compounded rejection felt like a sign from the universe that all her worst thoughts about herself were true and that maybe she was unlovable. I told her that's exactly how it feels.

Now, sitting here on the beach, I wonder why she didn't tell me that day she was pregnant. I thought I would be the first person she would tell. In truth, I don't feel mad that she's having a baby or worried that I'll be left out. I just feel terrible that my depression may have taken up so much space, she didn't feel there was room for her own good news.

By Christmas, Carmel is very pregnant. She is the most beautiful pregnant woman I have ever seen. Her rich brown hair is ten times glossier than it usually is and it is usually very glossy. Clothes look incredible on her perfectly round bump. Her skin looks radiant from underneath. She makes me realize that women can be pregnant and sexy at the same time. She makes me wonder what I would look like pregnant. Would I look this good? A small part of me wants to find out, but I remind myself for the millionth time that on the other side of pregnancy is motherhood, and I'm not sure I'm up for that. Multiple menstrual cycles have come and gone, and I never returned to the fertility clinic to see if the cyst on my ovary resolved itself. I have decided not to repeat IVF again.

As we string Carmel's Christmas tree with popcorn garlands and eat iced cake her partner has baked from scratch, I think to myself, *This time next year the baby will be here and she'll be nearly one year old. Life is amazing.* When I leave Carmel's Brooklyn apartment, she walks me downstairs to the front door of her building. She starts crying.

"No, don't cry!" I say without thinking, but immediately wish I had phrased it differently. What I meant was, "If you start crying, I'm going to cry," which I do, but I also start laughing. I am laughing because I am crying, but I'm also now worried Carmel might think I'm laughing at her because she is crying. What I wish I had said is what Reece said to me: *It's okay to cry.*

"I'm sorry," she says, wiping her eyes.

We hug, but I'm still laughing. It's a nervous, crying laughter.

"Our friendship is so important to me," Carmel says, sniffing back tears. "We've been friends for so long. I don't want us to be less close because I have a baby."

I don't want us to be either, but I know the fear and the tears we are both experiencing are because we can't guarantee what will happen after the baby. I'm afraid there won't be room for me, and she's afraid I won't want to be as big a part of her life. I'm afraid that once everyone in our group has children except for me, I'll be unimportant—the single, childless woman to whom they can no longer relate. I'm afraid I'll lose my community and my support system, and that fear is so intense that it comes out as laughter at the same time it comes out as tears.

We hug again.

"I'm so happy for you," I say, "and I know you're going to be the best mom. You'll always be my best friend, even when you have a baby."

As I exit the door, prepared for a long drive home, I say, "I promise we won't be less close," hoping, but not knowing, if it's a promise either one of us can keep.

Twenty-Seven

I'm walking along the edge of Prospect Park when I see Javier coming toward me. He's wearing white jeans, a white T-shirt, and a white chore coat that offsets his chin-length dark hair and light green eyes. His androgyny is captivating.

"Hi," he says, giving me a one-armed hug as if we already know each other. He points in the direction I've just walked from. "Let's go this way."

As we walk down Eastern Parkway toward Vanderbilt Avenue, I fill the silence with questions.

"Where were you born?"

"Mexico City, but we moved to Miami when I was twelve."

"Do you have siblings?"

"Yes, two younger sisters."

"Why did you move to Miami?"

"My parents worried Mexico City wasn't safe."

His answers are brief, with little elaboration. He looks straight ahead as he walks and talks. A native Spanish speaker, Javier doesn't have an accent, but his voice is mellifluous in the way Romance languages are. He asks me no questions in return. He seems very uninterested to be on the date.

"Let's try here." Javier stops outside the door of a very popular Brooklyn restaurant that never has reservations available online.

"You didn't make a reservation?" I ask.

"No."

Javier goes inside and comes back out a minute later. "We can wait ninety minutes for a table inside or they can seat us there right now." He points to one of the outdoor seating patios erected on sidewalks and in streets during Covid so restaurants had a chance to stay in business. Now these outdoor dining areas are permanent.

"Outdoor is good with me," I say.

We order drinks and a few small plates to share.

"Did you hear that?" he says, eyes wide. He's referring to the very audible rat squeaking within the wooden walls of the patio right by our feet.

"I did." I look under the table and then back at Javier. "Getting bitten by a rat on a first date feels like a bad sign of things to come."

"Yeah," he says. Then we sit in silence until I can't take it anymore and I start asking more questions.

"How long have you been single?"

"Since February."

"Have you been dating much since then?"

"No, this is my first date. You were the first person I matched with."

I'm surprised because something about him seems fuckboy-ish. "What happened in your last relationship?"

Javier looks away from me and doesn't make eye contact for the whole of his answer. He doesn't take a breath, either. "I made some mistakes I shouldn't have made and broke her trust and then tried to repair it but the damage was already done. I've done a lot of work on myself since then."

"You cheated?"

"Not exactly."

"Not exactly?"

"We broke up and then I slept with my ex from before her. Then when we got back together she asked me if I slept with my ex, and at first I said no, but then I came clean and told her I did and she was very mad." He's still not looking at me.

"Yeah, I'd be mad too."

"We were broken up!"

"So what's the work you've been doing on yourself since then?" I ask.

"Um, I guess just trying to be more truthful and open. And more direct about my feelings and what I need."

"Got it," I say, choosing not to push against the vagueness of his answer.

"I wish I had the courage to ask these same questions back to you," Javier says, tucking his hair behind his ears.

The scraps he's giving me, my inability to read his interest, the femininity of his movements all amount to intoxication. I want to choke on him. As I look at Javier across the table, doubts about my own value begin to surface. *Why would he like me?* I've had this same thought at the beginning of all my relationships.

"Want to go somewhere else and get a drink?" Javier asks as we pay the check.

I'm surprised, because for the past hour I haven't gotten any indication he wants the date to continue. "Sure," I say.

At the bar we also sit outside. We each order and finish a Paloma. We talk about books and film. We are sitting on plastic chairs, my legs resting across his lap, when the bartender comes out to tell us it's last call. Javier looks at me and says, "If I have another drink I'll be pretty drunk, but I don't want this night to end."

We go inside and have one more drink.

I dip into the bathroom multiple times to update my friends.

Me: Guys, he's an enigma. I can't tell if he's into me, but he's the most beautiful person I've ever seen maybe? I'm a little drunk.

Then later:

Amanda: You gotta give us one anecdote or something. What does he do for work?
Me: He's a cinematographer/director.
Sarah: HOT. He'll take great photos of you.
Me: I'm very drunk now.

Then later:

Carmel: Anna, are you making out with him??
Me: I don't think we will make out.

Then twenty minutes later:

Me: Ok we made out
Sarah: and ????
Me: GREAT

Javier and I sit on a bench outside the bar, sharing a cigarette. My head is on his shoulder, his head rests against mine. I tell him I will be out of town for the next two weeks. We won't be able to see each other again until early June.

"In two minutes I'm going to call a cab to my hotel," I say.

We sit quietly, neither of us wanting the night to be over.

"Has it been two minutes?" I say after five.

"No," he says, taking my hand in his.

In the two weeks following our date, Javier and I text a lot and even FaceTime a few times.

"I can't stop thinking about you," he tells me.

"I have the strong desire to text you just to say hello," he tells me.

"I want to see you again as soon as possible," he tells me.

I believe everything he says.

The first warning comes when I follow him on Instagram.

I can't follow you back, he texts me. My ex-girlfriend will see it and I know she will ask me if we are dating. I don't want to lie to her. She and I just got into a good place. I don't want to upset her.

I understand, I text back. No big deal.

What I was really thinking was, *If you are in such a good place, why would she be upset that you followed someone on social media? If you are in such a good place, why would you even consider lying to her about going on a date with me?* But I don't say either of those things. I don't want to push Javier away.

A day later he suggests we spend our birthdays together. They are one day apart. It seems like we are moving fast, but I like fast when it comes to love. If it moves fast it means the person really likes you. I can't trust anything other than fast.

That weekend I spend a few nights at Javier's apartment. I'm gone during the day, showing my photographs at an art fair. My work was so successful at the previous fair that the director invited me back to run a portrait booth at their four North American shows. Two years ago I had no income, now people come dressed in formal wear to have their photograph taken in "my style." It's surreal and amazing. At night Javier and I get drunk and fuck, an activity that moves with frantic speed and intensity. One minute his fingers are inside me, the next it's his tongue. He never stays in one place long enough for it to feel good. We both make a lot of noise, but we are just putting on a show for each other.

The following day I'm back home in Connecticut and we text a little.

Still want to do birthdays together? I text.

Yeah sure, whatever you want, he replies.

The next day he tells me he has to go out of town and will be gone for both our birthdays, but I can still use his apartment if I want to come into the city.

I ask my mom to watch Petunia for a couple days. In my fantasy I'm going to have a fun birthday weekend with no responsibility. I stay at Javier's apartment and watch his cat while he's out of town. A responsibility. Sometimes she nuzzles her head against my leg and lets me pet her. Other times she hisses and tries to scratch me. I spend my birthday alone reading in Prospect Park, pretending I like the solitude. I order takeout for dinner from a nice Italian restaurant as a treat, but by the time it arrives it's only slightly warm. Javier texts me once in the morning to say happy birthday, but then I don't hear from him again for the rest of the day.

Back at home in the days that follow, I don't hear from Javier at all. When we finally talk on the phone I question him about his obvious emotional retreat, and he breaks things off with me. I am devastated. I try to convince him he's making a mistake, clutching desperately to anything I can interpret as a door left open, like when he sends me a present—a white chore coat similar to the one he had that I loved so much—and includes a note that ends, "I hope I get to see it on you one day." I cry for two weeks, in part because I once again feel not special enough to be chosen by someone and in part because I feel so foolish for believing this time might have been different. I tell him how depressed I am and how much I miss him.

"No feeling is permanent," he tells me.

In the throes of sorrow I fall back on one of my more eccentric practices—consulting a tarot card reader. She's a woman I've known for a few years, who has uncannily forecasted specific and monumental events in my life. I don't believe that tarot predicts our future. I believe in free will, always. Yet I do believe in intuition and a greater spiritual binding that loosely holds the world together. Tarot cards often point me in a specific direction of self-exploration or remind me to be on the lookout for lessons.

"I don't understand why this happened," I say to the reader as she lays out the cards.

"I have good news for you," she says. "This is the person that allows you to break a relationship pattern you've been stuck in. This will be painful, but it will be swift. It is swords energy and ultimately a great gift to you. Here and now is where you discover your worth. If you can sit in the discomfort of this breakup, your entire view of relationships will change and a wound will be healed."

"It just hurts so much. I don't know how I got this one so wrong," I say.

"Life is painful in this way," she says. "It's impossible to know why someone comes into our life. Sometimes it's simply to teach us a lesson. From what the cards tell me, this is not the last time you'll hear from this person. They will come back around and you will have a defining moment where you get to make a choice for yourself, a choice to choose yourself. Choosing yourself breaks the previous cycle."

A few months later Javier asks to see me again. I say yes. I consider wearing the chore coat he sent me last year, but I don't, not wanting him to think I'm sending coded messages. We spend a day together microdosing mushrooms in Prospect Park. I ask him if I can sit on his jacket—I'm wearing white pants and we didn't bring a blanket. He says no, he doesn't want to get his jacket dirty. When we leave the park I have dirt stains on the butt of my pants. I see that Javier is paralyzed by indecision, not just about me but about small things, like where to get a sandwich—a meandering search that takes us on a miles-long, circuitous walk through Brooklyn. Pretty, but equally annoying. This indecision doesn't make Javier a bad person, but it makes him bad for me. As we walk, and walk, and retrace our steps, and then walk some more, I am able to let go of the imago I had constructed of him. I do not fill in the blanks with what I want him to be or what I assume he wants. Instead of thinking, *Will he want me?*, I coax my inner monologue to a new option: *Do I want him?* This is a question I have never considered in any of my relationships.

We sleep together that night, and in the morning when I'm leaving Brooklyn, I cry a little as we say goodbye. I don't want Javier. He is the type of person I can have as a friend, but not as a partner. My tears are not because I think I'll never see Javier again. I know I will. But no matter how freed I am by the power to recognize our incompatibility, and the power to not choose him, endings are, to me, inherently sad.

Over the next few months I mentally comb back through all the romantic relationships I've had over the course of my life and see the disturbing pattern of chasing men who are not interested in me, fueled by a belief that I can change their mind and by the belief that my own misery is inextricable from love. I chased Julian, Sam, Theo, and a list of other crushes throughout my adult life to the detriment of my own happiness. Now, at thirty-six, I have sobbed over the phone to Javier, a man I met on a dating app who I've spent a combined total of twelve hours with, pleading with him to see why we were perfect for each other. It's embarrassing and feels pathetic. My reexamination practice is mired in grief—for time I wasted, and for the woman I was who could not acknowledge her own worth. I have chased unrequited affection because to me, struggle is indicative of love. Volatility is indicative of love. Dismissal is indicative of love.

But that is not how I want to do love anymore.

* * *

Javier and I see each other again nearly a year later. We meet in Prospect Park. This time I bring a blanket. We lie on our backs and watch puffy clouds drift across the sky. We discuss the anxieties of life as working artists. When the sun turns gold we smoke a cigarette.

"Stand up," he says, pulling a camera out of his tote bag. "I want to take your photograph."

Twenty-Eight

Today is the day, I text Dr. Emily, Petunia's vet.

It is April and over seventy degrees. The magnolia trees in my front yard have ruptured into massive pink pom-poms.

When my mom arrives, she is already crying. She sits on the floor with Petunia, who is curled up in a fluffy blue bed.

"What do you want to do with her body?" she asks while stroking my dog's bony back.

I feel weird talking about this in front of Petunia, so my mom and I walk outside.

"I think I'd like to bury her under the magnolia tree. I want her to go back into the earth."

"I'm worried an animal will dig up her body."

"Yeah, I don't want that to happen. I guess I'll have her cremated."

"Let me see if I can dig a hole."

My mom takes a shovel from my garage and walks out to the magnolia tree. I sit with Petunia in my lap while I watch her hack at the earth from my kitchen window. My area of Connecticut is not known for its easy soil. It is littered with rocks. Some are tiny enough to pick up; some are too big to move even slightly. You can't dig more than a few inches without hitting both kinds. To get better leverage, my mom uses her foot to push on the back lip of the shovel. After two digs she stops and ties her long silver hair into a ponytail. These actions are meant to give her an advantage on the hole, but I don't think her foot or her ponytail are any match for the rocks.

I need to shake off this macabre scene: watching my mom dig my dog's grave while she's still alive. I go to my freezer and grab a pint of vanilla ice cream and a spoon. Petunia's soft, pink tongue laps the ice cream into her mouth hurriedly.

"Mmmm," I say to her. "Is that so good?" Because of her allergies, Petunia has never eaten ice cream before.

I spoon another heaping scoop out of the pint and hold it in front of her mouth. She looks at me, tired, and lays her head on the floor, closing her eyes.

Two years after I came home from the hospital, and nearly ten years after Petunia was first placed in my arms, I felt instinctively that something was severely wrong with her. Though blood work indicated no cause for concern, I knew my dog, and I knew she was sick. She started sleeping all the time; she had periods of confusion; she looked all-around depressed. I did every noninvasive test I could—EKGs, echocardiograms, labs—but due to her past medical history, she was not a good candidate for anesthesia, a necessary component of CT scans and MRIs. When her fur started shedding profusely and she stopped being able to walk without balance issues, I brought her to a cardiologist at a hospital in New York City, wondering if her heart issues were to blame. This vet had cared for her during many of her other emergencies.

"Petunia's heart disease has rapidly progressed," she began, "and it does not look good. But unfortunately, that is not the biggest issue going on. The neurologist took a look at her as a courtesy, because all the vets here could tell this was not the Petunia we knew. She determined that Petunia likely has a brain tumor or brain-stem disease. Without a scan it is impossible to tell which is the exact issue, but Petunia should not go under anesthesia, and to be quite honest, at this point, it doesn't really matter. I am so sorry to tell you she is at the end of her life."

Medical calamities had always been a part of Petunia's world. She had amassed two hundred pages of vet records, with five entries on pneumonia; chronic ear infections; not one, but two nose surgeries due to her face being literally concave; even a run-in with a snapping turtle who *leapt* into the air to snap her cheek. Until that day, I had no idea turtles leapt. She had degenerative disc disease in her spine. She had a heart murmur. She had permanent scarring on her lungs. She was allergic to almost everything. Her vet bills were exorbitant. Petunia's life only lasted as long as it did because I was in an incredibly privileged financial situation.

She bounced back from each ailment almost miraculously. Petunia was the Jesus Christ of dogs—pure resilience and a little magic. A large portion of my life became dedicated to her medical care, and it was exhausting. Though I had constant anxiety about her health, I leaned on the very real fact that she always recovered. This time, though, there would be no great resurrection.

"I don't think I can dig the hole!" My mom's voice is too loud as she bursts back into the house. I know her well enough to know that when she's frustrated or scared, she yells. I don't even think she knows she's doing it, but its effect engenders a feeling that I need to be the calm one. I have to hold it together while she falls apart.

"Don't worry about it. I'll have her cremated," I say.

"Maybe you can call your lawn people and they can come dig the hole?"

"It's really not a big deal." My voice is tranquil, hoping to mitigate my mom's guilt.

"Or I can go back out there and try again. I just don't know if I'll be able to do it alone. Your lawn people might have something electric that would move the soil really easily."

"I'm fine with cremating her. I don't want to spend the day figuring out how to dig a hole just because my first instinct was to bury her under the magnolia tree. It's not that important to me."

"Fine," my mom says. I can't tell if she's annoyed at me for not wanting to dig the hole anymore or at herself for not being able to. "What do you want to do now?" she asks.

"I'd like to take her for a walk in her stroller."

"Do you mind if I come with you?"

I want to be alone with my dog, but I don't want to hurt my mom's feelings. I know she loves Petunia too. "Sure," I say.

I bought a dog stroller for Petunia when she was still young. The summers were too hot for her to walk far but she loved to be outside. She was also a generally stubborn walker—willing to go in one direction as far as she could, but absolutely unwilling to walk back. When she didn't want to walk anymore, she would lie on the sidewalk with her back legs splayed out behind her. I called this move "frogging out." If Petunia decided to frog out, the walk was over. She had to be carried home, and it's hard to carry a twenty-one-pound dog several city blocks. I started walking her one way while pushing the empty stroller, and then when she frogged out, I would put her in it and walk her around some more. I knew she appreciated this by the way she watched the streets through the stroller's front mesh window with a human alertness.

When I walked Petunia in the stroller, I did so with the entitled confidence of a woman pushing her newborn. I said "excuse me" too loud and too exasperated at anyone blocking the graded curb of the sidewalk when I crossed the street. I didn't really believe these people should be mindful of an animal in a stroller, but I enjoyed seeing their reaction when they realized I was pushing a dog. I also enjoyed the way pushing Petunia around allowed me to cosplay motherhood.

On summer nights I would take Petunia to the parks along the West Side Highway of Manhattan. We would stop at a bench overlooking the Hudson River and I would unzip the top of the stroller, pushing it back so she could sit exposed to the world. I watched the soft current as Petunia's nostrils flared at the breeze and her tongue licked the air. "You're my best friend," I'd tell her.

Now, walking Petunia through my neighborhood feels like a death march. She doesn't sit up to look out the mesh window. She keeps her head on the soft pad, her legs stretched behind her. Frogging out. My mom and I don't say much because there is not much to say. Too soon we are back at my house. I lift Petunia from the stroller and look at the short white fur that has tucked itself into the crevices of the fabric over the years. I unclasp her harness and place it inside the bassinet where her body just was. This is the last time I'll ever take Petunia out of her stroller. In the months to come it will sit undisturbed in my garage like a reliquary of a life I once lived.

Dr. Emily and her vet tech Kate show up to my house at seven p.m. and we decide to do the euthanasia outside on my back patio. I don't want Petunia's soul getting stuck in the house. I want it to float up and out into the sky. Dr. Emily talks me through exactly how it will go. First Petunia will get a medication that will make her sleep. Once she's asleep she won't feel anything. Then she will receive medication to slowly and peacefully stop her heart. The whole thing should take around twenty minutes.

"Do you want a few minutes alone with her before we start?" Dr. Emily's voice is soft. She places her hand on my back. Both she and Kate have known Petunia for years, and like everyone who knows Petunia, they love her. Petunia will die surrounded by love.

I pick my beloved dog up into my arms and walk with her from room to room of our house, recounting all the things we did together in those sacred spaces.

In the kitchen I say, "This is where you watched me bake banana bread and licked spilled flour dustings from the floor."

In the dining room: "This is where we ate dinner. Remember how beautiful it looked the first night I lit all the candles?"

In the living room: "This is where we watched movies."

And in my office, my favorite room, the room where my new career and life have flourished, I say, "This is where we pulled tarot cards every morning. This is where you helped me sew lampshades. This is where you kept me company while I edited all the photographs."

Back outside now, the peepers are singing. Fireflies are beginning to dot my yard with their electricity. As the sun dips behind the trees, I see bats darting across the sky, their scalloped wings flapping vigorously. We put a blanket on the stone patio, which I sit on, Petunia cradled in my lap. Dr. Emily has positioned her so I only see her front half, not her back legs where the drugs will enter her veins. From a small speaker, *Saint Cloud* by Waxahatchee plays. It's an album I've listened to thousands of times over the past two years, dancing with Petunia in my arms to "Can't Do Much"; laying my head on her dog bed, tucked against her paws listening to "Lilacs." *I won't end up anywhere good without you . . . I need your love too*, I'd sing to her.

Petunia dies as she lived, defiantly and on her own terms. She clings to life just as she had all the other times it was nearly lost. Later I will learn Petunia required the amount of life-ending medication reserved for a full-sized Labrador retriever. This doesn't surprise me.

I feel her take her last breath and her whole body relaxes. The exact moment of death feels fast and unceremonious.

My mom, Dr. Emily, and Kate go inside and try to prepare a cheap clay paw-print kit my mom bought at Michaels craft store earlier that day. I stay outside holding Petunia. It is dark now and she is dead, but still I tell her how much I love her. I tell her how grateful I am for her love and companionship.

"I'll miss you forever," I say into her ear.

The paw-print kit is terrible. We take turns pushing Petunia's limp paw into the soft clay, but each time it barely makes a dent. None of us want to press too hard.

"It's fine," I say. "I don't need it."

"Let's just try one more time!" My mom's voice is sharp with anxiety, as it was when she couldn't dig the hole. I know she wants the paw print to work so she can feel like she contributed something, but I just want her to stop.

"Mom. I don't want to try again. It's fine. I don't need the paw print."

"Here! I bought two just in case. Let's try the other one."

"No," I say.

She has tears in her eyes when she acquiesces. Dr. Emily tells us the crematorium can make a paw print for us.

My mom carries Petunia to Dr. Emily's car and places her in the back seat, where Dr. Emily has already prepared a bed from a blanket. I pet Petunia's head one last time. She looks like she's sleeping. I hear Waxahatchee playing through Dr. Emily's speakers as she drives away. My mom and I hug, then she leaves too. I am alone in my house for the first time ever. No nails tapping against the floor, no snorting, just silence and the sound of the peepers in the woods.

* * *

In the weeks following Petunia's death I build her an altar on a ledge in my family room. I fill it with dried flowers friends have sent me as bereavement gifts. I fill it with trinkets that remind me of her: a small porcelain box with her fur, foam butterfly wings she wore one year for Halloween, her collar. I set the perfectly made paw print from the crematorium and the carved wooden box with her ashes on the altar. I put a photograph of her in a gilded frame on the altar. I sit in front of the altar most mornings and meditate. My mom tells me she meditates for Petunia too—a fourteen-day Buddhist practice for the dead.

I can still feel Petunia everywhere. I begin to worry her spirit has not crossed over. Though feeling her presence comforts me, I worry this is unfair to her. She deserves to pass through the liminal space between life and death fully, to complete her journey to the other side. The answer to this problem is clear. I contact a healer to facilitate a crossing-over ceremony.

"Petunia is ready to go, but she is afraid to leave you," the healer tells me. "She is afraid you won't be okay without her."

I begin to cry.

I tell the healer to thank Petunia for being my constant companion. I promise Petunia that I am okay and that I will be okay without her. I tell her how grateful I am to her for staying with me—for guarding me—until I was strong enough to survive without her.

The next morning I wake up to find I no longer feel Petunia in the house. This was my intention, but I panic at first, wishing for a moment I could take it back. I cannot. The portal is closed now. I am crushed. I am lonely. But I am okay.

I am okay.

Twenty-Nine

I sit at my dining room table with my laptop open. A large slice of sun pours in through old French doors that lead to my patio. This is where Petunia used to lie in the afternoons. At the door are two plant stands. One holds Caitlyn's jade plant, which is a foot tall now. I've had to repot it twice since leaving the hospital. On the other stand sits a large ceramic pot that holds the Cuban oregano plants—mine, Mary's, and Caitlyn's. After they each outgrew their small plastic cups, thin roots bursting from holes in the bottoms, I combined them. I am not good with plants. I usually kill them by underwatering and neglect. But I am very diligent about my jade and Cuban oregano. I water them once a week just like Sandy the horticulturist told us to.

It's been two and a half years since I left the hospital. A month after my discharge, I was sent my final report, which compiled the findings of my analysis. It was the contract I knowingly entered into: to talk and talk, to provide as thorough an overview of my life as was possible in two weeks, and then to allow a group of doctors to play blocks with that information, fitting experience on top of experience until they built a structure that amounted to a recognizable form.

However, the more days I spent in the hospital the less I cared about my assessment. My team of doctors did not treat me as though I were sick or insane, but as someone in crisis who, with help, could pull herself out of the depressive swamp and learn to tolerate diffi-cult, overwhelming emotions. Because of this, the importance of their diagnosis atrophied, so much so that when I received the formal document, I didn't read it. I had left Dr. Karr, started treatment with a new therapist, and done a year of intensive DBT therapy. I felt I had the information most pertinent to my recovery. I didn't need more.

But now that I'm nearly finished writing this book, my curiosity has finally gotten the better of me. I want to know what the doctors had to say about me. I want to know if it aligns with what I think about myself. I open the file on my laptop.

The report is quite short, only eighteen pages. The first two pages contain basic and uninteresting information under headings like "Identifying Data and History of Present Illness." So far it has a bunch of wrong information. It says I began cutting when I was in seventh grade and that my parents divorced at this time as well. It says I never wrote a suicide note—at all, much less while wearing a leopard-print Norma Kamali dress. It says I stated my self-injurious behavior was something I felt I could control, when what I actually stated multiple times, to multiple different doctors, was that I used self-harm as a way to feel *in control*. Same word, two very different meanings. Were the doctors even listening?

Everyone from my team—Dr. Samuels, Dr. Philips, Beth, the chaplain—submitted their own findings. Nearly half of the report is Dr. Philips's psychological report, which he and I discussed in-depth while in the hospital. The rest of it was written by Dr. Samuels, the head of the program. The formal diagnosis, the final word, is his.

The traits he attributes to me are oddly worded and inconsistent in tone. Some sentences read definitively:

ANNA HAS DEPRESSIVE EPISODES WITH DEPRESSED MOOD AND HOPELESSNESS.

ANNA HAS PANIC ATTACKS CONSISTING OF CRESCENDO ANXIETY, PALPITATIONS, DYSPNEA, AND LIGHTHEADEDNESS.

Other sentences read equivocally:

ANNA DENIES SYMPTOMS OF MANIA, PSYCHOSIS, AND ADHD.

ANNA DENIES ROUTINE USE OF ANY RECREATIONAL SUBSTANCE.

Dr. Samuels is reporting information I relayed to him, but why is some of it phrased like I'm trying to outfox him? The word *denies* particularly bothers me. It suggests that somewhere later in the report my "denial" will be exposed, which it never is. I *did* deny symptoms of mania, psychosis, and ADHD. When, during my assessment, Dr. Samuels found me void of these symptoms, he could have skipped the word *denied* and instead written *Anna* has *no symptoms of mania, psychosis, and ADHD.* Or he could have inserted here what he has written two pages later:

HER THOUGHT PROCESSES ARE SEQUENTIAL. THERE ARE NO DELUSIONS OR

HALLUCINATIONS.

I wish I could tell him to go back and make it uniform. Language matters.

When I reach the spiritual evaluation portion of the report submitted by the chaplain, I am excited to see I got way more freaky than I remembered.

ANNA IS A REIKI MASTER. SHE FEELS HER ENERGY IS BLOCKED IN HER HEAD

AND THROAT CHAKRAS.

So true.

ANNA PRACTICES AND STUDIES ASTROLOGY, AND GEMINI TENDENCIES

INFORM HER OUTLOOK.

Now, this woman listened.

The psychodynamic formulation section, written by Dr. Samuels, stirs my anger yet again—precisely because of how it focuses on my anger.

HER AGGRESSION PARTICULARLY SEEMS TO BE MANAGED WITH DIFFICULTY.
HER LIABILITY TO EXPLOSIVE OUTBURSTS IS LIKELY PARTLY DERIVATIVE OF
DEFENSES INADEQUATE TO MANAGE THE AGGRESSION IN A USEFUL WAY.

These statements lack any contextualization that my anger is largely directed at myself, or at larger social structures I find personally oppressive—misogyny, patriarchy, sexism. This makes it sound like I was freaking out and screaming at everyone. I was not. I had no altercations, physical or verbal, or even any mild disagreements with any of the doctors, any of the staff, or any of my fellow patients. I got along with and was respectful to everyone. Where, exactly, did Dr. Samuels see examples of unchecked aggression or explosive outbursts?

Perhaps he is referring to the crying. I cried *a lot*. It would be ludicrous of me to *deny* that. But it seems unfair to categorize sobbing as an explosive outburst of aggression. Would it be described as an "explosive outburst" if a man were sobbing? Or would he be described as "emotionally open" and "there to do the hard work"?

Or perhaps Dr. Samuels is referring to my cutting as explosive outbursts of aggression. *Implosion*, yes, but *explosion*? Not really. Moments of self-harm were often calm, dissociatively so. They were controlled in their uncontrolled-ness. They were ritualized. I described this to him. I wonder if he heard me, or if it even mattered for his assessment of me.

The report goes on to analyze my breakdown with Dr. Karr.

. . . CAUGHT IN A SADOMASOCHISTIC TRANSFERENCE-COUNTERTRANSFERENCE
ENACTMENT . . . THIS IMPASSE LED THE THERAPIST TO REFER THE PATIENT
TO THIS PROGRAM . . . IT SEEMS LIKELY THAT THE PATIENT MAY HAVE

EXPERIENCED THE THERAPIST AS A PUNITIVE, DEMANDING, AND REJECTING
FIGURE. HER READINESS TO STAY IN THE SITUATION MAY REFLECT AN ATTEMPT
TO RECAPITULATE HER ATTACHMENT TO ABUSIVE FIGURES IN HER PAST.

Readiness to stay in the situation? I didn't begin to sense a break-down with Dr. Karr until late 2019, and given she was my only long-term therapeutic experience, it took me time to realize something was off. True, I didn't want to acknowledge the rupture at first. Dr. Karr had, up until that time, been a hugely positive influence on my life, and I'm not the type of person who bails at the first sign of conflict. Plus, my gendered life experience causes me to second-guess myself before questioning the figure of authority. This is something women routinely do. Once it was communicated and validated by the other doctors at the hospital that Dr. Karr and I were caught in an unhealthy dynamic, I ended my work with her immediately. To me that sounds like a woman ready to get out, not a woman ready to stay.

I stand up from my dining room chair and pace around the table. In for three. Out for six. Where is the mention of Dr. Karr's role in this? The report omits what occurred at the case conference or my last meeting with her. It omits her suggesting she and I "get a divorce," and her outright accusing me of manipulating the male doctors. It says nothing of the doctors' wariness of Dr. Karr's behavior, though they were quick to express this to me behind office doors. The report says I chose to end my work with her as if this was a decision I came to completely on my own instead of mutually agreed upon by all as the right move, the only move, for the success of my future treatment. I look down at the carpet to see a path worn in its pile by my bare feet.

I sit back down and keep reading.

* * *

Soon I reach the most upsetting part of the report.

... GIVEN WHAT ANNA DESCRIBES AS NEGATIVE EXPERIENCES WITH MEN,
SHE SEEMS TO HAVE TO SOME EXTENT DEMONIZED MEN IN GENERAL ...
ONE WONDERS IF IT MAY BE POSSIBLE THAT ON THE SURFACE SHE IS READY TO
REJECT MEN AS A GROUP, BUT PERHAPS AT A DEEPER LEVEL HER RAGE TOWARD
MATERNAL FIGURES MAY BE FAR MORE POWERFUL.

If I may be so bold as to analyze this analysis of me.

What I see here is deflection and denial of the ways men have impacted my psyche. What I see here is that my rejection of and rage toward the patriarchal structures that govern nearly every aspect of life couldn't possibly be my authentic reality. No, there must be something else at the root, something that has nothing to do with men at all. Something that has to do with women. Let's blame women.

Even though this assessment is more than two years old, I feel misunderstood and misinterpreted in the now. I also feel something familiar, a bumping against the limitations of a man's point of view. In this assessment I see a portrait of myself drawn by a straight, white, cisgendered man; the standard against which modern psychology measures all else. I'm not saying there is no truth to what Dr. Samuels has written in my report. Of course there is. I *am* angry. But how my anger is categorized is reductive and without context. His inclination to substitute rage toward maternal figures for rage toward male privilege suggests an *either/or* where a *both* might exist. It flattens my own experience of my rage by implying it's so similar across demographics that I have gotten them confused. I have not. My anger toward male privilege is not confused or surface-level. It is cellular. I feel it in my body every day. It torments my thoughts. It has, for most of my life, dictated how I move through the world.

At the risk of sounding like a defensive narcissist, I would suggest the impulse to link my alleged demonization and rejection of men to an allegedly more real hatred of female figures is yet another example of a man's inability, unwillingness, or fear to fully consider the harmful impact men can have on women. Though isn't that the thing about pathology according to a system devised largely by men? To even suggest male fragility or male bias might be at play, I first must suggest my own defensiveness and narcissism. I doubt Dr. Samuels felt compelled to do this. Men, in my experience, usually do not feel compelled to do this.

Women displaying anger—even acknowledging anger—are deemed pathological. As a woman I know this and have acted accordingly. I have hidden my anger, buried it, for fear of being judged or persecuted—only to have it explode out of me later, after being pushed and pushed and pushed past my limits. What occurs then is a cyclical pattern of obfuscation and explosion, instead of steady acknowledgment, distress tolerance, and conflict resolution. Anger becomes a quality of shame rather than a workable emotion, one that can spark creativity, realizations, and transformation. Men have analyzed my anger, often forgetting or refusing to understand that part of what makes me so angry is having to contort through social dynamics and mores that they have created. Men have judged me and men have called me crazy, trusting in their own neutrality. But when neutrality is only accepted by the one who has created it, it is an illusion.

On the final page of my assessment, Dr. Samuels formally diagnoses me with generalized anxiety disorder, major depressive disorder, intermittent explosive disorder, and borderline personality disorder. The first two are givens, holdovers from a previous doctor, but the latter two are a shock. No one ever suggested these disorders to me while I was in the hospital, nor has anyone since. Dr. Samuels ends the report by suggesting that an addition of antipsychotic medication "may be helpful for explosive outbursts." I can't help but laugh at how his suggestion makes me seem like an unhappy 1950s housewife who needs to be kept under control. In the weeks to come my current therapist will read the report and will also be confused and surprised by the addition of intermittent explosive disorder and borderline personality disorder to my diagnosis; he will refute both.

As much as I am infuriated by what Dr. Samuels has written in the report, I am grateful to him. I am grateful to Beth, to the chaplain, and most of all to Dr. Philips. The help I received from them saved me in that it gave me the tools to save myself. Now I am a new person. Life has in no way gotten easier. In so many ways it has become harder. But I've become sturdier. I am now a sturdy person. Someone who feels tremendous emotions, but who knows how to acknowledge those feelings, sit with them, communicate them if need be, and then let them go. Usually. I don't cut or self-harm anymore. Ever.

I am messier than I once was, emotionally speaking, but I'm a little messier in life too. I don't always get everywhere exactly on time, I don't always respond to an email in a timely fashion, I'm not as concerned with potting the plant perfectly. I get tired easily. I like a lot of alone time. I'm not married anymore. I don't have a dog anymore. I won't live my life only to make someone else happy.

The anger I sometimes feel toward men is not usually as personal as it might seem. Some of the anger has to do with them, but I also know some of it is the product of a life experience coalesced long before I had romantic relationships. It is my early life, it is my parents, it is their parents, it is pure luck of brain chemistry.

I believe men have the ability to look outside themselves, to question how their actions affect the women around them, and to exist with more awareness to others' experiences, should they want to do that. I have been lucky to know a few men who do. They are sensitive and communicative and empathetic. They give me hope.

I don't hate men. I still want to fuck them. I still want to love them.

I've simply changed the way I relate to them and what of myself I'm willing to give. I no longer get lost inside the abyss of the other. There is space between us now. It's shocking how much faster I recover from an ending when I don't have to also disentangle my sense of self from the other person. I can at times feel mad at the me who came before this moment because I know for sure no man ever had to work so hard to disentangle himself from me. *You were so stupid,* I want to tell myself, but I redirect my thoughts to something more constructive. *You are so lucky to have learned this now; it will keep you safe and happy.* My brain makes a slight amendment: *Maybe not totally happy, but perhaps happier.* I'm still me, after all.

I do still feel like I'm dying after a breakup, and I want to normalize this feeling. It's okay to feel this way within a healthy context. The human desire to find meaningful connection is strong. There's a reason most of us pair up: Love is an enviable and powerful force. Only now I feel like I'm dying for one, maybe two days, instead of an entire week. Or month. Or months. That's progress. I've come to understand that the dying feeling comes after the anger wears off, when I'm left with the emptiness of knowing I must once again rely largely on myself for company. So I acknowledge my loneliness. I acknowledge the anger was largely created by fear: of rejection, of being unlovable, of lacking control, of having to begin the getting-to-know-you phase all over again with someone new—if I can even find someone new who I want to start the getting-to-know-you phase with. This feeling is temporary though. And it is universal, which brings me comfort.

I won't pretend that I'm miraculously happy now, that I never think about wanting to die. I do. But my old brain before the hospital would think: *I want to die. I deserve to die. No one will ever love me. Why am I even alive? Maybe I should act on this now so I don't have to feel this way anymore.* Now my brain thinks: *I want to die. Okay, what is this feeling, really? This is grief. Grief is one of the hardest feelings to feel. Why am I alive? I'm alive because I have jobs to do. I have to show up for my friends and my family. I have to take care of the new kittens I adopted after Petunia died, who I love and who depend on me. I have to make art. I have to write. I like doing these jobs. Doing them brings me joy, a sense of purpose, and best of all laughter. So is what I'm feeling really the desire to die? Not really. It's okay to grieve and to mourn right now. This feeling will end.*

It was a lot of work to get here and frankly annoying. But now I have the luxury to experience grief and to feel deeply without crumbling. I can pick myself off the floor without having to reassemble myself first. It's true, no feeling is permanent. With less time lost I start walking forward to meet the next joy, the next fit of laughter, the next success, and the next failure, and inevitably the next loss. I still don't know where my career will lead me, and this is frightening. But it is also exciting. I chose the path of writing this book, I stayed the course, I did not turn left, and that's something. Maybe more than something. Maybe it's a victory.

I close out of the report and shut my laptop. I sit at the dining table thinking about the girls. I wonder if Kristin has been back to the hospital. I wonder if Mary became a lawyer. I wonder where Caitlyn went to college. I miss them and I wonder if they remember me. I picture Shawn playing violin, and looking out the Dalby window to catch a glimpse of the turkeys, and her face when she took the rock I picked for her into her hands.

I look down at my own hands, at my body, at my feet. I thank them for where they have taken me, this wild journey. I remember the words Caitlyn wrote on the white plastic cup that first held her Cuban oregano: LOOK UP.

I do.

Acknowledgments

A deep and heartfelt thank-you to the following people:

Meg Thompson—my friend and literary agent. The kind of whip-smart, intuitive, loyal, deep-thinking woman you want to work with. Also, one of the most beautiful. Meg, I feel so lucky to have sold this book with you fifteen years after we first met.

Everyone at Simon & Schuster—Anne Tate Pearce, Tzipora Chein, Irene Kheradi, Amanda Mulholland, Jackie Seow, Emma Shaw, Rachael DeShano, Lauren Gomez, Stacey Sakal, Felice Javit, Carly Loman, Beth Maglione. As well as Jonathan Karp and Priscilla Painton.

Alexa Sparacio, who designed my book cover (and my initial proposal so long ago).

Nicole Garton and Ryan Stanier at The Other Art Fair, who first took a chance on me as an artist.

Eleanor Alter and Jennifer Montoya, who helped me navigate a challenging year.

My family—Mom, Jesse, Dad, and Joan—for their support in writing this book. I know stories have many sides and interpretations. Thank you for graciously allowing me the space and trust to write mine.

More women I love madly—Kim M., Sarah T., Jenny W., Bianca H., Yilin C., Joanna N., Jen D., Mimi E., Stephanie R., Laine C., Emily M., Mary Kate F.

Three important men (plot twist!)—Ben F., who has been my dear friend since I was sixteen years old. He makes me laugh out loud on a weekly basis and texts me without fail during every new episode of *The Real Housewives of Salt Lake City* for a real-time debrief. That's friendship.

My former therapist, MG, who saw me through the most challenging three years. In so many ways I owe the life I have now to you.

Last, but most, Sean Manning, my editor. Thank you for giving me this opportunity. Thank you for seeing what this book could be (even before I could). Thank you for knowing when to push me and for allowing me to push back when I needed to. Thank you for making me a better writer. Thank you, truly, for everything.